Best Laid Plans

The publisher and the University of California Press Foundation gratefully acknowledge the generous support of the Barbara S. Isgur Endowment Fund in Public Affairs.

Best Laid Plans

WOMEN COMING OF AGE
IN UNCERTAIN TIMES

Jessica Halliday Hardie

UNIVERSITY OF CALIFORNIA PRESS

University of California Press
Oakland, California

© 2022 by Jessica Halliday Hardie

Library of Congress Cataloging-in-Publication Data

Names: Hardie, Jessica Halliday, 1978– author.
Title: Best laid plans : women coming of age in uncertain times /
    Jessica Halliday Hardie.
Description: Oakland, California : University of California Press,
    [2022] | Includes bibliographical references and index.
Identifiers: LCCN 2022004933 (print) | LCCN 2022004934 (ebook) |
    ISBN 9780520297876 (cloth) | ISBN 9780520297883 (paperback) |
    ISBN 9780520970052 (epub)
Subjects: LCSH: Teenage girls—United States—Social conditions—
    21st century—Case studies. | Coming of age—Social aspects—
    United States—21st century—Case studies.
Classification: LCC HQ798 .H34 2022 (print) | LCC HQ798 (ebook) |
    DDC 305.242/20905—dc23/eng/20220307
LC record available at https://lccn.loc.gov/2022004933
LC ebook record available at https://lccn.loc.gov/2022004934

Manufactured in the United States of America

31 30 29 28 27 26 25 24 23 22
10 9 8 7 6 5 4 3 2 1

To my mother, Jean Margaret Lynch, who listened.

Contents

Illustrations

Acknowledgments

It is truly remarkable to be writing my thanks to the people who helped bring this book about when for a long time the prospect of a book seemed so daunting and unlikely. And indeed, it would not be here if not for the support I received from family, friends, mentors, colleagues, and editors. Books, like many endeavors, appear to be the product of a single person, but they require an entire support system.

Thank you, first and foremost, to the young women who shared their lives with me to make this book possible. I am so tremendously grateful for your time and for your willingness to describe your hopes and dreams, your daily lives, and your triumphs and disappointments. I hope that I represented you well. I am also indebted to the principals and teachers at the two high schools where I conducted this work.

Plans for the project that would eventually become this book began almost fifteen years ago, when I was a graduate student at the University of North Carolina at Chapel Hill. I owe so much gratitude to Lisa Pearce, my advisor at UNC, for her unending support and guidance. Lisa balanced insightful criticism with enthusiasm for my ideas and served as a model for conducting qualitative interviews. She has continued to be a source of support over the years. Barbara Entwisle served as my dissertation cochair at UNC and provided crucial advice in the early planning stages of this project. Both as an instructor in graduate research methods and as a mentor, Barbara taught me how to think deeply and critically about research design. Karolyn Tyson always asks the tough questions, and for that I am eternally grateful. Our work together taught me how to approach fieldwork, how to analyze qualitative data, how to be true to my research subjects, and how to push my writing to its best. Karolyn also read and provided much needed feedback on this book at an early stage.

The Sociology Department at UNC and the Carolina Population Center both gave me a home among a community of scholars. Thanks to Jan Hendrickson-Smith for her advice and for her work in creating a community among the graduate students and postdocs. A traineeship at the Carolina Population Center and UNC's Jessie Ball DuPont Dissertation Completion Fellowship supported my work for the final two years of graduate study. I am grateful to Deana Allman, who transcribed my first round of interviews, sending me weekly reports and checking with me when problems arose. Thank you to my fellow graduate students at UNC who shared their brilliance and humor over the years; in particular, JD Daw, Anne Hunter, Vanesa Ribas, and Ria van Ryn. I admire Amy Lucas's equanimity, and I am lucky to have her as a longtime collaborator and friend. Many thanks to the faculty at UNC who provided critical guidance, including Philip Cohen, Glen Elder, Guang Guo, Kathie Harris, Ted Mouw, Andy Perrin, Ron Rindfuss, and Cathy Zimmer.

An NICHD Postdoctoral Fellowship at the Population Research Institute at Penn State gave me the time and resources to follow up with the young women I had interviewed to update their contact information and launch new research projects. I am grateful to Nancy Landale, who was a wonderful mentor, both in her rigorous approach to scholarship and as a model for the kind of work-life balance I aspire to. I also benefited from presenting my work at the PRI brownbag lecture series and from the advice and support of several faculty at Penn State, including Gordon De Jong, John Iceland, Michelle Frisco, and Jeremy Staff. Molly Martin was incredibly generous with her time and advice. Thank you to Lori Burrington, Linda Halgunseth, Daphne Hernandez, and Anita Zuberi for their friendship and camaraderie. And many thanks to the Ladies Creamery Running Group for including me in their early morning runs through the hills of State College.

In 2010, I was named an Emerging Scholar by the University of Kentucky Center for Poverty Research. This gave me the opportunity to visit the center and present my work. I am grateful to the attendees of this talk for their feedback and in particular to Ed Morris, Brea Perry, and James Ziliak. In 2011, I received support from the Work and Family Researchers Network as an Early Career Work-Family Scholar. Thanks especially to Stephen Sweet for coordinating professional development workshops during this time and providing career advice.

My first academic home as a faculty member was at the University of Missouri–Kansas City. While there I received the University of Missouri Research Board Grant, which funded my second wave of interviews with the young women of this book. Deborah Smith and Sookhee Oh were both wonderful faculty mentors during my time there. Michelle Smirnova was an enthusiastic and thoughtful colleague, and we continue to commiserate over navigating motherhood and book writing. Thanks to Lori Sexton and Erika Honisch, who started with me at UMKC and were such important friends as we managed long-distance relationships while learning how to be proficient teachers and researchers.

It was not until I settled into the sociology department at Hunter College that the plan for this book truly took shape. I received feedback from the department when I presented my fledgling ideas at our colloquium series and my colleagues' comments pushed me to broaden my thinking about the contributions of this work. Many thanks to Lynn Chancer and Erica Chito Childs, who have both served as chair during my tenure and have been such important cheerleaders and mentors. Margaret Chin, Nancy Foner, Calvin Smiley, and Peter Tuckel have been my hallway comrades for many years now. They make going into the office enjoyable. Thanks to Peter for equitably sharing control over our window blinds. Michi Soyer learned the faculty ropes along with me and has been a steady source of support and encouragement. I appreciate her demystifying the book process for me. Thanks to Tom DeGloma and Don Hernandez for their guidance over the years and to Mike Benediktsson for his camaraderie during the tenure process. I also received feedback and support from my fellow Mellon Faculty Fellows at Hunter, James Cantres, Xuchilt Pérez, Calvin J. Smiley, and Tricia Stephens, and our senior faculty mentors, Milagros Denis-Rosario and Victoria Stone-Cadena.

Thanks to my colleagues in the sociology department at the Graduate Center and CUNY's Institute for Demographic Research. Leslie McCall's work was an inspiration to me as a scholar before I met her and has been a sounding board for this book. Thanks to Richard Alba, Neil Bennett, Mary Clare Lennon, and Van Tran for being so welcoming to me. Deborah Balk has been incredibly generous with her time and resources; I'm so glad to be her colleague. Amy Hsin, at Queens College, invited me to present my research in her department. The feedback from Amy and others in attendance pushed me to articulate my ideas around family support and schooling.

I have been lucky enough to be a member of two fantastic writing groups with people I consider dear friends. Kristin Turney and Anita Zuberi have been incredible friends and writing teammates for almost a decade. We have seen each other through joys and heartaches over the years, have read one another's messy drafts and polished ready-to-submit articles, and have always been on each other's sides. I would not have published half as much without them. Thanks to them for providing detailed feedback on my original book proposal and many chapters over the years. After beginning this book in earnest, I joined Sarah Damaske and Carrie Shandra in a book-focused writing group. It is no exaggeration to say that this book would not exist without them. For one, I delayed committing to a book until describing the material to Sarah at a conference. Her enthusiasm for my ideas and suggestions for the book's structure got me started. Weekly meetings with Sarah and Carrie kept the work sustained for three years. All my thanks to them for traveling this journey with me and for always pushing me to do my best work. Thank you, also, to Joanna Pepin for reading a chapter of the book at the last minute, for the brainstorming sessions, and for the friendship she and Chris Olah have provided over the years.

I have presented portions of this book at conferences and published work from my first round of interviews in two journals. I am indebted to the feedback I received in these venues. Thanks to the anonymous reviewers at *Social Problems* and *Teachers College Record* for their engagement with my work. Two students have contributed to the analyses included in this book. Asia Orr, a master's student at UMKC, helped create profiles for each of the young women. I have turned to her insightful notes on each participant throughout my time writing this book. Alec Cali, an undergraduate student at Hunter College, contributed to transcript coding.

I couldn't believe my luck when Naomi Schneider agreed to take this project on. I am immensely grateful to her for her belief in my work. Thanks to Naomi, too, for pointing me to Carolyn Bond, an extremely talented and kind developmental editor. I have learned so much about writing from her. Thanks to editorial assistants Renee Donovan, Summer Farah, and Benjy Malings for their work and to the entire UC Press production team. I am grateful for Sharon Langworthy's copy editing of this manuscript and to Scott Smiley for completing an index. Thanks to Yasemin Besen-Cassino, Jen Silva, and the anonymous reviewers for providing feedback on the book proposal and manuscript.

My mother, Jean Lynch, paved the way ahead of me as a sociologist, queer woman, activist, and mother. She was my first model for how to listen to other people and truly see them. She and Helenka Marculewicz, my stepmother, always believed this book would come about, and they read early chapters with enthusiasm. I am immensely grateful for their belief in me, and I wish I could share the final product with them. My father, Andrew Hardie, and stepmother, Madeline Hardie, are steady sources of support and encouragement. I am grateful for their love and humor. To my daughter, Eleanor, you fill me with joy. I am immeasurably lucky to watch you grow and engage with the world. I hope you always keep your sunny spirit, your fists of fury, and your passion.

To my wife, Alison, I love you. Thank you for being my teammate and love for twenty-one years. Who else could I spend a pandemic working from home with and yet lament that we do not have enough time together? I am so incredibly grateful for your unceasing belief in me and your encouragement, for the fun we have together, and for your amazing parenting skills. Thank you for always making space for my work, but more importantly making space for our life together.

Introduction

In the 1980s, sociologist Ruth Sidel interviewed young women between the ages of 12 and 25 to understand how the new ethos that women could "have it all" was shaping their outlooks and hopes for the future.[1] She found that many young women fully embraced the American Dream. In her book, *On Her Own: Growing Up in the Shadow of the American Dream*, Sidel wrote, "Many of these young women are optimistic, adventurous, and, above all, individualistic. They see the future as bright and full of promise. They focus on career, on upward mobility, and on the need to be independent. They believe success is there for the taking; all they need do is figure out the right pathway and work hard."[2] Young women looked forward to futures in which they would live in the "house on a hill" and enjoy an upper middle-class life.[3] Sidel cautioned readers that these young women would soon face constraints: the imperative of two incomes in modern society and the gendered nature of family obligations. She cast doubt on the likelihood that these young women's futures would be as bright as they anticipated, arguing that they had not taken stock of the barriers women faced in the labor market and at home. To the young women she interviewed, however, nothing stood in their way.

Two decades later, on the precipice of the Great Recession (2007–2009) and after years of mostly stalled progress for women and increasing inequality between the rich and poor, I set out to interview middle-class, working-class, and poor high school–aged girls about their aspirations for the future and plans for fulfilling these aspirations.[4] Given the social and economic changes impacting women over the preceding years, would I find the same optimism among the girls I spoke to, and would they be prepared to follow through on these aspirations? I conducted these interviews with sixty-one young women interested in the health field in particular; these jobs offered relatively high wages, steady employment, and a predictable career path (i.e., clear educational credentials, training requirements, and job duties). Five years later I interviewed them again to follow their progress as they went to college, worked, and formed families in their early twenties. My goal was to understand why young people who start off with high aspirations fall short of their goals, particularly among the poor and working class, and what we can do to better support young people in fulfilling their aspirations.[5] By following those who were interested in health, I was able to see how plans for "knowable" career paths (i.e., occupations that have very clear educational and training expectations) differed both in their details in high school and in their pursuit in young adulthood. I anticipated the girls I interviewed would hold lofty, unfocused goals for the future, as much of the research on adolescent aspirations had prepared me to expect that adolescents' aspirations would be unrealistically high and poorly planned, much like those of Sidel's young women.[6] Moreover, prior research suggested this poor planning—that is, having "limited knowledge about their future occupations, about educational requirements, or about future demand for these occupations"[7]— would be what stood in their way. Both media accounts and researchers were clear: if only young women could prepare for the future better, they would accomplish more.[8]

Yet to my surprise, I found neither excessive optimism nor poor planning among those I interviewed. They were not Sidel's young women with stars in their eyes and no roadmap to the future. Certainly their aspirations for school and work were lofty: most wanted to complete at least a bachelor's degree and work in professional jobs. However, most of the girls' aspirations were reasonably well planned. They had researched the jobs they hoped to hold and knew the basic steps needed to attain these occupations. Many had reached out to professionals in their intended careers, although this was more successful for some than for others due to class- and race-based differences in both how much access they had to adults knowledgeable in these fields and the willingness of adults to offer help.

Would these plans be enough to successfully move them to adulthood? As I followed the girls into young adulthood, I found that it was much harder for them to enact their plans than anticipated. This was true for all of them, but especially for poor and working-class young women, for two main reasons. First, plans were not enough; they needed extensive guidance to prepare for college and career, beginning (but not ending) with an understanding of the college options that would lead them to the jobs they wished to hold. This was partially due to the vast complexity of the postsecondary system, encompassing a range of college and degree types and often unclear connections between college degrees and jobs. Second, they needed substantial financial and practical assistance to navigate college and job preparation in the transition to adulthood. Middle-class young women typically had both, not only through their parents but also through their communities and, once they reached college, higher education programs. Working-class and poor young women, however, were left largely on their own to navigate college while working long hours in low-wage jobs and providing emotional, practical, and sometimes financial support to their families. Indeed, I found that among the middle class, even poor planning sometimes led to relative "success" in the early transition to adulthood, while good planning among the working class and poor sometimes led to early exits from college and difficulty obtaining a steady job.

In *Best Laid Plans*, I argue that planning alone is not enough. Tangible and intangible resources—including advice and information, economic security, and family stability—also shape young women's plans and their transitions to adulthood and, ultimately, their likelihood of success. These resources provide roadmaps through and buffers along a college and labor market landscape that is complex and uncertain. This does not mean that plans are unimportant but that plans, to bear fruit, need to be forged through class-based resources, require resources to enact, and are constructed in relation to what young people envision for their futures more broadly. In other words, what sociologists call structure, or the sets of resources and schemas (mental maps or frameworks for understanding the world) that enable and constrain action, cannot be fully disentangled from the process of planning and enacting plans.[9] By understanding how planning for the future and attempting to follow through on those plans is enabled and constrained by structural forces, we can better understand the role of both structure and agency (i.e., the capacity to enact one's will) in the transition to adulthood and class mobility.

My argument builds on a sociological literature on how parental social class is replicated across generations, in other words, what is known as the intergenerational transmission of inequality or the tendency for middle-class adolescents to become middle-class adults, working-class adolescents to become working-class adults, and poor adolescents to become poor adults. Prior work has suggested that either working-class and poor young people do not aspire to lofty enough goals or, conversely, their aspirations are too high and poorly planned. I discuss these arguments in the next section and why, I argue, they are incomplete. As I show throughout this book, plans without resources not only fail to produce the desired results, they put young people further behind. In subsequent sections, I situate the need for both planning and resources in light of the increasingly vast and complex higher education landscape and the changing opportunities and constraints for women in the labor market and increasing levels of inequality and uncertainty in the twenty-first century.

THE ROLE OF ASPIRATIONS IN THE INTERGENERATIONAL TRANSMISSION OF SOCIAL CLASS

Over three million high school students graduate each year and continue on to college, work, the military, or other pathways; many take more than one such path at the same time.[10] Some follow the plans they laid in high school, while others deviate. Whichever path they take and however closely they hold on to their high school plans, the first few years out of high school are rife with uncertainty. Suddenly, the dual pillars of school and family shift from obligatory and predictable to voluntary and individualized. Data from the High School Longitudinal Study (HSLS) reveals that in 2012, in the first few months after graduating from high school, 92%

of middle-class girls and 70% of working-class and poor girls planned to enroll or had enrolled in college that fall.[11] Most of these young women also planned to start or had already started working, although this was true of less than half of the middle-class young women (40%) and almost two-thirds (60%) of working-class and poor young women.

Plans to complete a college degree do not always translate into a degree, however. Following a cohort of young men and young women who graduated high school in 2004 and went on to enroll in college, research shows that only slightly over half of first-generation college students completed a degree by eight years after first enrolling, compared to almost three-quarters of those whose parents had attended postsecondary school.[12] Type of degree completion varied as well, with less than one-quarter of first-generation college students completing a bachelor's degree, 13% completing an associate's degree, and 17% completing a certificate. Among those whose parents had at least some college education, over half completed a bachelor's degree, with 8% and 7%, respectively, completing an associate's degree or certificate. Racial differences emerge, too, and are not fully explained by social class.[13] The path to completing a degree, therefore—and particularly a bachelor's degree—is highly unequal by social class and race.

Why do we see these disparities in educational attainment by class background? A classic sociological model of inequality, called the status attainment model, suggests that the social class of one's parents passes on to the social class of children via aspirations. The idea behind this model is that parents' occupational and educational attainment is related to their children's attainment, and that much of this association is explained by "social psychological" factors: parents' and teachers' encouragement to go to college, peers' college plans, and aspirations.[14] Put simply, this model suggests that young people who grow up in higher-status families aspire toward higher-status goals, and young people who grow up in lower-status families aspire toward lower-status goals. These aspirations become plans, leading young people toward disparate educational and, subsequently, occupational attainment.

The status attainment model offers a tidy explanation of how the social class of parents passes down to the social class of their children in the intergenerational transmission of inequality: disadvantaged adolescents are not encouraged to go to college or seek professional jobs, and therefore they are less likely to hold or pursue those goals for themselves. Instead, they pursue the kinds of education and jobs they know: those of their parents. Early research into the process of status attainment led many to believe that to improve poor and working-class young people's chances, we needed to raise their aspirations. Media accounts still imply this, pointing to the role of high aspirations in rags-to-riches stories.

This model of inequality, however, failed to explain how the intergenerational transmission of inequality persisted even as aspirations grew more lofty for adolescents of all social classes, and as aspirations to go to college and pursue semiprofessional or professional careers became nearly universal.[15] Moreover, it failed to explain how aspirations are better predictors of attainment among middle-class and White young people than among working-class and poor and Black young people.[16] Black youth, in particular, have long expressed loftier educational goals than White youth of similar class backgrounds, but these aspirations have not translated into higher (or even equal) attainment.[17] If holding high aspirations is the key to educational and occupational attainment, we would expect everyone with high aspirations to complete college and obtain a good job. But that doesn't happen. Why do aspirations work differently for some groups than for others?

Some attempts to answer this question have focused on the aspirations themselves. Sociologist Roslyn Mickelson argued that Black youths' high aspirations did not match their achievement because, despite holding strong abstract beliefs in the value of education overall, they did not believe in the viability of education for their own and their family members' success.[18] According to Mickelson, this difference between concrete attitudes and generalized beliefs arises because Black young people share in a collective understanding of education as a means of success generally but see those around them—family members, neighbors, and community members—struggle against barriers to success. They therefore express doubt about their ability to follow through on their aspirations, which in turn dampens their academic performance in school. White young people, particularly those in the middle class, in contrast, see evidence that "success in school is rewarded by good jobs, higher salaries, and promotion."[19] Thus, what allows aspirations to become a vehicle for achievement for middle-class Whites is evidence that education has worked for the people they know.

Other scholars have also focused on plans, arguing that if young people plan carefully, align their occupational aspirations with the correct educational plans, and exhibit good decision-making, they should be able to attain their goals.[20] In Schneider and Stevenson's *The Ambitious Generation*, the authors chronicle how mismatches between young people's early, lofty educational and occupational aspirations and their knowledge of how to pursue these goals lead young people to pick colleges and college courses poorly, finishing college but often not obtaining a useful degree—at least for their chosen careers.[21] These researchers concluded that if young people planned better, specifically choosing more realistic career plans and the appropriate amount of schooling needed to fulfill those plans (what they call "aligned ambitions"), then they would be more likely to accomplish their goals. The ability to construct aligned ambitions reflects "planful competence," as sociologist John Clausen calls the ability to make rational goals that will "lead adolescents to make more realistic choices in education, occupation, and marriage."[22] In essence, these scholars argue that having good plans is key to successfully attaining one's goals. This suggests that social class and race disparities in goal attainment might be due to differences in planfulness and holding aligned ambitions.

By focusing on the content of young people's aspirations and plans and not the contexts surrounding their development and pursuit, however, these arguments lend too much power to individual agency and too little to how structures—both schema and resources—shape the status attainment process. This does not mean that we must ignore the ways individual actions matter; however, it does suggest that by uncovering the structures that enable some actions and constrain others, we can see the full extent of young people's agency. It is possible to be *planful*—to put in the work needed to plan for future schooling and careers—and still not have all the "right" information or resources to put those plans in motion. Young women's plans for the future are molded by both the world as it is and the world as they see it; they may hold ambitious plans to go to college and graduate school, eventually obtaining a professional job, but they must also grapple with questions of where to go to college and how to fund this goal. Gathering information to answer these questions and constructing and enacting a plan requires substantial resources, including information and money, neither of which is plentifully available to those in the working class or who are poor. Their pursuit of their goals, too, depends both on their own persistence and the degree to which institutions reward, deter, or even punish this persistence.

NAVIGATING THE HIGHER EDUCATION LANDSCAPE

Young people who aspire to white collar and professional occupations must complete a college degree. Yet there is a dizzying array of pathways possible under the "college" designation. The postsecondary system comprises a landscape that young people must understand in order to plan for. There are colleges (primarily but not entirely undergraduate serving) and universities (including both undergraduate and robust graduate offerings). Some colleges offer only associate's degrees and postsecondary certificates or only bachelor's degrees, while others offer a range of degrees. There are public institutions (funded in part by states and thus costing less for in-state residents) and private institutions (not directly funded by states and thus carrying higher tuition).[23] There are not-for-profit colleges and universities, which may be either public or private but do not have profit as a motive, and there are for-profit colleges and universities, which aim to earn profit for shareholders.[24] Some of these for-profit institutions are online schools, while others are not, and still others are hybrid online and in-person. Many not-for-profit colleges and universities also offer online learning, whether for a segment of their class offerings or for entire programs, in order to accommodate working students and those with family responsibilities, a trend that will likely increase in the wake of the coronavirus pandemic. Some programs these institutions offer are accredited, meaning that they have been certified by state or federal agencies as comprising the appropriate training for a particular career or providing a comprehensive liberal arts education, whereas others are unaccredited programs, which have not been reviewed or have not been approved by any larger government agency.

Best Laid Plans shows how the diversity of the higher education landscape matters for both young people's planning and their pursuit of those plans. The complexity of this landscape makes careful planning necessary and makes the information young people receive key to that planning.

And when these young women move into early adulthood, the multiple types of institutions and programs in which they enroll create vastly different contexts for how successfully they pursue their goals. Within many large universities, there are colleges and programs that admit smaller, selective groups of students. Some of these are honors programs while others offer preprofessional training, such as health or business programs. These smaller, internal programs can be worlds unto themselves, offering students significantly greater resources, access to more sought-after courses, tailored advising, internship opportunities, and daily contact with likeminded peers.[25] Young women admitted to these programs, or tracks, within these colleges are provided with support to move them toward their career goals. Others, whether at for-profit institutions or more traditional college environments, are left to fend for themselves without adequate institutional support.

These for-profit and less selective not-for-profit institutions, which rely more on student tuition to offset costs than do selective colleges and universities, are dependent on selling their product (educational degrees) directly to students.[26] This creates incentives to produce marketable programs for entering students but little motivation to invest in retention programs, which are expensive and which move students from less costly (to the institution) introductory classes to more costly advanced courses.[27] Taken together, the increasing reliance on student tuition, the responsiveness to market forces, and the need to keep the cost per student low create incentives for colleges to produce professionally oriented certificate and associate's degree programs that attract students but do not require extensive expenditure on the part of the college.[28] Unfortunately, many of these programs do not translate into occupations that are worth the investment even when they are completed. Although a college degree is the best bet for obtaining full-time, well-paid work, many college graduates still struggle to secure these "good jobs."[29] This is particularly, but not exclusively, true for for-profit colleges that market to young people desperate for credentials that will improve their chances of finding a good job, yet with little time or money to pursue such a degree.[30] These for-profit institutions are expensive relative to comparable public not-for-profit colleges, and graduates do not see the same income returns as those who complete their schooling at not-for-profit institutions.[31]

Not only do some degrees not pay off, but many students do not complete the postsecondary degrees and certificates they pursue, particularly when their institutions do not provide adequate retention programs. Although college enrollments have risen quickly over the past five decades, college completion rates have not increased much, especially among low-income students.[32] The stakes of not completing college are high for young people, particularly those from working-class and poor families. College students have increasingly relied on student loans to pay their way in recent decades.[33] For those who do not complete a degree, obtaining stable and high enough paying work to pay down their student debt is difficult.[34] Higher education, therefore, creates an obstacle course for many young people; getting through this obstacle course offers a likely but not guaranteed reward, while anything less may set them back further than not enrolling at all.

As we will see in this book, aspirations can lead working-class and poor young women into postsecondary programs that promise more than they deliver and leave many in debt without a degree. In other words, *aspirations provide the fodder for the growth of postsecondary institutions*, unconstrained by government oversight. Well-laid plans do not provide insurance against this because even well thought-out and informed planning can come undone when young women receive little institutional or financial support while in college. Needing to work long hours, struggling on their own to meet coursework demands, and feeling obligated to provide care for family members, working-class and poor young women are stretched thin between obligations to school, work, and family.

PLANNING FOR THE FUTURE IN AN AGE OF UNCERTAINTY

The social and economic conditions in which young people grow up also shape their attitudes toward the future.[35] The young women I spoke to were more cautious than Sidel's young women, both in their assumptions about their role in family life and in their elevation of jobs that provided stability; middle-class families, in particular, encouraged their daughters to prioritize occupational stability and flexibility. Working-class and poor girls also expressed a desire for stability, in response to what they saw in their own families: the weight of insecure work, mounting bills, and interpersonal tensions. We can better understand the differences between the goals of the girls I met and the goals Sidel's young women held when we compare the times in which they lived. Sidel's young women entered adulthood on a wave of expanded opportunities for women in the economic, political, and social spheres; when wage inequality—though rising—was low relative to today;[36] and when a college degree offered a ticket into the middle class.[37] In contrast, the young women I interviewed entered the transition to adulthood following the Great Recession, when economic inequality was at its height, when a college degree was no longer an all-but guarantee of a stable future, and after the "gender revolution" that started in the 1960s had stalled in the late 1980s and early 1990s.[38]

Many of Sidel's young women were buoyed by the enormous changes that had swept the country over the preceding decades. As early as 1976, *Time* magazine declared American women "Man of the Year" for 1975, stating, "They have arrived like a new immigrant wave in male America. They may be cops, judges, military officers, telephone linemen, cab drivers, pipefitters, editors, business executives—or mothers and housewives. . . . The belief that women are entitled to truly equal social and professional rights has spread far and deep into the country." The *Time* article depicted women as finally achieving equal status with men. Indeed, between 1960 and 1990, the number of women participating in the paid labor force more than doubled, with 35% of women employed at the beginning of that period and 54% employed at its close.[39] This movement of women into the labor market rapidly changed the face of the occupational structure; women entered into male-dominated professions like law, business, and medicine at an accelerated pace.[40] Women's wages rose, too, relative to men's, narrowing the wage gap between men and women by 20 percentage points between 1975 and 1993.[41] Women also made tremendous strides in educational attainment; they only earned 35% of all bachelor's degrees in 1960 but surpassed men in this marker of attainment by 1982.[42]

Women gained bodily autonomy and civil liberties as well. The Federal Drug Administration first approved the use of birth control pills in 1960, giving women greater control over their sexual and reproductive activities. The Presidential Commission on Women, led by former first lady Eleanor Roosevelt, helped to pass the Equal Pay Act in 1964.[43] That same year, the Civil Rights Act, which prohibited discrimination on the basis of sex in addition to race, ethnicity, and national origin, was passed.[44] The 1970s saw the passage of the nation's first no-fault divorce law in California[45] and the Equal Credit Opportunity Act, which prevented creditors from discriminating "on the basis of race, color, religion, national origin, sex, marital status, or age."[46] When applying for credit, a woman could no longer be asked for a male cosignatory, have her income or employment discounted, or be asked about her marital status or childbearing plans. In the courts, women won expanded employment protections[47] and the right to have an abortion.[48] In sum, from 1960 through 1989, women's status in the economic, social, and political spheres grew markedly. This could be seen both in measurable advancements, such as labor force data and the passage of bills, and in an ethos of optimism around women's place in the world.

This wave of expanded opportunity, however, did not last. Although women's educational attainment continued to grow relative to men's, their occupational and economic status vis-à-vis men plateaued. Within postsecondary institutions, women had been breaking barriers by increasingly majoring in male-dominated fields such as engineering, chemistry, and economics throughout the 1970s and 1980s, yet this slowed to a crawl after the late 1980s, leaving gender segregation in college majors nearly unchanged. Indeed, the proportion of women majoring in the physical sciences, math, and engineering did not change much for decades, and actually declined between 2000 and 2010.[49] In turn, the movement of women into male-dominated jobs and of men into female-dominated jobs decelerated.[50] The increase of women in the paid workforce also stalled after 1990, leaving the female employment rate mostly flat for the last thirty years.[51]

These fluctuations in women's status occurred alongside and, in part, were spurred along by, widespread political, social, and economic changes in the United States. Income inequality rose as a result of political and institutional forces that benefited college-educated workers and drove down wages among the working class.[52] Beginning in the 1970s, jobs that had offered many working-class families a chance at the American Dream— secure, unionized, highly paid industry jobs—began to disappear.[53] At the same time, the service sector—comprised of jobs that involved caring for others (e.g., home health aides, childcare workers, cleaners)—grew.[54] This expansion of work in traditionally female-dominated occupations increased the demand for female labor, yet these jobs were less often unionized than work in manufacturing had been and were poorly paid.[55] The 1980s also ushered in a conservative era in which employers and politicians sought and secured legislation to weaken pro-union labor laws.[56] These economic and political changes had two important repercussions for those in the working class: jobs were both less well paid than in the past and less stable. Together, expanding (if low-paid) labor market opportunities for women alongside contracting employment conditions and wages for men created conditions in which women's work was a crucial component of the family economy.

Alongside labor market changes that squeezed working-class family incomes, rising demands for workers with technological skills rewarded workers at the higher end of the educational distribution.[57] As a result, wages in the United States polarized, leaving many workers struggling to make ends meet while those at the top of the income distribution amassed larger fortunes than ever before. Even college-educated workers were not protected from this job polarization, with some struggling to secure jobs with middle-class wages.[58] These labor market changes expanded the gulf between the upper and upper-middle class and the working class and poor.[59] Changes to the family compounded these inequalities.[60] Rates of divorce and nonmarital childbearing left many working-class and poor women raising children alone on their meagre and unstable incomes while higher-earning and college-educated women were more likely to marry and to marry men who were similarly educated and well paid.[61] The size and stability of the middle class steadily eroded, leaving many families struggling.[62] The American Dream became more and more difficult to attain.

Not only has the United States become more unequal, but it has also become riskier for individuals and families. College is no longer the insurance policy it once was; particularly for those who are from low-income families and take out loans, the wage benefits of some college degrees may be minimal or even negative.[63] And according to Yale political science professor Jacob Hacker, changes in public policy and the labor market have shifted risk onto workers by offering fewer job and wage protections and demanding more work.[64] Employers are increasingly taking advantage of labor market flexibility by hiring part-time and contingent staff, making use of layoffs, or using freelance labor, which is typically less regulated.[65] Although some forms of flexible work, such as telecommuting and high-demand freelancing, can be a boon to well-educated workers who can demand high wages, lower-wage workers are disadvantaged by these practices. Workers can be easily disposed of by corporations, and the unemployed tend to blame themselves rather than their former employers.[66] Furthermore, these changes in the value of a college degree and work have only accelerated since the Great Recession.[67]

As sociologist Richard Settersten has observed, "Times of rapid social change can suddenly alter the landscape that young people are navigating and the possibilities that lay in front of them."[68] Social scientists have shown how increasing instability and inequality have affected families and individuals, demonstrating how even the wealthy feel intense pressure to protect their children from downward mobility,[69] how working-class young adults have constructed new markers of achievement in the absence of attaining "traditional" markers of adulthood,[70] and how the working class and poor hustle to survive in an untenable context.[71] Research focusing on college-age young adults has also uncovered the kinds of structural barriers that stand in the way of entering college and completing a college degree. Work by Ranita Ray, for example, shows how even poor youth who make all the "right" choices—by avoiding drugs, violence, and early parenthood—still face very real barriers to success due to poverty itself.[72] Laura Hamilton and Anthony Jack have also shown how elite colleges and universities are oriented toward wealthy students at the expense of poor, working-class, and even middle-class students.[73]

This book builds on this prior work by showing how, together, notions of gendered responsibilities, fears of economic insecurity, and the resources garnered through social ties shape young women's plans for the future and attempts to follow through on these plans. Although I first interviewed them during the crash of the market in the fall of 2008, I do not argue that these young women were aware of rising inequality or the Great Recession as we know it in retrospect; they were not. Instead, the young women responded to the ways the recessionary period impacted their families. Many middle-class young women received messages from adults they knew to prioritize well-paid work that could be modified around family life (whether or not this flexibility actually existed in the occupations they identified). Working-class and poor young women, and some in the middle class, saw more viscerally the repercussions of the labor market on their families and constructed their plans in response. Furthermore, in following these young women over time, I demonstrate how social mobility and social class replication operate in the early transition to adulthood as young women navigate school, work, and family and find their plans enabled, stalled, or blocked. I find that inequality between and within postsecondary educational institutions produces substantial differences in institutional support. These differences in institutional support, coupled with differing levels of labor market attachment and demands from family members, produce vastly different young adult lives and future prospects for maintaining or improving class standing.

THIS STUDY

The data for this book comes from two waves of in-depth, semistructured interviews conducted with young women from Glenbrook and Kensington, two mid-sized towns in the East North Central region of the United States, a region overlapping with most of the "rust belt" states that were hit hard by the decline of manufacturing over the later twentieth century. Sixty-one junior and senior high school girls were interviewed in the first wave, which took place in the fall of 2008, just as the Great Recession was unfolding across America and in many of the girls' homes as well, when parents or other family members lost their jobs. Five to six years later, in 2013 and 2014, I reinterviewed 41 of these young women to understand how their lives had unfolded and their plans had changed or remained the same.[74] At this point, they were between the ages of 21 and 24 (see the methodological appendix for more detail).

I selected young women who aspired to work in the health field in order to minimize other forms of variation. This allowed me to more easily compare the young women to one another and to compare their educational aspirations to the education standards that these jobs demand. A high proportion of young women across the country were expressing an interest in the health field, making it by far the largest occupational sector of interest for young women of high school age at the time.[75] And because the health field was (and still is) booming, getting a job primarily requires the right credentials and experience.[76] Thus, unlike sectors in which the labor market is tight and hopeful entrants must rely on a prestigious set of social connections and luck in addition to hard work and credentials to land employment (e.g., the arts, academia), following young women who plan to enter the health field allows us to see how planning matters or does not matter in a field many young people can realistically expect to enter.

The young women I interviewed attended either Glenbrook High School or Kensington High School, each of which served as the only public high school in its town.[77] Both towns are politically and culturally conservative. Residents of Glenbrook and Kensington reliably vote for Republicans in national, state, and local elections, and Christianity is the dominant religious orientation. However, Glenbrook, a primarily working-class town, is a former manufacturing town that had suffered some population losses in recent decades due to job scarcity, whereas Kensington, a middle-class suburb of a mid-sized city, had recovered from the loss of a major manufacturing plant in the 1980s and is thriving. I provide some descriptive statistics for these towns, alongside national averages, in table 1.[78]

Glenbrook and Kensington High Schools reflected these town differences. Glenbrook High School was older, with fewer resources, and its students were lower performing than those at Kensington High School. Despite these differences, it would be overly simplistic to describe students at Glenbrook as disadvantaged and at Kensington as privileged. Both schools educated students from a variety of class backgrounds, from poor to upper middle class, and I interviewed students from a range of class backgrounds at both schools. At Glenbrook, I interviewed eight middle-class girls, one of whom was upper middle class; 12 working-class girls; and ten poor girls. At Kensington, I interviewed 17 middle-class girls, five of whom were upper middle class; 13 working-class girls; and one poor girl. Both schools and their towns have some racial diversity but are Whiter (82%) than the nation overall. To achieve greater racial diversity in my samples, I purposely overselected Black young women to interview. Ultimately, I interviewed 19 Black or self-identified Black and White biracial girls, 39 White girls, and 3 Latina or self-identified Hispanic and White girls.

Table 1 Aggregate Statistics for Glenbrook, Kensington, and the United States, 2007–2009

	Glenbrook	Kensington	United States
Population	50,000+	42,000+	—
Race/ethnicity			
Black	12%	11%	12.1%
Hispanic	2%	4%	15.4%
Other	4%	3%	7.0%
White	82%	82%	65.4%
Finances (households)			
Median household income	$37,000	$55,500	$51,369
Poverty			
Families below poverty line	15%	5%	9.9%
Families with children below poverty line	28%	8%	15.5%
Employment status (age 16+)			
Employed	54%	64%	59.9%
Unemployed	6%	4%	4.9%
Educational attainment (age 25+)			
Less than high school degree	19%	16%	15.1%
High school degree/GED	40%	34%	29.0%
Some college/associate's degree	27%	27%	28.2%
BA/BS degree or higher	14%	22%	27.8%
Marital status (women, age 15+)			
Never married	26%	26%	28.2%
Married	43%	48%	47.8%
Separated/divorced/widowed	31%	26%	24.0%
Household units vacant	14%	8%	12.4%
Foreign-born persons	3%	8%	12.5%

SOURCE: American Community Survey 2007–2009.
Numbers in the table are rounded to obscure the towns' identities.

CLASS, RACE, AND GENDER

This book considers how plans are constructed, pursued, and amended among a cohort of primarily Black and White middle-class, working-class, and poor young women. These interlocking class, race, and gender identities all matter for shaping the planning and attainment process, in ways that are visible in this book and that are not. Because my focus is on explaining the intergenerational transmission of inequality among White and Black young women, the explanations contained herein focus most predominantly—but not exclusively—on social class background. We will see the role of race and gender in constructing plans most clearly among high school–aged girls, as they are gently pushed to consider female-dominated occupations and as middle-class White young women are spontaneously offered information and resources useful for planning by both close ties and acquaintances, while middle-class Black young women and their families find that the resources available to them through social ties are much more limited.

As these young women graduate high school and enroll in higher education, enter the labor force, and form families, their paths diverge, and identifying the ways that gender, and particularly race, intercede is more difficult. This does not mean that gender and race do not matter in this period of the life course. Copious research tells us that women earn lower wages than men, particularly after becoming mothers.[79] Young women also endure harassment and sexual violence in multiple settings, which impacts their mental and physical health and sense of safety.[80] And these barriers are even greater for Black young women than for White young women. Most colleges are predominantly White (or "predominantly White institutions," referred to as PWI), which can be alienating spaces for Black students to navigate. Discrimination in the labor market impacts Black women in ways that are distinct from White women (and Black men).[81] And Black women face a different set of calculations than White women for both working and raising children once they are mothers.[82] By focusing on the role of resources via class background and institutional affiliation, my aim is not to erase other important mechanisms of inequality but rather to add to our understanding of the mechanisms by which social class origins become social class destinations for Black and White young women.

OVERVIEW

If the media, "dress for success" books, and attainment scholars are correct, projecting confidence and establishing ambitious and aligned future plans should be sufficient for young people to successfully navigate the transition to adulthood. Yet in an era of social and economic upheaval, both the free market and changing family forms make planning for and pursuing goals labyrinthine; the higher education landscape is vast and highly stratified, workplaces offer few protections to employees, and families both provide support for and make demands on young people. *Best Laid Plans* provides an in-depth look at high school girls' imagined futures for college, work, and family life and follows them as they enroll in school, obtain jobs, and start their own families. What we find in following these young women is that most middle-class, working-class, and poor girls worked hard to construct reasonable plans for the future while they were in high school. The efficacy of good plans in predicting attainment depends, however, on a system that rewards such planning. Instead, differences in institutional and interpersonal resources by class, and within the middle class by race, shaped young women's pathways out of high school and into school, work, and family lives. For many young women with good plans but without the resources to support their plans, the pathway through higher education became a cycle of accruing more debt but not a degree. Under these conditions, class origins often become class destinations despite young women's best efforts.

This book is divided into two parts. Part I, consisting of chapters 1 through 3, focuses on the girls' aspirations and plans for work, school, and family life based on the first round of interviews with them when they were in high school. Chapter 1 outlines both similarities and differences by class in the girls' school, work, and family aspirations. On the surface, these aspirations appeared uniform; nearly all aspired toward a middle-class future with a college degree, good job, and marriage and children. However, key differences emerged by class in how they articulated their plans for the future. Middle-class girls aspired toward what I call *packaged futures*: the futures they hoped for replicated the home life they knew, making the future seem familiar and the pathway clear. Working-class and poor young women aspired toward the same outcomes in their own lives. Yet for them these were what I call *repackaged futures*, constructed not so much from their own experiences but from what they saw around them in the media, their extended families, and their communities.

Chapters 2 and 3 focus on how high school girls construct plans for the future, how they seek out and receive information about their hoped-for futures and how they make plans to achieve these goals. I argue that most middle-class girls (chapter 2) and working-class and poor girls (chapter 3) showed planfulness by gathering information and making reasonable plans for their school and work goals. However, differences in class-based and, within the middle class, race-based, resources translated into unequal preparation for the future among middle-class compared to working-class and poor girls, and between middle-class White and middle-class Black girls. These differences in resources—that is, the information, advice, and opportunities available for planning—contributed to the girls' unequal preparation for the future. In these chapters, I also discuss how assumptions about gendered tasks and romantic relationships informed these girls' desires to be economically self-sufficient before cohabitation or marriage.

Part II of this book catches up with many of these high school girls, now young women in their early to mid-twenties, to take stock of how their high school plans translated into their early adulthood experiences of school, work, and family. Chapter 4 outlines the three pathways these young women took in their transition to adulthood: some were *on track* to fulfill their plans, others were barely *holding on* to their hopes of moving toward a middle-class future, while still others were *navigating rough seas* amid fraught family ties and insecure attachments to school and work. It delineates each of these pathways and how the young women ended up on these pathways. Social class is sticky, such that many middle-class young women were in the on track group, many poor young women were in the navigating rough seas group, and working-class young women were more spread out but often in the holding on group.

Chapters 5, 6, and 7 follow the young women who are on track, holding on, and navigating rough seas, respectively. On track young women had enrolled in college after high school and stayed enrolled and were now on their way to finishing (or had finished) bachelor's degrees. These young women were often ensconced in college programs that operated like tracks and helped keep them progressing toward a career path, moving them smoothly from high school student to credentialed professional with remarkable efficiency. Those who were holding on, on the other hand, found themselves caught between their goals for college, a good job, and middle-class stability and the realities of school, work, and family commitments that created roadblocks to their success. These young women had substantially lowered their goals but continued to work toward post-secondary credentials and stable employment. Finally, young women navigating rough seas had drifted far from their high school goals and were struggling to find work, to return to school, and to gain an economic foothold. Most of these young women would be categorized as "disconnected youth" by researchers, defined as youth between the ages of 16 and 24 who are neither enrolled in school full-time nor employed.[83] Although most planned to enroll or reenroll in college or vocational training and to secure steady work, they were stymied by family responsibilities and numerous health and personal setbacks—what sociologists Clawson and Gerstel refer to as life's "normal unpredictable" events, which are much more frequent and more difficult to handle in contexts where resources are low.[84]

In the conclusion, I return to the questions that motivate this book: how do plans matter, how does uncertainty shape the transition to adulthood today, how is intergenerational mobility conditioned by class-based resources, and how do notions of gender frame young women's imagined futures and present obligations?[85] The stories in this book, of hopes and plans, opportunities and constraints, provide answers to and elaborations on these questions. What we learn, most of all, is that we must provide structural opportunities for all young women to thrive—whether they go to college or not, work or stay home to care for children, and follow a path to a professional career or not.

PART I Reconsidering Aspirations

1 High School Girls' Plans

Much has been made, in social science literature and media, of the importance of aspirations and their role in stratifying young people's circumstances.[1] There is the assumption that if we can raise poor and working-class young people's goals, then they will rise above their class origins. Indeed, in casual conversations and presentations, I'm often asked what would be different if disadvantaged young people dreamed bigger or focused their sights on college.[2] At the same time, other scholars have worried that young people are overly ambitious and that they do not construct reasonable plans to achieve their lofty career aspirations.[3] The solution, they argue, is that young people should plan better, matching their career ambitions to appropriate educational credentials.

The young women I interviewed held similar goals whether they were in the middle class or working class or were poor. When describing the futures they saw for themselves, they depicted the prototypical middle-class life. They all wanted a good education, career stability, and a happy family. Furthermore, they saw these goals as interconnected. Their educational aspirations were oriented toward their occupational goals, and their family and work aspirations were frequently shifted to accommodate one or the other. They saw education, work, and family as elements of a set which, if put together correctly and in the right order, would comprise an idyllic future. All three aspirational domains were tied to a vision of themselves in the future, typically envisioned as a strong, stable family life supported by work and community. Ideally, many hoped to have the flexibility to take time off from work or at least work fewer hours in order to take care of their children.

In this chapter, I summarize middle-class girls' and working-class and poor girls' school, work, and family aspirations, highlighting both the commonalities between them and some of the differences. In the chapters that follow, I focus separately on how these middle-class girls (see chapter 2) and working-class and poor girls (see chapter 3) planned for the future. As I discuss in chapter 3, I describe working-class and poor girls together because their experiences of planning for the future and the barriers they faced in doing so were very similar.

HOW MIDDLE-CLASS, WORKING-CLASS, AND POOR GIRLS ENVISIONED THEIR SCHOOL, WORK, AND FAMILY FUTURES

When I sat down with 16-, 17-, and 18-year-old girls in the fall of 2008, I asked each of them: "What do you think your life will look like when you are 30 years old?" Their responses were strikingly similar and primarily focused on education, careers, family, and homeownership.

KATHLEEN: I want to own my own home. I guess be married, and since I want four kids . . . I want my kids after I get out of school, and after I do my [medical] internship.

BETHANIE: I'm going to be out of school. I'm going to have a good career, and maybe be married. . . . Maybe I'll have kids. Or adopt.

ISABEL: I would like to be married, have two kids, working, church, a good husband—a good husband who is Christian.

ALLISON: I think I will be married [and] have a kid. . . . I'll be successful in my job. . . . And I think I will have a nice house, a nice car, and I will be very stabilized.

JEAN: I'll have my doctorate. I'll have a job, be married, have a house and a car.

ALICE: Hopefully, I'll have one or two kids. I'll be married, have a big house, do what I like and have time for things.

These sentiments—quoted from middle-class and poor; White, Black, and Hispanic; straight and queer young women—were echoed in numerous interviews. Deviations occurred, of course, particularly in the family realm. Some young women did not want to have children or marry, wanted more or fewer children, or were unsure of their family plans. Yet the elements remained the same: a home, family, career, and stability.

Pathways to these imagined futures were also similar across social class. All the young women I spoke to anticipated attending college and obtaining at least a highly skilled white-collar job. Ten young women aspired to complete a two-year college degree, compared to seventeen who wanted to complete a four-year degree, and twenty-five who anticipated finishing graduate or professional schooling. The remaining nine wanted to attend college but either did not state a specific degree or were undecided. Similarly, 25 of the 61 young women I interviewed aspired to work in a "high professional" career (e.g., doctor, physical therapist), and 16 aspired to a "low professional" career (e.g., nurse). Seven aspired to work in skilled technical fields (e.g., respiratory therapist) and thirteen aspired to occupations in more than one category or were undecided on their exact goal. No one I interviewed aspired to a job that did not require at least some postsecondary training. There were some differences by social class; more working-class and poor girls aspired toward fewer years of college and skilled or low professional occupations, whereas middle-class girls mostly aspired to attend graduate or professional schooling, and more aspired to work in high professional careers. In general, however, all of them, whether from middle-class, working-class, or poor backgrounds, aspired to jobs that required a college education and that would garner stable incomes.

The 16- through 18-year-olds I interviewed also expressed a considerable degree of uniformity when asked to select major events they hoped would occur in their early lives and the order in which they hoped these events would occur.[4] Most aspired to leave their parents' home when they were 18 and go to college, graduating at age 22, and attend graduate or professional school at some point in their early to mid-twenties. Young women from both the middle class and working class and poor anticipated marrying (either a man or woman), buying a house, and starting to have children in rapid succession.[5] Not all girls aspired to marry and have children, but most did. Even those with less typical family goals still embraced family as an important part of their lives, including one young woman who said, "It means a lot to me, the family that I have. . . . I don't think I could ever be away from my cousins, and uncles, and stuff." Most anticipated having children within the fairly narrow five-year window between ages 25 and 30. Very few anticipated marrying before they had completed college. Overall, there was remarkable uniformity in aspirations, with the girls' early through mid-twenties reserved for full-time study, followed shortly by entry into work, romantic relationships, marriage, homeownership, and children.

There were some differences in the anticipated timing of certain life events, however, reflecting what scholars have observed regarding working-class and poor young people taking on more responsibilities at younger ages and feeling subjectively older compared to middle-class young people.[6] These differences were driven primarily by White working-class and poor girls. On average, White working-class and poor girls said they would start working at age 19, compared to age 22 for Black working-class and poor girls, 23 for White middle-class girls, and 24 for Black middle-class girls.[7] White working-class and poor girls also anticipated moving in with their significant others two years earlier than middle-class girls of either race and three years earlier than Black working-class or poor girls, with engagement occurring around the same time. Working-class and poor girls anticipated longer engagements than middle-class girls did, by about a year, and therefore anticipated marrying and having children at the same time, on average, as middle-class girls within both racial groups.[8] Black girls anticipated marrying and having children at slightly older ages than White girls within each social class grouping, however. Although there were few differences in the timing of education and home buying by social class, within each social class, Black girls anticipated ending schooling and buying homes later than White girls did. Finally, while most girls anticipated having children between the ages of 25 and 30, five of the six who anticipated having children earlier, including one who was already pregnant, were working class and poor. The only middle-class girl who anticipated this timeline was Mormon.

As we will see in coming chapters, the young women justified these timelines in relation to idealized connections between work and family life. They hoped to complete schooling and establish themselves in a career before marrying and having children, although their reasoning for doing so varied by social class background and lived experience.

ENVISIONING A (RE)PACKAGED FUTURE

Sociological research on adolescent aspirations often focuses on one aspirational domain at a time: educational aspirations, occupational aspirations, or family aspirations. This approach is puzzling, because copious research shows that these domains are interdependent throughout the adult life course. Educational attainment strongly predicts occupational attainment and earnings as well as cohabiting, marital, and childbearing outcomes.[9] In addition, having children lowers women's labor market participation and income in the aggregate.[10] So why not assume that young people also see these domains as interdependent?[11]

The young women I interviewed spoke about their plans in concert with one another. In fact, they showed a surprising degree of awareness that school, work, and family life were interconnected. Their educational aspirations were entwined with their occupational goals, and they discussed their family and work goals in light of each other, sometimes amending one to facilitate the other. All three aspirational domains were also tied to a vision of themselves in the future that typically envisioned a strong, stable family life supported by work and community.

Although this vision of the future as interconnected across school, work, and family domains was expressed by girls of all class backgrounds, class differences emerged in the way the girls constructed these imagined futures and in how they planned to achieve them. Middle-class girls envisioned packaged futures, as I call them, whereas working-class and poor girls imagined what I refer to as repackaged futures. The packaged futures middle-class girls aspired toward were replications of their current lives, with minor changes. These girls had ready examples of what their futures would look like within their own families, making their aspirations a package that could be handed down to them. And they were well supported in these goals, with adults around them who had forged these paths before them. This made the way clearer and more comfortable; not only was college a "given," but the steps to get into and attend college were well understood. Working-class and poor girls, on the other hand, looked ahead to repackaged futures. They dreamed of the homes, workplaces, and educational institutions and sometimes families they had seen on television or heard of at school but had not experienced. In planning for their futures, they took elements of their own lives (sometimes pieces they wanted to replicate and sometimes as examples of what they did not want) and the lives of others and arranged the pieces, "repackaging" them, to make a coherent whole. Yet the details of how to get to these futures were less clear to them, making planning a more difficult task. Although most working-class and poor young women I spoke to worked actively to piece together a plan, they had to rely on limited information. As we will see in the coming chapters, social class mattered less for what the girls aspired to and the work they put into planning than it did for the contexts in which they planned—the help they received from others, the stressors they encountered in their daily lives, and the support they received through institutions—which ultimately shaped those plans and the resources they had for following through on their plans.

2 Anticipating a Packaged Future

INTERVIEWER: Have you talked to anyone about your plans
to go to college?

CASSIE: Everyone. Everyone asks me about it.

INTERVIEWER: Why do you think they ask?

CASSIE: They know I want to be something.

Cassie was a small, stocky, middle-class White 16-year-old brimming with energy. I first met her before she was selected for an interview, when she volunteered to help me find a classroom as I wandered the hallways at Kensington High School. Then, as during the interview, Cassie spoke quickly, verbosely, and with obvious confidence. As we spoke while sitting on two folding chairs in the hallway outside her music classroom, she sat cross-legged, shoes slipping on and off as we talked.

Cassie aspired to a career as a nurse anesthetist, a job requiring a master of science in nursing degree and paying, on average, $160,000 a year, a sum higher than her father's $140,000 salary as a computer programmer.[1] Like most middle-class young women, she had detailed plans for pursuing her goal. Everything in her life supported a presumption of future success; now a high school junior, she was enrolled in mostly honors courses, maintained a 3.5 grade point average, and participated in elite extracurricular activities. Regarding the latter, she had been admitted to her school's award-winning audition-only show choir; the Tri-M Music Honors Society, an honors group for chorus, band, and orchestra students; and the Connect Cultures program, which selected 80 students from the region to travel abroad for a month in the summer. The program chose

31

the "fastest and brightest . . . [t]hey look for risk-takers, for people who are adventurous," although she acknowledged that selecting participants "is mostly about whether you can afford it."

When asked to list adults she felt close to or could turn to for advice, Cassie had more than a soccer team's roster comprising 12 adults: family members, school faculty and administration, her doctor, and others in the community.[2] This group included her parents, who were still married, were college educated, and worked in professional jobs. More importantly, these adults offered her concrete advice and information about how to position herself in a future career. In short, Cassie was a middle-class young woman with a strong support network and a seemingly bright future ahead, like most of the middle-class young women I interviewed.

.   .   .   .   .

There is no universally agreed upon definition of *middle class* in the United States. Self-identification of middle-class status has historically been high, with over 60% of Americans defining their class status in this way, though this has decreased in recent years to just half of all Americans.[3] Self-identification, of course, may be related to one's income, education, work, neighborhood, or subjective experience. Sociologists also have different definitions of social class, usually drawing on some combination of education, occupation, income, and income-to-needs measures.[4] I classified young women as members of the middle class if at least one parent worked in white-collar, managerial, or professional jobs and had attended, and usually completed, college.[5] A total of 25 young women fit this criterion (see table 2).

The label *middle class* included young women in a range of family circumstances, from those whose two biological, married parents had obtained graduate degrees and worked in professional occupations to those who lived with a single college-educated parent working in a managerial position. What most of these young women shared, however, was access to resources that helped prepare them to make the transition to adulthood. These resources included both economic security based on family income—which in turn produced household and family stability—and access to information and career-building activities through adults they

Table 2 Composition of Middle-Class High School Girls in Sample

	White Middle-Class[a] (N = 14)	Black Middle-Class[b] (N = 11)
Family structure		
Biological/adoptive parents	9	1
Stepfamily or joint custody	5	3
Single parent or extended family	0	7
Educational aspiration		
Graduate/professional schooling	8	8
Four-year college degree	5	2
Two-year college degree	1	0
College (vague or undecided)	0	1
Occupational aspiration[c]		
High professional	7	8
Low professional	4	2
Skilled technician	0	0
Mixed/unclear	3	1
Social ties		
Mean number	9.3	7.0
Majority college educated	13	9
Know someone in desired occupation	10	6

NOTE: Information in the table was compiled in fall 2008 from surveys completed prior to sample selection (racial/ethnic identification and aspirations) and from interviews (aspirations, family composition, and social ties).
[a] Includes one biracial Latina and White participant.
[b] Includes two biracial Black and White participants.
[c] Examples: high professional = doctor, veterinarian; low professional = nurse, health teacher; skilled technician = vet tech/assistant, respiratory therapist; mixed/unclear = two or more occupations that fall into multiple categories.

knew. Networks of adults, most centrally their parents, supported these young women emotionally, practically, and financially. These networks informed and shaped the girls' plans for the future and offered them the confidence that others believed in them. They were sheltered from outside responsibilities; few mentioned household chores or obligations to family members such as caring for younger siblings or contributing to the household income, and those who worked for pay did so at a moderate intensity that was easily balanced with schoolwork and extracurricular activities. This is not to suggest that these young women had not faced hardships. Cassie, for example, had undergone fourteen surgeries in her young life to correct abnormalities in her ear and nose. Her mother struggled with a chronic illness for several years, although she had stabilized since Cassie was in high school. Few lives are seamless. Yet the privileges of class allowed these young women's families and social networks to smooth over the difficulties, maintaining stability in the face of hardships.

In interviews with middle-class girls about their lives, their future plans, and the adults they felt close to, five themes emerged. First, middle-class young women aspired toward *packaged futures*, consisting of goals for high educational and occupational attainment and a middle-class family lifestyle that typically mimicked the one they grew up in. Second, *packaged futures* incorporated a period of financial independence before marriage that was primarily expressed as a way to show that they could be independent before starting a family and sometimes also as an insurance policy against the risk of depending on a spouse. Third, these young women were strongly supported by a network of ties—including parents, schoolteachers and administrators, friends' parents, parents' friends, church co-congregants, neighbors, and other adults they knew—that recognized their talents and interests and offered them encouragement, advice, and career-building opportunities for planning for the future. These were forms of *social capital*: resources transmitted through relationships with other people and institutions that can be further invested for personal gain.[6] Fourth, racial differences stratified the middle-class sample. Black young women had access to fewer highly educated, career professional ties than White young women and were less often able to secure resources from the ties they possessed. These differences, what researchers have referred to as access to and mobilization of social networks, meant middle-class Black young women had less social capital available to them in planning for the future than did middle-class White young women.[7] The fifth and final theme I draw from these interviews is that middle-class young women experienced a remarkable degree of stability in their lives, in their relationships with others, their families, their schools, and their communities. Stability itself was a resource that minimized life disruptions and gave these young women confidence in the future.

PACKAGED FUTURES

The packaged futures that middle-class girls aspired to included a college education, stable work, and a middle-class family life. Out of 25 middle-class girls, 16 planned to complete graduate schooling, and 7 planned to obtain a four-year degree. Only 1 aspired toward a two-year degree, and 1 had not decided what type of degree she wanted to complete. Fifteen aspired toward high professional careers such as becoming a physical therapist or physician, and six aspired toward a low professional career such as a nurse. Four were less certain of their goals and were deciding between two or three careers, all of which fit into high or low professional occupations. They envisioned stable family lives as well, with most hoping to marry and have children, although they were wary of depending on a spouse for financial support. Thus, they wanted to establish themselves with educational credentials and a job before marrying and having children. The majority (22 of 25) aspired to marry and have children.

These young women's goals were usually well planned. Janice, for example, was a middle-class biracial (Black and White) student at Kensington who ultimately graduated with a grade point average of over 4.0. Janice lived with her mother, who had attended but not completed college and now worked in a salaried retail store management position; although retail work often involves low pay, Janice's mother had been working as a manager in higher-end retail and at times at the district level. Like Cassie, Janice belonged to the elite school show choir and had been selected for the summer travel abroad program. She was also a member of the school's symphonic choir, the art club, and a school group devoted to discussing issues around diversity and was active in theater. She planned to become a psychologist, explaining: "I'm going to go on to college to major in psychology, and . . . I'm going to get a PsyD degree. Which is kind of like PhD, except for it's less research oriented. It's more like the practical application of psychology." She had learned about this type of graduate degree while visiting one of the colleges she planned to apply to, an in-state private university. It was one of four she was considering; two others were private and one was public. All were rated selective or more selective by *U.S. News & World Report*.[8] Although Janice's mother would not be able to pay full tuition, they had attended financial aid information sessions and planned to apply by November in order to meet scholarship deadlines.

Janice knew a great deal about the pathway to the career she wanted. She understood the distinction between types of colleges and that private colleges offered the small classes and picturesque campuses she felt would be a good fit. Although they were not wealthy, she and her mother had access to information and resources to assist them in securing scholarships. Janice understood differences between the various graduate degrees and was able to match her work interests to the PsyD (doctorate of psychology) degree. She also had the academic preparation for college; Janice earned nearly straight As and secured SAT and ACT test scores above the eighty-fifth percentiles. As she noted, the only thing standing in the way to her attending college was finding time to complete the applications between her choir and theater commitments.

Not all young women had such detailed plans. Christina, a middle-class White senior, reported that she was interested in becoming either an X-ray technician or a photographer. Her knowledge of these occupations, and others she had considered, was vague, however. Her father had suggested she pursue X-ray technology because "it pays well and it's not boring, it's interesting." Christina agreed, and planned to go to college to pursue this goal, although she acknowledged, "I didn't want to go to college, because I'm not too fond of school. But you need to go to college in order to get a decent job now." Christina therefore didn't have the internal motivation to attend college, and this appeared to dampen her enthusiasm for planning her future. Yet her aspirations were still aligned (she knew the amount of education needed to accomplish her goal), and she had a road map for attaining them. Christina was also fairly unique among the middle-class girls. Most expressed enthusiasm for college and future careers and could articulate the general pathways to achieving their goals.

The young women I spoke to were cognizant of the demands of work and family on women, and in some cases, this awareness altered middle-class girls' occupational aspirations. Almost all aspired to continue working after having children, reflecting broad societal shifts in women's labor market participation, yet several (N = 8) acknowledged that they chose their occupational aspirations partly based on their family goals and anticipation of childcare responsibilities.[9] Gail, a middle-class White senior from Kensington, explained that while she had considered pursuing a medical degree, she didn't think she could fit it within her family goals: "I was afraid that if I became a doctor, and I had kids, first of all, I wouldn't have kids until very late in my life. . . . Plus I was afraid that I would lose my job being a doctor if I took a year or two off to have kids. I was afraid I wouldn't have a job to go back to." Although Gail acknowledged that she didn't know if she could take time off from her current ambition of being a pharmacist, either, she *perceived* it as more flexible and family friendly.

Jocelyn, a middle-class White senior from Kensington, also aspired to be a pharmacist. She initially intended to pursue law like her father, but her mother admonished her: "She goes, 'Well, think about it. You can't be.' Because my dad wants me to be a lawyer because he's a lawyer, and she goes, 'Now, Jocelyn, you realize that he's gone from five to five every day.'" Jocelyn explained that her mother encouraged her to get a job in which she could work part-time in anticipation of raising children. Later, when I asked her about her family goals, she replied:

> I want to be married, have kids. And that's one of the things that they talked about when I was shadowing people. . . . Pharmacists [can] work part-time in pharmacy. So, it's easier because . . . you can only work Monday, Tuesday, Wednesday, and you'll have Thursday and Friday with the kids at home. And, working from home . . . they work with you, so you don't have to be completely away from your family all the time.

The professionals Jocelyn shadowed encouraged her to consider pharmacy in light of the flexibility that the job offers, and in response to their and her mother's advice, Jocelyn altered her goals to pharmacy.

Others did not say that they adjusted their career goals to accommodate having children but did report that adults they knew had encouraged them to consider "flexible" jobs or had mentioned that their jobs would be conducive to having children. When I asked Pamela, a middle-class Black young woman, about whether she would take time off work to have children, she explained:

> That's kind of something I've been going back and forth with. . . .The rich people who have nannies raise their children, that's not something I would want. I would want to raise my kids. . . . I don't know if I would want to take a year off or anything, but, have something where it could be flexible. Where

I could raise my kids, or, when they're in school, I'll be working and something, and when they get out, I'll be out.

Interestingly, Pamela aspired to a very demanding job. She hoped to be an
obstetrician, although she also considered going into law. Her childrearing goals had not dampened her occupational aspirations, at least so far.

Ultimately, middle-class young women aspired toward packaged futures, with their school, work, and family goals stemming both from individual interests and from a holistic vision of what their future lives might
look like. Of course, these young women envisioned futures that looked
much like their own pasts because that is what they knew and already
enjoyed. They hoped to replicate their current experiences or make small
adjustments. As a poignant example, when I asked Christina what her
vision of her future was, she reported wanting to live in a subdivision and
have a kid because, "I've grown up in a subdivision all my life, so it's what
I'm used to." And gendered assumptions about their role in their future
family lives were woven throughout these young women's pasts and anticipated futures. In many cases they had grown up with mothers who had
greater responsibility for their care, fathers who worked long hours, and
other families around them who echoed these models. This was certainly
not exclusively the case; four young women (all Black or biracial) were
raised by single mothers who had worked long hours to provide for them.
For most, however, school, work, and family life were answerable to one
another and to gendered assumptions about family life.

FINANCIAL INDEPENDENCE FIRST AS
A MANIFESTATION OF INDEPENDENCE

In *The Unfinished Revolution*, sociologist Kathleen Gerson found that the
young men and women she interviewed preferred to form egalitarian relationships in which both partners balanced their work and family commitments equally. Yet they faced contradictions between their idealized goals
of egalitarian home lives and the structural barriers that impeded seeing those goals through.[10] Gerson found that in the face of domestic and
career uncertainty, many of the young women she interviewed expressed

"fallback positions" of self-reliance; they would go it alone if they couldn't find a co-equal partner.

The young women I spoke to also expressed a desire for self-reliance, although for them, self-reliance was not a fallback position. Instead, they intended to finish school and start work before getting married and having children in order to secure financial independence first. Many young women saw financial independence symbolically, as a way to show themselves and others that they were self-sufficient. These young women typically planned to temporarily stop working or work fewer hours after having children and therefore wanted to show that they could support their families first, before scaling back.

Gail, for example, aspired to be a pharmacist and had already applied and been admitted to MidCity University, a large public university located in a midsize city, and planned to enter its six-year bachelor's to PharmD (doctor of pharmacy) program. She had her life mapped out. She would take six years to finish her degree and then begin working, then two years later, she would marry, and two years after that, at age 28, she would begin having children. Ideally, she would marry her boyfriend of a year and a half, Doug, a senior and football player at Kensington. Yet in thinking about her future, Gail explained the importance of making enough money to support herself and her family in the future:

> After I'm out of college, I want to earn enough money to really support me and my family. Pretty much ever since I can remember, I've wanted to be more of an independent person. That's why I wanted a job that would give me enough money. . . . That was a factor, I'm not going to lie. That was a factor in picking my job, but, then again, I'm into science. So, this was kind of perfect for me. I wanted to be able to be, like, if I don't have a husband, I would be able to make it on my own. I don't need anyone else's income. I'll be fine by myself.

Like Gail, many young women framed their aspirations as a *manifestation of independence*. Pamela, a senior, explained that she would want to "start a career" as an obstetrician before having children so that she could "make a life for them." She was also conflicted about how to juggle a family life with this career and considered becoming a nurse instead or looking for "flexible" work. Jean, a middle-class White junior from Kensington, chose her occupational aspiration (physical therapist) based on the availability of jobs in the area and salary in addition to the flexibility it would offer once she had children. Jordan, a middle-class Black young woman, explained that she wanted a "steady job" before having kids, "so I can be able to provide for them." These young women wanted to prove their ability to provide for themselves prior to starting a family. They saw the period before marriage and family as a time to complete their education, establish themselves in careers, and buy a home.

The desire to have children, coupled with the expectation that they would be the primary caretakers, meant that many young women did not anticipate relying solely on their own income for very long. Many expected to cut work hours or leave work entirely to have children. In this way, their desire for financial security was in part symbolic: if they earned credentials and experience in a career that offered a good salary, they didn't need a relationship or husband and were not reliant on either and therefore could "choose" to sacrifice their career and earnings at a later date.[11] They valued the manifestation of independence: a job that could provide a steady income and predictable future, one that allowed them to support themselves and their families. At the same time, many anticipated relying on a spouse's income for a least some time while their children were young. Independence, then, did not have to be ongoing for these young women. It had to be established in young adulthood and remain—at least theoretically—available to them throughout their lives. Relying on a spouse or partner was acceptable as long as independence had been symbolically achieved.

Finally, some middle-class girls worried that marriage might place them in a vulnerable financial position and explained their desire to obtain a steady job in relation to providing themselves with extra security if a marriage failed. This explanation, which I call establishing financial security as a *bulwark against risk*, was a more common explanation among the working-class and poor but not absent among the middle-class girls. Liz, for example, was a middle-class White junior at Kensington who split her time between living with her mother and her father, both of whom had remarried. She anticipated attending college and graduate school before beginning work at age 25, then getting engaged at age 26 and married at 29. When I asked her why she preferred this order of events, she explained that she would complete schooling first and then, "I would rather have a steady job before I get into, like, a serious relationship. . . . So, I can give myself a mile and two feet [in case] the relationship didn't work out." For Liz, and other middle-class girls who had seen the impact of divorce on their own families, a stable career would give the "mile and two feet" they needed as a bulwark against the risk of marriage and children. We will return to this explanation in more detail in chapter 3.

THE ROLE OF NETWORKS OF ADULT TIES IN THE FORMATION OF PACKAGED FUTURES

Middle-class girls' social networks, starting with their parents and extending out to other key adults, informed their plans for college and occupational goals. Liz split her time between her mother, a funeral services manager, and her father, a lawyer currently employed as a law book editor. Both parents had remarried. Liz was short and of medium build, her blonde hair pulled back into a ponytail with a thin, white headband keeping stray hairs out of her face.

Liz was an honors student with a 3.8 grade point average; in middle school, she was selected for a gifted and talented program that sequestered 40 students together for three years as they completed advanced coursework. In the ninth grade, the gifted program ended, and she and her cohort took their own paths, mostly into advanced and pre–advanced placement (pre-AP) coursework, leading to advanced placement (AP) coursework in the final year or two years of high school. Liz aspired to be an orthopedic surgeon. She became interested in this career through volunteering as a sports trainer with the football team. She enjoyed it, and she said she could see herself doing it long term. Her grandfather was a pediatrician, which motivated her. She explained, "I'm pretty much his token grandchild. . . . I'm the one that, if there's anybody in the family that's going to do it, it would be me." He and her parents supported her goals: "[My parents] always pushed me to really do well with grades and stuff. And then, more recently, we've talked about different schools, and [they have] taken me to college fairs to get information. Make sure that I'm looking and planning." They planned to go on college visits the summer between her junior and senior years, which would take them out of the state; Liz was one of a handful of students who was primarily interested in colleges outside of her state. She had also talked to her parents about her occupational goals.

In addition to her parents, several adults Liz knew supported her goals. She had spoken to her high school football team's volunteer doctor, a surgeon, who offered to let her shadow him: "He's talked to me about [shadowing] him for a day, or spending time with him, watching what he does." Her father also put Liz in touch with his best friend, a doctor living in North Carolina, who had invited her to spend a week with him and his family and shadow him at work. Liz also talked to the school sports trainer about her goals, who advised her on colleges to consider, and her school counselor talked to her about selecting colleges and wrote recommendation letters for her when she needed them.

Parents laid the groundwork for college early; most middle-class young women said they had "always wanted" to go to college. Gail explained: "I've always wanted to go to college, even before I really understood what it all entailed. There was never really a choice. It was always go to college, that's just what you do." When asked whether this came from her parents, Gail was ambivalent; she said it must have come at least in part from them, but that they had never "nagged her about it." Similarly, Kathleen, a middle-class Black young woman, stated that she had always wanted to go to college and that her parents had encouraged this goal. Yet when I asked how they had encouraged her, she responded:

> I don't think it's really "encouraged" me. It's just like a fact that I'm going to go to college. [Just like] graduating from high school. It's a fact that I'm going to graduate. . . . They never actually had to tell me that I was going to go to college. . . . That was just what's going to happen.

Kathleen struggled with explaining her parents' role in shaping her educational aspirations. This was not uncommon. Within many middle-class families, college was treated as an extension of compulsory education; it was "just what you do," "just what's going to happen." The question was not about college. It was about *which* college, *which* occupation, and *which* pathway to the future.

Guidance from both parents and other adults was not unusual among the middle class. Large networks of well-educated and successful adults shaped and informed middle-class girls' aspirations. This went beyond encouragement, as the status attainment literature has long emphasized.[12] Instead, parents and others in the young women's networks offered concrete resources to them in planning for the future. This guided the young women's goals in important ways and taught them how to plan for the future and how to ask for help in doing so.

RACE DIFFERENCES IN SUPPORT FROM ADULT TIES AMONG MIDDLE-CLASS GIRLS

There were clear differences in the kind and amount of support Black and White girls within the middle class received. Middle-class White girls had access to larger and better-educated networks than did middle-class Black girls, and middle-class White girls more often reported receiving information and resources from these networks. This sometimes occurred after White girls' parents (most often their mothers) had sparked connections between friends or colleagues and their daughters, and at other times appeared to occur spontaneously, with adults asking these White young women about their future plans and offering help. In comparison, middle-class Black girls and their parents frequently worked harder to forge productive ties, yet with less success. Middle-class Black young women reported that their parents, like middle-class White parents, connected them to knowledgeable adult ties. However, middle-class Black parents possessed smaller and less well-educated social networks than middle-class White parents and so had to reach further into their social networks, to weaker ties who offered less sustained assistance.[13] No middle-class Black girls reported that an adult outside of their family spontaneously offered to help them in their planning.

Jean, who had long, straight blonde hair and large blue eyes, aspired to be a physical therapist and had constructed detailed, well-informed plans based on advice from a number of adult ties. Her father, who had a PhD and worked as a scientist for a multinational corporation, discussed her plans with her. She explained, "He says to look for the stable jobs, and he says that the health sciences are stable. He says I can do anything I want, but he will talk through the pros and cons with me." When Jean began planning for college, her brother, who was a PhD student in chemistry, sent her a thirty-page list of scholarships that he had compiled during his own college search, along with information about preparing for the SAT. When we spoke, Jean had already taken her second PSAT exam and planned to take the SAT and ACT later the same year, explaining, "I'll probably take them twice to make sure I get a good score. And this summer I will go on college visits. I'll decide by the end of the summer." She planned to pursue a doctorate in physical therapy after college, explaining that while this degree was not currently required for working as a physical therapist, the guidelines were changing such that soon physical therapists would require a doctorate in order to work independently of a doctor's supervision; she had been told about this upcoming change by physical therapists she had met during her father's PT appointments.[14]

Jean's social capital, defined here as the resources available and received from relationships with others, can be characterized like those of other middle-class White girls, as "sponsored."[15] I consider this social capital to be sponsored because adults in her network supported her by initiating conversations with her about her future and mobilizing resources, such as additional social ties and information, on her behalf. Even adults she did not personally know—such as the physical therapists she met when accompanying her father to his appointment—offered her information useful for pursuing her goals. She planned to return to that office to volunteer and had talked to the doctors there to receive permission. Her advantages came from the wide range of well-educated adults she came in contact with and from how these ties were mobilized by her and on her behalf.

This ability to secure resources through social ties was common among middle-class White girls. Gail, who aspired to be a pharmacist, obtained detailed advice and support from her uncle, school counselor, and boyfriend's college friends. Maggie, a middle-class White junior from Glenbrook who aspired to be a veterinarian or zoologist, received help securing an internship at the zoo from an elderly man in her church who took an interest in her career plans and received a shadowing opportunity through her pastor's wife. Cassie came to know her doctor (a surgeon) well enough that he visited her when they both happened to be traveling internationally in the same country, and he offered to set her up with internships at his hospital in the future.

Not every middle-class White young woman had such productive social networks, but most did. These stories bring to light several themes apparent in my interviews with White middle-class girls. First, they had access to large social networks of educated adults, claiming an average of over nine adult ties. Second, all but one said that either all or most of the adult ties they knew had attended college. Third, and most essentially, these ties offered them resources vital to planning for their futures. This last component was what made the girls' social capital "sponsored"; adults they knew recognized them and their goals as important and offered information, advice, and assistance. As a result, most of the middle-class White girls I interviewed had acquired detailed information about the careers they hoped to obtain and about college applications and programs, and they had taken advantage of or were currently arranging opportunities to shadow a professional working in their intended careers.

Middle-class Black girls' social capital was "insulated;" they boasted smaller social networks of about seven ties, and these ties had lower levels of educational and occupational attainment than middle-class White girls' ties.[16] Jordan, for example, aspired to complete college and graduate schooling, pursue a career in pharmacy or finance, and eventually live a family life complete with "a husband and kids and a dog." An honors student with a 4.02 grade point average, Jordan exuded confidence and had a notably well put-together appearance for a 16-year-old. She and her sister, Kathleen, whom I also interviewed, lived with their mother, a pharmacist and manager at a branch of a national drugstore chain in a large home in a middle-class suburb. Their father, who had recently retired from running a small business, lived nearby. Although never married, Jordan's mother and father remained friends and co-parents of the girls. Both parents were protective of Jordan and her sister; in fact, each of the girls called her mother "overprotective" in interviews.

Jordan described a relatively small network of adults compared to middle-class White girls. She named four adults she felt close to and could turn to for advice: her mother; her father; her great aunt, who ran a day-care center from her house and had taken care of Jordan and her sister when they were young; and Ms. Sackett, her mother's best friend and their hairdresser. Only Jordan's mother was both close to Jordan and worked in an occupation that required a college (in her case graduate) degree.

Jordan's mother supported both her and her sister in their occupational goals. She discussed college options with them and encouraged them to keep up their grades. She had secured a shadowing experience for Jordan, who was considering going into pharmacy, and she had told Kathleen she would sign her up to shadow a doctor she knew through her work. However, the ties she tried to mobilize on behalf of her daughters didn't appear to be as useful as those initiated by middle-class White parents. Jordan ultimately shadowed a friend of her mother who worked as a pharmacy technician rather than a fellow pharmacist, and she knew much less about the occupational opportunities available for pharmacists than the White young women who aspired to the same jobs did. Gail, for example, recounted several options in pharmacy, including working at a drugstore, hospital, or manufacturing plant. Jordan, on the other hand, described pharmacist work solely in relation to being at a drugstore, and when I asked her what pharmacists did at work explained, "They analyze scripts and I don't know exactly what they do. I know more what the technicians do because they count pills."

Jordan also hoped to learn more about working in finance, a job she matched with using the Kuder career assessment tool in her class on college and career planning.[17] Although she wanted to shadow someone working in this field, she explained that she had trouble figuring out where to go because financial analysts "work in corporations, but I don't know where corporations are." A teacher suggested she try calling local banks to ask whether she could shadow someone there. Her sister Kathleen also garnered less support from professionals she spoke to than many middle-class White girls. When I asked her whether she had told her pediatrician about her interest in the field, she replied, "I told her I want to [be a doctor], but there weren't really facts exchanged or anything." Thus, while some middle-class White girls reported that professionals they met volunteered information and opportunities, such offers were not forthcoming for the middle-class Black girls I interviewed.

Although Jordan's occupational plans were in flux, she was well prepared for college. She had researched colleges as part of an assignment for school and was particularly interested in St. Francis University, a selective private university with popular business and health programs. St. Francis was also her mother's alma mater and fit her mother's preferences of being nearby and small. Jordan had signed up to attend the school's upcoming "experience day" and another day on which she could meet college representatives in a more intimate setting. She had recently taken the PSAT and was planning to take the ACT in May. Altogether, Jordan was prepared to go to a good college that would offer her options to pursue the careers she was interested in and that would facilitate the kind of lifestyle she anticipated for her future.

Middle-class Black girls' social ties were also insulated because when they did reach out to professionals working in fields they wished to enter, they did not receive as useful or detailed information as White girls received from similarly positioned ties. Pamela, for example, aspired to be an obstetrician and was supported in her college planning by her father but by few others. Her father, who had recently completed law school and was studying for the bar, encouraged Pamela to talk to her own doctor about her goals, but when I asked about the conversation, she described her doctor's advice as: "She said take a lot of math and science type of classes. So, just little things like that." Pamela, like other middle-class Black girls, did not receive much advice from the professionals she reached out to. As a consequence of these differences, middle-class Black young women were usually well prepared for college but had less detailed plans regarding their occupational futures than middle-class White young women did.

Jordan, Kathleen, and Pamela were well supported by their parents, who monitored their academic progress, helped them plan for college, and endeavored to forge connections with other adults who might help their daughters succeed. Yet these young women had smaller adult social networks and received fewer offers of support from ties outside their immediate family members than middle-class White girls did. These middle-class Black young women reported being strongly supported by their parents and sometimes other close adults; indeed, they often described their parents taking a more direct role in their college and career planning than White girls did. At the same time, their social networks were insulated relative to their White middle-class peers. This appears to be explained by two factors. First, middle-class Black girls had less access to well-educated, professionally employed adults working in the fields they wished to enter than middle-class White girls did.[18] Second, middle-class Black girls did not receive the same degree of information and resources from the ties they did have. This was due to differences not in the young women's effort or intent but in the willingness of ties to offer extended help and mentoring. Some of this, of course, may be explained by limitations in what their parents were able to do "behind the scenes" to leverage their own social ties compared to White parents. However, there were also clear differences by race in the kind of support middle-class young women were offered by professionals they met in work settings, such as Liz by the physical therapists she met and Kathleen and Pamela by their doctors.

One aspect of middle-class White and Black girls' lives that did not differ was their plans for packaged futures. Most middle-class young women, regardless of race, dreamed of marriage and children along with a successful career. Sheryl, a middle-class Black young woman, explained that she wanted to "finish school and get a good job, that all [comes] first. Be able to just be on my own for a while. And then, after I feel comfortable with that, and start a different life, [a] family." When I asked her why it was important to finish school and get a good job before starting a family, she explained, "Just because most, some marriages don't work. So, just in case something like that happens, I'll know that I can take care of me and the family that I built on my own." This is quite similar to Liz's desire to give herself "a mile and two feet" or Gail's desire to be able to "make it on my own" without a husband. Across race, these middle-class young women dreamed of being educated and financially stable before marriage and childbearing, and they depicted marriage as an important but potentially risky institution.

MIDDLE-CLASS STABILITY

One striking component of the interviews I conducted with middle-class young women was the relative stability of their lives. This was thrown into sharp relief by the much more chaotic lives of their working-class and poor peers—an issue I discuss in detail in the next chapter. However, even without direct comparison, it is clear that being a member of the middle class presents an advantage for living a stable life. Only 6 of the 25 middle-class girls (two of whom were sisters) lived with a single parent. Several lived with stepparents or split time between two parents. For most middle-class young women, two biological or adoptive parents were a steady part of their lives, even if their parents were divorced. Only two reported unusual household structures: Karai, a Black young woman whose boyfriend and his mother moved in with her and her father after experiencing financial difficulty, and Shantel, who was also Black and lived primarily with her adult sister, with their mother occasionally joining the household. In addition, middle-class girls described long-term residential stability, typically living in the same town and even the same house for their entire lives. Only four reported having moved to Glenbrook or Kensington in the past five years, with only two reporting multiple moves. This is important because residential stability lent consistency to their lives, their institutional affiliations (school, church, and other activity groups), their friendships, and their neighborhood ties.[19] Notably, both young women with unusual household structures and all four who reported recent residential moves were Black.[20] I discuss these racial differences in more detail later.

During interviews, I took note of any significant and potentially disruptive events that these girls reported when recounting their lives. At the end of each interview, I also asked an open-ended question about whether anything important—bad or good—had occurred during or since middle school. Many middle-class young women did not report any events that had had a long-term or dramatic impact on their well-being. The most common type of negative event among this group was a grandparent's death, followed by close family members' health problems. These events were no doubt important, but the girls did not describe them as particularly disruptive to their lives.

There were, of course, exceptions to this. As I recounted earlier, Cassie's own health and that of her mother was a near-constant source of concern. Bethanie, a middle-class White junior from Glenbrook, also described the emotional toll her family life took on her:

> My stepdad is a very smart man. But he has no common sense. I mean, he kind of did something, and hurt my mom. [It] wasn't anything physical. But he kind of went off and found him a lady friend. And my mom has been really upset over it, and it's kind of caused me to be upset. I'm very emotional towards it still, and it really affects me in a lot of ways.

Shortly after learning about her stepfather's cheating, Bethanie got into an altercation with a football player at school and was taken to the school office. She explained: "Once I got in there, and Mr. Charles had calmed [me] down, he could tell something else was wrong. So, he asked me. And, he's going to try to put me in some counseling." After this, Mr. Charles continued to check on Bethanie, bringing her into his office when she appeared overwhelmed or upset.

Other disruptions may be so severe that they are life altering. Allison, a middle-class biracial (Black and White) senior from Glenbrook, suffered from mental health problems in her junior year that culminated in her attempting suicide and spending a week in a mental health clinic. Although Allison described her weeklong stay in a mental ward as helpful and her mental health problems in the past tense (e.g., "I had mental health problems I had to deal with myself"), these were the kinds of problems that would likely follow her for years to come. In the short term, they also took a toll on her grades, which dove sharply from a grade point average of above a 3.5 to one semester in which it was 1.7. Although Allison felt she had recovered from her mental health problems when I spoke to her in her senior year, and her grades had recovered, this certainly was an important and consequential life disruption, one that would likely linger throughout her life.

Some middle-class girls went through difficult times, whether experiencing parental divorce, a close family member's health problems, or a death in the family. Yet these major disruptions were rare, and most of their consequences were softened by the adults in these young women's lives—whether parents, a school administrator, or a counselor. Thus, class served as both a barrier to difficult events and a buoy, keeping young people afloat when turbulence hit. At the same time, class was not a panacea. Mental health problems and trauma can arise within the middle class and are unlikely to be smoothed over by class resources.

Notably, middle-class White young women appeared to have more stable home lives than middle-class Black young women. Only one middle-class Black young woman lived with both biological, married parents, compared to almost two-thirds of middle-class Whites. Over one-half of middle-class Black girls lived with single parents, while no middle-class White girls lived with only one parent. Both young women who lived with adults other than their parents (Karai and Shantel, described earlier) were Black, and all four who had reported recent residential moves were

Black. This is important because stability is a resource for young women, particularly at a time in which they are planning to move into adulthood.

In addition, several Black parents had only recently reached middle-class status. Pamela's father had just completed law school and was studying for his bar exam. Janice's mother (who was White; Janice's father was Black) had worked her way up to a management position, despite leaving college to have her first child in her early twenties. Although some parents were solidly middle class, only one middle-class Black girl reported that her extended family members were also middle class, suggesting a great amount of recent upward mobility. This is consistent with the literature on middle-class Black families, which finds that they are not equivalent to middle-class White families in wealth and neighborhood characteristics.[21] Therefore, it reflects important distinctions between the realities of Black and White middle-class families' experiences.

When middle-class girls did experience difficulties in their lives, these disruptions had consequences. As happened to Allison, instability can lead to poor grades when young people are distracted from the everyday demands of schoolwork. As in Bethanie's situation, they can lead to conflict in or outside of school, possibly culminating in disciplinary procedures. Family and household stability may be taken for granted when considering only middle-class girls' lives, but it is an important resource for planning. Stability meant fewer transitions to new places and institutions; less bureaucracy in making it through the school year (e.g., fewer course changes needing visits to the school counselor); greater consistency in grades and track placement; and a higher degree of confidence in the future because the basic facets of their lives, such as their homes, presence of family members, and economic stability, were less likely to change.

3 Hoping for a Repackaged Future

INTERVIEWER: Who has encouraged you to go to college?

CORTNEY: My dad and my granny ... the economy
too. ... I look up to my managers, and the
older people I work with, and I don't want to
be here for the rest of my life. I want to be
able to afford nice things and not be strapped
down, like my dad. And not have to work
crazy hours like my dad. I just want to be
able to have a nice, set job, and make good
money.

Cortney was a well-tanned, thin working-class White young woman wear-
ing a stylish black zip-up jacket, large hoop earrings, and a sparkly silver
scarf whose edges she played with idly during the interview. Cortney was
close to her father, her only parent after her mother had drifted out of
her life when she was a child. They talked about her goals, school experiences, and relationship with her boyfriend. In recent years he had encouraged her to pursue nursing or X-ray technology, two jobs he sometimes
observed in his capacity fixing air conditioning and heating in local hospitals. Cortney heeded his advice and aspired to get an associate's degree
to become an X-ray technician and get married, maybe to her high school
boyfriend of three years, with enough income to afford a "good-sized"
home and nice cars.

Cortney's grandmother, an X-ray technician herself, also encouraged
her to go to college and pursue X-ray technology. Cortney explained, "My
granny works [at the hospital]. ... She works nights, so over the summer I would go and stay with her some nights just to get a feel for it, see
what it was like." Cortney attended a health festival at her grandmother's

workplace, where she learned about their forgivable loans program that helped pay back college loans for young people who worked for them for three years after obtaining a college degree. She planned to graduate from high school early—in December of her senior year—and work at the hospital to save money, then enroll in college in the fall. During her junior year, Cortney signed up to meet with her guidance counselor, who gave her pamphlets from a local private, not-for-profit nursing college whose tuition ran about $30,000 per year. At this meeting, Cortney learned that nursing and X-ray programs were two years full-time, although when discussing this with me, Cortney never mentioned an associate's degree.

Cortney had both goals and a plan. Her plan was a good one in its broad strokes; she knew the educational expectations of her career goal, if not in name then both in terms of time and a local college she could attend. She had observed her grandmother working at the hospital, and she was aware of and intended to take advantage of a loan forgiveness program. These plans coincided well with her hopes for the future; she wouldn't be wealthy as an X-ray technician, but she could be steadily employed (given projected growth) in a job that paid over $40,000 a year. If she married someone who earned a similar salary in her low cost of living area, they could be comfortable.

Cortney faced barriers to achieving her goals, however. Although she took mostly college preparatory classes and received As and Bs, she struggled in math and chemistry, which would be required in any pre-health college program. In addition, she had not taken the ACT by the fall of her senior year because her father could not pay for her to do so. The previous year she had signed up late for the ACT and incurred a fine of $85 that her father could not pay: "My dad kept saying, 'Next paycheck, next paycheck,' and before I knew it, it was gone." Cortney worried about how she would afford college. The loan forgiveness program was contingent on maintaining a baseline grade point average and completing a degree. If she faltered, she would be on the hook for a lot of money and without the credentials needed to obtain a good job. Cortney's decision to graduate high school early and work could also be a risk; although she could save money, the time away from school and investment in work could deter college enrollment. Despite having a plan, Cortney's future was far from certain.

· · · · ·

In this chapter, I discuss working-class and poor girls' aspirations and preparation to follow through on their goals. All of the working-class girls' parents were high school graduates, and about two-fifths had attended college or postsecondary technical school.[1] They worked in primarily blue-collar or service jobs, such as custodian, secretary, or retail sales worker. Only two working-class girls had parents who were currently unemployed, and in both of those cases a second parent was working. Among the poor girls' families, on the other hand, unemployment was the norm.[2] Eight of the eleven lived in families in which there was no parent currently working for pay, and the remainder worked at a nearby factory.[3] Slightly more than half of poor girls' parents had not received a high school diploma, and the remainder were high school graduates.

In some respects, these two groups map onto Joseph Howell's distinction between "settled living" and "hard living" working-class families.[4] In his book, hard living families had nonunion jobs that paid low wages and were unstable and consequently had insecure housing and volatile family lives. Settled living families, on the other hand, had union jobs that offered steady wages and secure employment; these families typically owned their own homes and were active members of community organizations. Indeed, among those I interviewed, poor girls' lives were often chaotic and their families all struggled financially, whereas some working-class girls reported more stable or financially secure family lives. Yet major structural changes in the United States have depleted the kinds of jobs available to working-class families and, as a consequence, their family stability.[5] Nearly all of the working-class girls' families shared some characteristics with those Howell describes as "hard living," such as the almost two-thirds who lived with single parents, a parent and stepparent, or extended family members. Very few of their parents worked in jobs that were likely to be unionized or that offered high wages. In addition, working-class and poor girls were alike in the ways they planned for the future and the resources they had access to. Therefore, the similarities between these groups outweighed any differences, and I discuss them together.

Four themes emerged from the interviews with working-class and poor girls. First, similar to middle-class young women, working-class and poor young women's goals encapsulated a future comprised of educational attainment, stable jobs, and a fulfilling family life. I describe these goals as repackaged futures because the girls pulled together these imagined futures from what they observed of the lives of those around them. Rather than hoping to mostly replicate their own experience, they were attempting to imagine a future they had only glimpsed in pieces. Second, working-class and poor girls, like middle-class girls, hoped to establish financial independence before marriage. Their reasons for doing so, however, were more heavily weighted toward securing a bulwark against risk than among the middle-class girls, although some also sought a manifestation of independence. Third, working-class and poor girls were supported by a network of ties, much like middle-class girls. These ties provided emotional, practical, and material support but were limited in their ability to offer resources useful for constructing future plans. In addition, working-class and poor girls often reported providing *reciprocal support*—usually emotional or practical but occasionally financial—to adults they knew as well. Fourth, working-class and poor young women experienced a greater degree of instability and more life disruptions than members of the middle class. This included major life disruptions—what Marianne Cooper has referred to as destabilizing events—like frequent moves; nonimmediate family members sharing living space; drug and alcohol problems; incarceration of family members; physical, emotional, or sexual abuse; and serious health scares.[6] These disruptions affected the girls' level of stress and emotional well-being and interfered with their ability to plan effectively for their futures.

REPACKAGED FUTURES

The repackaged futures that working-class and poor girls aspired to were not so different from middle-class girls' packaged futures on the surface. They, too, hoped to complete a college degree, secure steady work, and live a middle-class family life. Of the 36 working-class and poor girls (see table 3), 19 aspired to at least complete a four-year college degree (9 of whom aspired to complete graduate or professional schooling), 9 aspired to complete a two-year college degree, and 8 aspired to complete some form

Table 3   Composition of Working-Class and Poor High School Girls in Sample

	Working-Class/Poor (N = 36)
Race/ethnicity	
Black/biracial	8
White	26
Latina[a]	2
Family structure	
Biological/adoptive parents	11
Stepfamily or joint custody	6
Single parent or extended family	19
Educational aspiration	
Graduate/professional schooling	9
Four-year college degree	10
Two-year college degree	9
College (vague or undecided)	8
Occupational aspiration[b]	
High professional	10
Low professional	10
Skilled technician	7
Mixed/unclear	9
Social ties	
Mean number	6.4
Majority college educated	8
Know someone in desired occupation	13

NOTE: Information in the table was compiled in fall 2008 from surveys completed prior to sample selection (racial/ethnic identification and aspirations) and from interviews (aspirations, family composition, and social ties).

[a] One young woman was a recent immigrant from Mexico, and the other was second-generation American with Cuban ancestry.

[b] Examples: high professional = doctor, veterinarian; low professional = nurse, health teacher; skilled technician = vet tech/assistant, respiratory therapist; mixed/unclear = two or more occupations that fall into multiple categories.

of postsecondary degree but had not decided how much schooling they wanted to complete. Ten aspired to a high professional occupation (e.g., psychiatrist), ten to a low professional occupation (e.g., health teacher), seven to a skilled occupation (e.g., dental hygienist), and nine to more than one occupation of different statuses (e.g., nurse or doctor). These plans were mostly aligned, where the girls aspired to an appropriate level of education for the job they hoped to hold. Even when they did not know the name of a particular degree they planned to obtain, they knew the length of time the degree took (two years versus four) and often knew of local colleges that offered such a degree. Nearly all aspired to marry and have children in the future. Only one working-class girl said she did not intend to marry or have children, and one aspired to marry but not have children.

However, the imagined futures that working-class and poor girls aspired toward were different from middle-class girls' packaged futures in that working-class and poor girls repackaged elements of their own lives and the lives of others around them, borrowing from what they admired and rejecting the parts of their lives they disliked, to envision their futures. Their descriptions of the future were peppered with references to the way they imagined others lived, saying they wanted to "do the 'take child to work day' thing," have the "TV lifestyle," or have a family the "way it's supposed to be."

Neke, for example, was a poor Black senior at Glenbrook High School. She lived with her twin sister and her mother, who had completed a GED and was currently unemployed but usually earned a living cleaning houses. Neke envisioned her life at age 30 to consist of "two to four kids, a husband with a good job, who can cook. A nice car, a nice house. Money to pay the bills and for food. Do the 'take child to work day' thing." Many of Neke's goals were jointly shaped by the lives of adults she knew and what she saw on television. In describing what she saw as the ideal family life, she explained that one adult she knew had a happy family life because "her daughter is mature, and respects her. She has a job, and time for the kids." Another woman she knew had four kids, and "they go to a Christian church, and have time for the kids." Both parents played sports with their children, she noted. Neke's educational and occupational plans came from watching television. She had become interested in being a detective when she was younger from watching *Law & Order: SVU*, and her understanding of what it would be like to be a doctor—her current aspiration—was informed by shows like *Grey's Anatomy* and *Scrubs*. She learned about the MCAT exam for medical school admission and the internship year of medical training from these television programs. Neke, therefore, had a vision of what she wanted her future life to look like, but it was refracted through her glimpses of others' lives, real or fictional, rather than a known quantity.

Working-class and poor girls also intentionally rejected elements of their own lives that they disliked when imagining their futures. Describing her desire to attend college, Kim, a working-class White junior, explained, "I wanted to make something of myself, and, basically, I want to get out of this town. . . . The only way to do that is to go to college and make something of myself so I don't have to live the life I've lived." Similarly, Tara, a poor White senior from Glenbrook, explained her aspiration to go to college:

> I've seen people struggle who didn't go to college, and I don't want to live my life like that. I don't want to live my life working at Bob Evan's being a wait-ress, making less than minimum wage for the rest of my life. . . . Because I grew up on welfare, and all kinds of stuff so I know what it's like. I don't want to be there. I don't want to be the adult in the situation. The one that actually feels worthless. . . . [My mom] felt like crap because she couldn't provide for us the way that she wanted to. So, I just don't want to be in [those] shoes [feeling] hopeless.

The desire for freedom from economic struggle was expressed by most working-class and poor young women I spoke to. In the future lives they described for themselves, they depicted a stable job, financial security, and happy home life as the ideal future.

Working-class and poor girls believed that college would open up oc-cupational opportunities that would be more secure and enjoyable than those their parents had. Thus, part of the package of these girls' aspira-tions was the link between education—making it—and a secure future.[7] Postsecondary educational institutions held the key to a better life with less of the struggle, disappointment, and helplessness they saw their par-ents encounter. Jennie, a poor White junior at Glenbrook High School, was enrolled in honors classes and earning mostly As and Bs. A confi-dent, assertive young woman with dyed red highlights in her hair, Jennie was well-known and popular. She lived with her mother, stepfather, and brother in a small, two-story home in a rundown neighborhood in Glen-brook. Her mother and stepfather were members of a local construction union and took jobs cleaning the slab furnace and occasionally other ap-pliances at the local steel mill factory on a contract basis, collecting unem-ployment benefits when they were not needed.[8] Jennie explained why she wanted to go to college:

Everybody in my family, they've always dropped out or they went back to high school [for a GED]. And they've made ends meet. They've survived. . . . I don't want to be the kind of [person] who has to work hard, work every day of my life [when] I can just go to college for about four years, and come back, you know, actually have a job that I like and get paid.

Jennie, like most poor and working-class girls, saw college as a way out of the hard living of those around them.

Despite these differences, working-class and poor girls expressed similarly aligned educational and occupational plans as did middle-class girls. Nearly all knew the level of education (two- or four-year degree, or graduate/professional schooling) needed for the jobs they wished to hold in the future, and many planned accordingly. The challenges they faced were not, therefore, difficulty in constructing "aligned aspirations," but barriers that interfered with the feasibility of their plans and the availability of detailed information. Feasibility was a concern because college is expensive, and most working-class and poor girls anticipated needing to work while enrolled in school, in some cases helping their families to pay bills in addition to paying their own way through school. Anticipating these problems, they expressed some concern that their repackaged futures might not happen. Their discussions of these futures were peppered with words like "hopefully" and "don't know." The girls and their families also lacked information about how to plan for college and careers. Access to information and resources was scarce. In many cases young women knew they would need a particular type of degree, such as a two-year college degree in radiology, but not what postsecondary programs were the most promising based on quality of instruction, time to completion, and cost. As I describe in a later section, working-class and poor girls didn't have the same access to knowledgeable social ties that middle-class girls did. As a result, they gleaned information piecemeal, sometimes from overheard conversations, from television, or from for-profit college marketing campaigns.

Like middle-class girls, working-class and poor girls incorporated family plans into their repackaged futures. Yet the specter of unhappy home lives shaped some working-class and poor girls' aspirations for the future and appraisals of the possibility of these aspirations. To be clear, many working-class and poor girls' home lives were stable and happy (and some middle-class girls' home lives were unhappy). However, many were difficult; economic hardship and its attendant problems engendered strife and disruptions.[9] A working-class White young woman compared an idyllic future to her current home life, explaining:

> DANA: The perfect family would be, you'd have dinner and you'd all eat together. And do family things together and everything like that.
>
> INTERVIEWER: Why is that important to you?
>
> DANA: I guess it's because I've never really had that, so I want that.

As we will see in the next section, experiences with family dissolution made many working-class and poor young women distrustful of marriage. These young women described witnessing marital breakups not only in their immediate families but among those around them in their extended families, neighborhoods, and family friends. Thus, while they wanted to marry and have children, many expressed caution regarding these plans.

FINANCIAL INDEPENDENCE FIRST AS A BULWARK AGAINST RISK

Many working-class and poor girls viewed marriage with some suspicion while still in high school and hoped to establish their own financial independence before getting too involved in romantic relationships and marriage. They often described this caution about marriage as a response to the marital conflict they saw at home or in other family members' homes; they were wary of becoming trapped in an unhappy marriage and saw a job and steady income as a way to protect themselves. For them, establishing financial independence was a bulwark against risk because depending on a spouse or partner who could leave them was a risky proposition.

Beth, a working-class Black senior at Kensington, said she had aspired to marry in the past, but that her parents were "going through some things"; she added, "I felt like people got married because they felt like they need somebody to support them. And to me, I feel like I can support myself." Beth explained that college was necessary for financial

independence, so that she would not have to depend on a husband financially. Thus, she depicted educational attainment, and the occupational
success it would support, as a defense against the potential instability of
marriage.[10] Beth and other girls who viewed financial security as a bulwark against risk aspired to complete college and obtain "good jobs" that
would earn them decent incomes, particularly in a low cost of living area,
giving them insurance against divorce, separation, or no romantic relationship at all. Blake, a poor White senior at Glenbrook, explained that
she didn't want to get into any kind of romantic relationship before becoming a nurse:

> You hear about [how] they'll go to college, and they meet this guy the first
> year of college, and they get married, and then, you know, then later on they
> get divorced, and they can't support themselves because they didn't finish
> college, and they can't pay for college because they're divorced. So I would
> definitely wait until I was an RN so that if anything were to happen, I would
> have my nursing degree and I could support myself.

In this way, Blake was cautious of romantic relationships both because
they could divert her from her college and career plans and because a relationship could later unravel, leaving her financially vulnerable.

Poor and working-class girls like Beth and Blake were particularly
attuned to the risks of being financially insecure. College and jobs were
therefore a bulwark against risk not only because of relationships but
also because of the realities of being poor and working class. Michelle,
a working-class Black senior at Glenbrook, explained going to college as
necessary for her own economic security and that of her future children.
"I don't want to be working at fast food restaurants all my life. I want to
have a good job and I want to be able to take care of myself. And, if I have
kids, I [don't] want them to be how I was." Michelle's plans were informed
by her experience of being raised by a single mother in economically precarious circumstances. Her hopes for a good job were tied to her goals for
raising children in a stable and secure household.

Working-class and poor girls were somewhat less likely than middle-
class girls to use the manifestation of independence explanation, in which
they saw establishing independence before marriage as a demonstration
of their ability to support themselves but ultimately anticipated taking

time off from work to be with children or scaling back hours as part of their goals for the future. Still, more than half of working-class and poor girls said they would want time off after establishing their careers to care for children. Shana, for example, a working-class Black junior at Glenbrook who aspired to be a psychologist, explained, "It seemed right to me to finish school first and then have a personal life, get a good job after college and get my career started so I can have kids. I need money to have a kid, because they cost a lot." Shana planned to work fewer hours after having a child but hoped to first get a good job and earn an income that would help support her family. Notably, Shana's parents were married, and her mother had worked in a more flexible occupation (hairdresser) when Shana was young. Many young women looked to their own families when anticipating the kinds of work and family lives they might have and how best to prepare themselves.

THE ROLE OF NETWORKS OF ADULT TIES IN GIVING AND RECEIVING SUPPORT

Most working-class and poor girls did not know many college-educated adults, and this limited the amount and quality of information they received about how to apply to and enroll in college and how to pursue careers that required a college education. Certainly the adults they knew, particularly their parents, encouraged them to go to college. However, they rarely reported that these adults initiated conversations about the careers they wished to pursue, nor did they ask for this kind of advice. Instead, they engaged in reciprocal forms of support wherein they discussed family problems (their own and that of their ties) with the adults they knew, received financial support to address immediate needs, and helped out with household tasks like cleaning and caring for younger siblings.

Michelle aspired to work as an ultrasound technician. She was a dancer and looked like one; she was lithe and athletic, with long hair pulled into a ponytail at the top of her head. Michelle's mother encouraged her to go to college and discouraged her from going into dance. However, when I asked whether her mother wanted her to pursue a job in ultrasound technology or something else, she explained, "I told her about it, but . . .

she isn't going to plan my future." Michelle's mother was encouraging but not intimately involved in her career planning. It was unlikely she could have provided much information Michelle could use for planning; she held a high school degree and worked as a receptionist.

Michelle was close to two family friends who worked at a local hospital, Kit and Tenisha. Kit worked in administration, and Tenisha was a nurse. Both women encouraged Michelle to "dream big." When I asked whether she had discussed her goals for becoming an ultrasound technician with them, she said she had and explained:

MICHELLE: They always tell me, everybody always tells me, do something bigger.

INTERVIEWER: Why?

MICHELLE: I guess to make more money, and they want everybody to do something bigger.

At the same time, these women didn't talk to Michelle about her career aspirations in detail or share their own experiences. When I asked what Tenisha did at the hospital, she replied, "I don't really know. And Kit, she just works at the front desk, so I really don't know what she does either." Thus, while Kit and Tenisha encouraged Michelle to dream big, she received few details from them that would help with planning. This was not an indication that they didn't love or care for Michelle; both women gave Michelle money for senior pictures and her graduation cap and gown. They cared about her deeply. It was likely that they didn't discuss details of college and pursuing a career in ultrasound technology because they did not know the process for applying to college and attaining this career themselves, or because they assumed Michelle's school would take care of this kind of advising.

Other working-class and poor young women reported receiving similarly sparse information from social ties. In some cases, like Michelle, these young women received encouragement and other forms of support but not the information vital to planning for college and future careers. Holly, for example, was a working-class White senior at Glenbrook. She aspired to attend college to become a physical therapist or social psychologist, a field she had heard about from her sister, who was attending a public university about four hours away. Holly preferred to stay close to home and was considering a local commuter college. Her parents encouraged her college goals but did not help her plan. Holly explained they didn't know enough about college to help her. Instead, she relied on a teacher and school counselor for advice regarding colleges and financial aid. However, she was unable to secure detailed information about the careers she hoped to pursue and therefore knew very little about what these careers would be like. As a result, Holly felt uncertain regarding her occupational aspirations.

It was common among working-class and poor young women to say that they did not talk to adults close to them about those adults' work experiences. In fact, a striking difference between middle-class girls' knowledge and that of their disadvantaged peers was the degree to which they knew the job titles, responsibilities, and daily tasks of many of the adults they knew. This is not simply due to differences in girls' interests or initiative; middle-class girls, especially those who were White, reported being approached by their ties to discuss both their goals and how these ties' work experiences intersected with those goals. Working-class and poor girls, on the other hand, rarely reported such encounters. It is possible that working-class and poor young women's ties, who were also primarily working-class and poor, did not enjoy reminiscing about their workplaces to the same extent as middle-class adults, or that they viewed this kind of information as the purview of schools.[11]

The social capital of working-class and poor girls like Michelle and Holly was "restricted" by a relative lack of ties to college-educated, professional adults and by the difference in approach taken by the adults they were connected with.[12] Working-class and poor girls had smaller social networks than middle-class girls (6.5 ties on average compared to 8.2 among the middle class), and the adult ties they knew or came in contact with often did not have the resources to help them plan for college and careers. About one-fifth of working-class and poor girls said that the majority of their adult ties had attended college, compared with three-fourths of middle-class girls. Furthermore, when their ties did possess resources that could have been helpful, working-class and poor young women were less likely to receive such help. This suggests two sources of disparity between the social capital of working-class and poor girls and that of middle-class girls: less access to potentially helpful social ties and less mobilization of resources from the social ties they held.

Working-class and poor girls' ties to adults—and subsequently, their social capital—should not be viewed solely as impoverished in comparison to middle-class girls' networks and social capital. Instead, working-class and poor girls' social networks were different in form and function from those of middle-class girls. While the resources middle-class girls received through interactions with adults were unidirectional (i.e., adults giving help to girls and not vice versa), working-class and poor girls had reciprocal relationships with adults that focused more on emotional and practical needs and were often give and take; these young women could be sources of help and support for their families, friends' parents, neighbors, and other acquaintances in addition to receiving help. And these exchanges were generally oriented toward current concerns rather than the future.

Sandra, a poor White senior at Glenbrook High School who aspired to be a nurse, spent a great deal of time caring for her family, and this showed in the way she spoke to me about her life. She talked at length about her young cousins' play habits and family dynamics and was less animated and engaged when discussing her aspirations and plans. Sandra lived with her mother, father, sister, and two cousins, whom her family was helping to raise due to her aunt's lingering medical problems from breast cancer and an automobile accident. In addition, Sandra's mother was disabled; she no longer worked and had trouble understanding and remembering things she was told. Sandra played an important role in keeping the family system functioning. She took half a day of high school classes, and after school she would "go home, clean the house, then go to work."[13] She also helped take care of her 19-year-old brother's new baby. She explained, "He always brings it to our house, and I take care of it, or my grandmother does. The other day, I was talking to my grandmother, and the baby started crying. I asked [my brother] to go take care of it, and he got mad. We all started fighting, so now he's leaving with the baby. We'll probably fight for custody." Additional family exchanges occurred as well. Sandra's aunt lived nearby and was paying Sandra's father to fix mold and disrepair in the new home she was renting.

Sandra's family members sometimes helped her out. She was close to her grandmother, who had gone back to school in recent years and was working at the hospital doing clerical work.

SANDRA: I talk to her a lot, if there's fighting at home or I have homework problems. And she can help with doctors' appointments. In my first pap smear, a few years ago, they found abnormal cells. They thought it was cancer. They still don't know what it is.

INTERVIEWER: And she helped with that?

SANDRA: Yeah. She has to understand words doctors use, for her job.

Her grandmother had also promised she would help Sandra find scholarships to help with college tuition, "but she's always working." It was easier for Sandra to receive help with more immediate concerns than with long-term planning.

Sandra, like many other poor and working-class girls, was enmeshed in reciprocal relations of exchange with family members that involved offering and receiving emotional and practical support. Sandra helped keep the home clean and took care of her aunt's and brother's children. Her grandmother helped her understand the medical close call she had experienced and listened when Sandra needed a confidante. These exchanges were valuable, yet also presented opportunity for conflict. A request to have her brother help care for his child led to a potential custody battle. In another incident, another brother moved out of the family home after Sandra and her parents threatened to "beat up" his girlfriend because she was still in contact with a former boyfriend. These enmeshed lives, though necessary to maintain household well-being in some domains, could turn sour quickly.

Shannon, like Sandra, contributed to her household's well-being. A tall, heavyset girl with dyed red hair, Shannon was a working-class biracial (Black and White) senior at Glenbrook who was enrolled in advanced and honors classes and maintained a 3.5 grade point average. Her parents, a commercial truck driver and stay-at-home mother, had custody of her two nieces due to her sister's drug problems, and Shannon helped out by taking on extra responsibilities at home. This added some friction to the household when she felt her mother had less time for her:

I've been sick, and I've been trying to do everything around the house, and trying to get doctor's appointments, and can't really do anything without

her, because I'm not eighteen. But, I understand because . . . I'd rather [my
nieces] be with us . . . so I kind of just sacrifice it.

Shannon felt responsible for helping out around the home and managing her own health care rather than demanding her mother's time and
attention.

Shannon and her parents also helped out Shannon's friends at times.
They had taken in one friend twice over the past few years when the
friend's mother was struggling with drug addiction. When I interviewed
Shannon, her girlfriend was living with them because her parents had
kicked her out of the house and stopped paying her college bills once they
discovered she was a lesbian (her girlfriend was a year older than Shannon). Shannon helped her girlfriend pay back room and board fees from
her brief time in college, "I told her, anytime I have extra money. . . . [be-
cause] I hold my checks, and if my mom needs it, and she needs help with
bills. . . . I'll just give it to her." Thus, Shannon helped both her mother and
girlfriend with bills while still a high school student.

The kind of help these young women provided—especially emotional
support, childcare, and house cleaning—is both gendered and classed. A
rich sociological literature shows that women contribute the lion's share
of unpaid labor in family life, caring for family members, contributing a
greater amount of the household work, and operating as kin-keepers.[14]
The greater need for these kinds of support systems among disadvantaged
and Black communities has also been documented.[15] And young people
are not immune from these expectations. Sociologist Linda Burton described the process by which poor families come to rely on children to
serve in adult roles, including one or more forms of being privy to adult
concerns, helping around the house with minimal supervision, being
treated by parents as a peer, and parenting siblings or parents, as "adultification."[16] Many of the working-class and poor adolescent girls I spoke
to appeared adultified in the ways that they recounted their roles within
their families and households. Moreover, they learned from these experiences. They saw themselves as independent and capable caretakers, and
this informed their aspirations and orientations toward work and family.
Like Shannon, many said they "like[d] helping people" and took pride in
their ability to do so. Jobs in the health field appealed to them because

they could take these experiences caring for family members and apply them in the larger world.

The reciprocal support these girls engaged in comprised important forms of social capital exchange. Childcare and home upkeep have monetary value, although this value is often overlooked or ignored.[17] Similarly, gifts received by them or their families from family friends, grandparents, and other relatives (e.g., clothes, money for school pictures, housing support) are economic in value, thus fitting traditional theories of social capital and its value. Yet these exchanges are often hidden when we seek to find only the kinds of social capital useful to young people's educational and occupational goals.

INSTABILITY IN WORKING-CLASS AND POOR GIRLS' LIVES

When considering the role of social class in educational attainment, there is a tendency to focus on what money can buy: homes in better school districts, tutoring, and immersive programs outside of school, for example.[18] Focusing on purchasing power, however, neglects the role of economic resources in maintaining stability and therefore ignores other aspects of working-class and poor families' lives that matter to the well-being of youth. For example, residential instability, characterized by multiple residential moves, has negative consequences for youth. Young people who have recently moved have higher chances of poor behavioral outcomes and academic disengagement.[19] Household instability, or the movement of other adults and children into and out of the residence, also has a profound impact on adolescents.[20] Residential and household instability frequently coexist, potentially compounding negative outcomes.[21] In addition to this, working-class and poor parents are at higher risk of financial setbacks than middle-class parents due to lost jobs and incarceration, factors that can drastically impact young people's lives.[22] These kinds of disruptions can trigger or exacerbate mental and physical health problems, family violence, and substance abuse. Thus, it is important to understand how working-class and poor young women's home lives differ from those in the middle-class, and how this might matter for their future plans and chances of following through on those plans.

Household instability was fairly common among the working-class and poor girls I interviewed. In some cases, this was due to changing household compositions. Brit, a poor White junior from Glenbrook High School, was a straight-A student enrolled in mostly general coursework. Dressed in a goth-inspired manner, with dyed black hair, pale skin, and baggy dark clothes, Brit had a constrained friendliness, talking openly and at length, but rarely smiling. At 16, she lived with her mother, grandmother, aunt, cousin, cousin's boyfriend, sister, and sister's baby. Her uncle planned to move in with them when he got out of jail, as he had in the past, and her cousin would move in when he got out of rehab. Her mother's boyfriend sometimes stayed over as well. Her mother, who had a high school degree, usually worked as an office assistant for trucking companies but was unemployed when we spoke.

Brit dreamed of a future with "no chaos, no drugs, no problems with paying the bills, just easy." This stood in stark contrast to her current home life: "I hate my life right now. At home everything's terrible. We just got our water shut off. I had to take a bath this morning with a gallon of water. It's just too many people live in our house, too many people aren't willing to help." Her family members were loud, making it difficult for her to sleep, and she had little privacy. Her uncle, who was currently in prison, lived in the room next to hers when he was around and would sometimes bring men over whom Brit found frightening: "One time I came home and I was changing my clothes, and I turn around and there's just some crack head sleeping in my bed, and I ran upstairs. I didn't even know him. [It's] really scary." Her uncle's friends also stole from her repeatedly; her family had purchased her a safe for Christmas the previous year to prevent these thefts. Brit ranked getting out of the house as the most important post–high school transition she could make.

Brit's frustration was palpable, and understandable. In addition to coping with her uncle and his friends, she was responsible for much of the household cleaning. Her aunt sometimes helped her out, but she struggled with alcohol and would often drink herself into a stupor. Brit missed her mother's ex-boyfriend, now in prison for robbing a bank, who was the only one of her mother's boyfriends to treat her like family. Although Brit planned to go to college and become a dental hygienist, she was unsure she would be able to enroll and attend full-time immediately after college;

if her mother was still out of work, Brit anticipated that she would get a job to help with household bills.

Residential instability was another source of life disruption for many girls. For some this amounted to frequent moves with their immediate family or to extended relatives' homes for purposes of schooling or even discipline.[23] Others, like Bernice, could be categorized as what experts on homelessness call "precariously or marginally housed."[24] Bernice was a poor Black senior at Kensington who aspired to attend college and work as a registered nurse in the future. She was enrolled in general education classes and an intervention class, which was for students who had individual education programs (IEPs) and needed extra support, and she received Bs and Cs.[25] When I first spoke to her teacher about excusing Bernice for an interview, the teacher explained that Bernice had been out of school for a few days with heart palpitations and suggested she take a few minutes to catch her breath before heading with me to the library.

When I spoke to Bernice, she was in her senior year and living with her mother in her mother's friend's apartment along with the friend's two daughters. The summer before, she had spent a month living at another friend's home before joining her mother. Her father and younger brother lived about fifteen minutes away in Bernice's oldest brother's apartment. This was not the first time her family had split up to live in different homes:

> Let's see, [in] ninth grade, we lost our place. It was me, my mom, and my dad, and my brother, and we all had to separate for a little bit. And then . . . tenth grade, I had to stay with my older brother. . . . And last year, we all were together again. And now we're pretty much separated again.

This series of moves began after the family lost their home, spurred by a number of health and economic setbacks. When Bernice was about 14, she was hospitalized with what doctors initially feared was cancer, although she was eventually diagnosed with lupus. Shortly thereafter, her father was laid off from his job of fourteen years as a truck driver. Although he obtained another job building automobile parts, he was laid off again not long before I interviewed Bernice and was receiving unemployment benefits. Her mother had also been laid off from her last job working at a factory and had been diagnosed with fibromyalgia.[26] She still received some income, most likely from disability (Bernice did not know). Overall, however, it was clear that household instability had been a constant presence in Bernice's life since early high school. Although she was able to remain enrolled in the same high school, these moves meant that she was frequently encountering new household members, physical spaces, and neighborhoods.

Other young women experienced disruptions in their schooling due to moves or school transfers. Tiffany, a working-class White senior who was seven months pregnant when I interviewed her, lived with her mother and half sister. The self-described "head of household," Tiffany took care of her younger sister, managed the family's bills, cooked, and "[made] sure things got done" while her mother worked long shifts as a licensed practical nurse (LPN). Tiffany was completing her final high school credits online through the Glenbrook adult education center after her doctor advised that she not attend school for full days because of recurrent kidney infections, which could lead to preterm labor.[27] This was not Tiffany's first change in schooling. After her freshman year of high school, she had transferred to a local charter school, Skills Academy, where she had heard she could complete high school faster than at Glenbrook High. She soon found that the school did not live up to expectations. Although the students took courses solely through computers, "the classes took about three months per semester to get done, which is like regular school, but then it was still setting me back a year for some reason. I don't know [why]." Tiffany had attended Skills Academy for about a year and a half when her mother had a meeting with the principal, who told her that Tiffany shouldn't take the SAT because it would be too difficult for her (there was nothing in Tiffany's academic records to suggest this was true). Tiffany's mother transferred her back to Glenbrook High School to complete her schooling, but at that point she had already fallen behind in credits and would not be able to graduate when she had planned or take the entrance exam for the nursing school she was interested in.

Some young women reported abuse in their homes when they were younger.[28] Alice, a poor White junior from Glenbrook, aspired to work in child psychology but also loved to write. She became interested in writing during a time when she and her mother lived with her mother's abusive boyfriend: "My mom was in a relationship with this emotionally abusive man. And when he was in the room with us, we weren't allowed to speak to each other. So I started writing little notes. And I would sneak them to her. And then I started to write all the time—I have notebooks full of writing." Margaret, a poor Cuban junior at Glenbrook, also reported abuse in her household: "When I was little, my dad was still around, and my dad would kind of beat my mom, and he would get drunk, and he would beat me too. And, he did drugs too, and I would see my mom getting beat up and stuff. And we were always far away from our family." Their problems did not end there. Margaret's mother saw a man shot in front of her, and a few years later her son, Margaret's brother, committed suicide. As a result of both experiences, Margaret's mother experienced mental health problems and was not able to hold down work.

Household instability, health problems, interpersonal conflicts, and abuse took serious tolls on girls' school engagement, grades, and commitment to future goals. Tonya, a poor White senior from Glenbrook, lived with her mother, stepfather, and stepsister. When Tonya was 12, her mother began partying late at night and doing drugs: "You know, things like Oxycontin and Vicodin, and Percocets, and Xanaxes. And I shouldn't know those . . . but I do." Tonya became responsible for her younger sister, still a toddler, while simultaneously caring for her mother. When Tonya was 13, her mother's drug use and health became worse:

> When I was 13, [my mom] had a seizure. And my stepdad wouldn't let me call an ambulance because he had a warrant. . . . I had to sneak and call the police, or call the ambulance, because he didn't want to go to jail, but my mom could have died. And if I hadn't taken Health that year, she probably would have, because she started choking on her tongue, and I knew exactly what to do. Because they told us about it. So, you know that's hard to deal with when you're 13, you know?

Although Tonya complained to extended family members, they waved off her concerns as typical adolescent complaints.

Eventually, Tonya asked her grandparents if she could move in with them in Arizona. This lasted less than six months, after which she returned to Glenbrook. Tonya moved back in with her mother, but after their electricity and hot water were shut off, she spent extended periods living at her best friend's home and with her father. After her father got drunk one night and threw a radio at her head, she called the police on him and moved out. When I interviewed her in her senior year, Tonya was living in Glenbrook with her grandfather and stepgrandmother, who seemed to offer relative stability.

These disruptions took a toll on Tonya's plans for the future, emotional well-being, and school engagement. She planned to go to college to work in the medical field and had spoken to her family members about this, looked up colleges online, and met with her high school guidance counselor several times. Many of her sessions with the guidance counselor, however, were devoted to addressing bureaucratic issues with course credits from her online school in Arizona. Her counselor had promised Tonya that they would discuss colleges and the SAT after her credits were resolved, and she waited eagerly to "be called down" for this discussion. Tonya also described going through periods of depression during her mother's addiction and while living in Arizona. School friendships fell apart, most drastically when a former close friend began a rumor that Tonya was a lesbian, leading to ostracism from the group. It is no surprise, then, that Tonya's goals and school performance were rocky. She frequently missed homework assignments, sometimes skipping school altogether on days she took her sister to school. Although enrolled in a mix of advanced and general courses, her grades fluctuated from failing courses some years to the honor roll and a 3.7 grade point average her junior year. Thus, the very serious disruptions in her home life were consequential for her plans, school life, and academic performance.

Kim, a working-class White honors student who was being raised by her single dad, also struggled with depression in the wake of family instability. Her mother, who was bipolar, left her father—and the family—for another man when Kim was in the eighth grade. Her father was often not at home, so Kim was raised primarily by her 21-year-old sister and her grandparents, who lived nearby. Her grandparents were both emotional support systems for Kim and financial benefactors for her father, providing money for house payments, food, and clothing. Kim described feeling ashamed at the state of her home, describing it as "dirty" and "not nice," particularly in comparison to her friends' homes. These family problems and emotional concerns wore on Kim, and when her grandfather died suddenly at the beginning of high school, Kim began to struggle with depression. When I asked her what her biggest obstacle to going to college was, she explained:

Starting my freshman year, I bec[a]me depressed and it was pretty much a battle. And then a lot of things happened, and I didn't know where my life was going, and basically hated myself. . . . And sometimes I just, I don't see myself making it to college . . . because nothing really matters to me anymore, and I don't like anything as much as I used to. So it's just, I don't know if I could make it through school after high school. High school is hard enough. Sometimes I can't make it through the day in high school.

Kim had trouble maintaining her motivation for high school and goals for college. Although she was earning straight As in her honors classes, she struggled to remain engaged in school and hopeful about the future.

The working-class and poor young women I spoke with were passionate and ambitious and worked hard to construct plans from all available sources. Yet they dealt with life circumstances that inhibited their ability to prepare for the future and follow through on their plans. This was not simply due to poor academic preparation; several reported being enrolled in honors or college preparatory classes and receiving good grades.[29] Instead, these young women faced significant barriers to planning for their futures. Their day-to-day lives could be chaotic and unpredictable. In these circumstances, planning for the future was difficult: immediate concerns like housing and healthcare took precedence. Even for those who encountered more mundane disruptions, such as parental divorce and residential mobility, these disruptions added bureaucratic hurdles to their own lives, primarily within the school setting, and could set them back both academically and with planning for the future. And when they did try to plan for college and careers, their access to information from adults around them was restricted. They dreamed big and did their best to gather information for themselves, but they faced serious barriers to successfully planning for—and pursuing—their goals.

PART II Traversing the Transition
to Adulthood

4 Dreams Unfurled

In 2013–2014, I reinterviewed two-thirds of the young women with whom I originally spoke.[1] My goal was to understand how their social class origins (the social class of their families in high school) and plans for the future intersected to shape their early transitions to adulthood. In this chapter, I outline the three pathways young women took through the early transition to adulthood and the role of plans in these pathways. In chapters 5 through 7, I delve more deeply into these pathways, showing how institutional constraints and resources intersected with class-based resources and plans to drive young women into very different circumstances. In doing so, I illuminate the early stages of intergenerational mobility, or how class origins become class destinations. *Class origin* is the social class in which one grew up, with its attendant resources. *Class destination* is the social class one occupies in adulthood, also comprised of a set of resources. *Class replication* occurs when class origin and destination are the same, while *mobility* occurs when they are not. In between class origin and class destination is the transition to adulthood. Current social class status in this period is less clear because most young adults are still partially dependent upon their parents, and thus social class origin still matters. At the same time, young adults' school engagement, labor market activity, and family status during this period are all strongly associated with their social class destination. In tracing young women's pathways from high school through the early transition to adulthood, we can see how class replication and mobility begin to take shape.

To be clear, one's social class destination cannot be perfectly predicted in young adulthood. I use class destination to mean the social class status they appeared to be headed toward, based on their pathway when I interviewed them.[2] These young women's prospects may change: they may marry someone with more earnings potential than themselves, they may drop out of college unexpectedly, or they may return to school and obtain a four-year (or more) degree and secure a high-paying job. However, circumstances in young adulthood, particularly postsecondary school enrollment, are strongly related to one's life chances.[3] These early adult years matter and are important indicators of social class in mid-adulthood.

PATHWAYS INTO ADULTHOOD

The pathways these young women took were numerous, complex, and sometimes unexpected. This does not make for easy analysis. Complete class replication would be easy to describe, making for an uncomplicated tale of inequality: middle-class young women would be finishing their bachelor's degrees and preparing for the labor market; working-class young women would be employed but struggling to make ends meet; and poor young women would be unemployed or churning through low-wage jobs. Instead, the young women I interviewed shared stories of disruptions and challenges at every level, with both inequality of opportunity and a fair degree of early adult mobility. Some middle-class young women dropped out of college and struggled to make ends meet. Some working-class young women appeared headed toward professional careers. And this is what makes their stories interesting: each of these young women had a class origin and early plans constructed while in high school, both of which intersected with institutional constraints and opportunities that shaped their early pathways toward a class destination. These pathways consisted not only of what they did (went to college, obtained a job,

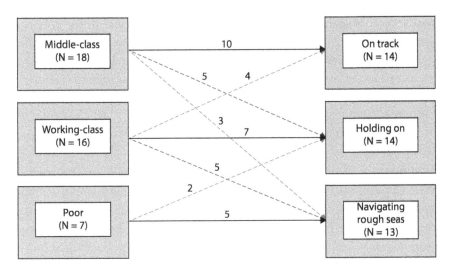

Figure 1. Class Origins and Destinations in the Transition to Adulthood

married, and so on) but also their revised plans and identities. In other words, class origin carried forward, but presumptive class destination also mattered. In the following chapters, I investigate the space where class origins and class destinations intertwine at a crucial point in young adulthood.

I found that there were three primary pathways these young women traversed in the years after high school: those who stayed on track in the pursuit of their goals, supported by college and family resources that provided the frameworks (tracks) upon which they moved toward their planned destinations; those who were holding on to their tenuous economic stability by juggling school, work, and family obligations while continuing to pursue their aspirations for a middle-class future; and those who found themselves navigating rough seas that buffeted their daily existence, leaving them no closer to—and often further from—their adolescent ambitions. In total, 14 young women were on track, 14 were holding on, and 13 were navigating rough seas.

Family social class was strongly related to young women's pathways. As shown in figure 1, 10 of the 18 middle- or upper-middle-class young women I interviewed in Wave 1 were on track in Wave 2, 5 were holding on, and 3 were navigating rough seas. Of the 16 working-class young women, 4 were on track, 7 were holding on, and 5 were navigating rough seas. Finally, no poor young women were on track, but 2 were holding on and 5 were navigating rough seas. The shading of the lines in figure 1 indicates the relatively more common pathways (darker shading) and less common pathways (lighter shading).

The most common pathways are depicted in parallel lines on the figure, with middle-class young women on track, working-class young women holding on, and poor young women navigating rough seas. The second most common pathways slope downward, with middle-class young women holding on and working-class young women navigating rough seas. Finally, the least common pathways slant upward or drastically downward, leading working-class and poor young women to relatively more advantaged post–high school positions or leading middle-class young women to rough seas. Overall, the figure shows a stronger trend toward potential downward mobility than upward mobility.[4] Middle-class young women fell farther than poor and working-class girls moved up, and the distribution of pathways suggests the class destinations may be more heavily weighted toward the bottom than class origins were in 2008.

DID PLANS MATTER?

Plans can be helpful in accomplishing one's goals, yet they are not sufficient by themselves. I found that the young women who followed through on their aspirations, or successfully amended them, did so because of not only the plans they held but also the support systems around them. To put this in sociological terms, both agency and structure mattered in shaping young women's pathways into adulthood. When young women had both good plans in high school and the resources to help them achieve those plans—that is, to choose the right colleges, gain access to volunteer or shadowing experiences, and receive advice from college-educated adults—nearly all ended up on track. Yet middle-class young women's high school plans had not (and could not have) anticipated all contingencies, and still most were on track. And poor and working-class young women with strong plans in high school were more likely to be holding on or navigating rough seas after graduating from high school than they were to be on track. As we saw in part I, social ties and economic stability are important resources for planning. As we will see in part II, institutional and social ties, economic stability, and good planning are all important for translating plans into reality.

5 On Track

JORDAN: I've definitely grown a lot as a person since I was in high school. I have become more confident in myself and in my abilities since I was in high school. I think I always expected myself to do well and be involved and do things. I've always had that go-getter personality.

Trains run over 140,000 miles of track in the United States, taking customers and cargo from point of origin to point of destination.[1] Their movement is mirrored in the on track young women's early transitions to adulthood. Like the trains, these young women's movement toward a career is preplanned and moves forward steadily, although with several stops. We can imagine each of these young women as the conductor of her own train, directing herself toward college, then college graduation, possibly further schooling, and a career. And once she is a college student, each is responsible for her own journey in important ways. Yet much like train conductors, these young women's pathways and movements are heavily guided by larger structures. Train conductors, in fact, do little "driving" of trains on most modern railways. Trains move from station to station by following the tracks set into the ground, which control the train's movement. Trains' paths may alter via switches, where two or more tracks meet and where the train can either move forward on its own track or onto a new track to the left or right. These switches, however, are supervised remotely via train dispatchers, who also monitor the train movements and advise conductors regarding traffic ahead, speed, and weather conditions. The trains' pathways, therefore, are guided by actors and arrangements outside the train conductors themselves: the tracks, signals, switches, and dispatchers all play crucial roles in getting trains to their destination.

Like train conductors, the young women who were on track to fulfill their teenage aspirations were often ensconced in larger systems that helped keep them affixed to a career path, moving them smoothly from high school student to credentialed professional with remarkable efficiency. Their colleges and college programs provided guidance, serving as the track that propelled young women along their paths. Parents played the role of dispatcher, watching remotely and helping the young women switch pathways when needed.

. . . . .

We met Jordan, an outgoing and confident middle-class Black junior at Kensington, in chapter 2. Jordan and her sister Kathleen, whom I also interviewed, were raised by their single mother, a pharmacist, although their father, a retired small business owner, was also very involved in their lives. Jordan was uncertain of her exact career plans while in high school, thinking she wanted to be either a pharmacist or financial analyst, the latter of which was appealing because it would allow her to work in a nice office with a "fancy desk" and dress in a suit for work. She had no ties to the corporate world, however, and little knowledge of this career path. Yet she had already begun visiting colleges, planning for college entrance exams, and gathering information on scholarships while still a junior in high school.

After high school, Jordan enrolled in Saint Francis University, a small, selective, Catholic college near Kensington, and majored in accounting. She excelled at college. She was in the honors program at Saint Francis and was deeply involved in the life of the college. She belonged to a number of student of color–centered organizations, including a sorority, the Black Student Association, an accounting association for Black students, and a college club for women of color.[2] She was also a member of the college accounting honors society, served as vice president of the school's accounting club, and belonged to an organization that facilitated business internships for students of color. That last affiliation landed Jordan an internship with a major bank in her first year of college.

Jordan was well supported by mentors at her college and in the business world. She had two academic advisers through her major, her accounting adviser and her honors program adviser, both of whom she met with regularly to get advice about classes. She also had an outside mentor through her participation in the mentoring program at Saint Francis, an associate director at a large multinational corporation. Jordan felt particularly close to this woman, explaining that she would go to her about career questions and guidance on issues such as whether to pursue a certified public accountant (CPA) certification. She explained:

> She's very honest, which is why I would go to her more so than I would go to someone else, because she gives me the honest opinion of how she thinks. She is definitely helping me become a better business professional, because I don't like really fancy food. [For example], I love chicken tenders and fries. And she said, "Well, in the business world, sometimes they give you, like, filet mignon, and you have to know that it's not undercooked hamburger. And you have to like different kinds of food." So, she is definitely teaching me how to be in the business world.

Although comfort around new foods might, at first glance, seem minor, Jordan's mentor engaged in explicitly teaching her cultural capital relevant to the business world.[3] Being familiar with the customs of professionals in the career she intended to enter would both increase her own comfort and confidence in business settings and signal to others that she fit into that milieu.

Overall, Jordan was on track. She was pursuing one of the careers she had considered in high school. Except for her first semester of college, in which her grade point average slipped to a 2.9, she was maintaining a 3.5 average. She was a leader at her school, deeply invested in the success of other students of color and the place of Black students within her university. She had secured two internships over her first three years of college, and through these experiences she had narrowed down her career aspirations. As she explained, "I used to think I wanted to go into public accounting, but I think now I want to go into private accounting. . . . It would be hard for a woman in public accounting to be able to move up in the company while still having a nice work-life balance, which is something that I really think that I want in life." Jordan worked 8:00 a.m. to 11:00 p.m. routinely at her public accounting internship and saw first-hand how difficult this would be to square with marriage and children. In direct comparison, her private accounting internship provided steady hours and less fast-paced work.[4]

On track young women moved efficiently from high school to college and continued to pursue the goals they had held in high school or amended them slightly. All had completed or were close to completing a bachelor's degree or higher. In this chapter, I discuss how these young women either sustained or successfully amended their high school plans and what their early pathways into adulthood looked like. First, I argue that on track young women were assisted in accomplishing their educational and career goals by institutional ties: their connections to academic programs and faculty that provided tailored support to students. These ties provided structural opportunities to receive mentoring, facilitated access to internships, clarified academic requirements, and demystified pathways to their intended careers. Second, I describe how most on track young women navigated academic difficulties by drawing on their institutional and family ties. This is particularly notable because, as we will see in subsequent chapters, other young women who faced similar challenges often transferred institutions or dropped out of college. Third, I discuss differences between the experiences of middle-class and working-class on track young women. Although all of these young women had completed or were close to completing a bachelor's degree, working-class young women faced impediments that slowed their progress and pushed them into lower tracks within colleges. In the fourth section, I show how middle-class parents were on hand to help out; although not actively involved in these young women's college lives, they provided support when their daughters were floundering. Working-class young women, on the other hand, were at times distracted by worries from home. Fifth, I describe how financial support eased on track young women's pathways through college, particularly by minimizing their engagement in paid work. In the last section, I show how on track young women's plans for the future continued to include both a career-building period and time to pull back from work in order to take care of children.

THE ROLE OF INSTITUTIONAL TIES
IN STAYING ON TRACK

Being on track refers to two qualities: first, that in young adulthood these young women were moving steadily toward a career that would likely garner them at least middle-class status, and second, that they were guided and moved along by institutional structures—or tracks—that eased their way. Good planning in high school aided many of them in being on track, but so did economic stability (both in high school and now in college) and institutional and social ties. Jordan, for example, did not have especially strong occupational plans in high school, partially due to having a relatively small and less well-educated network than many middle-class White girls, as discussed in chapter 2, but she had clear plans for college, substantial support from her mother in finding a good college, and a middle-class background. Once enrolled in college, Jordan was guided by her accounting major within the business college and the university honors program. These college programs were institutional ties that facilitated her path forward and also provided more individualized social ties, such as those between Jordan and her mentor. I return to the topic of economic support in future sections. In this section, I discuss the role of institutional ties in keeping young women on track.

In total, 8 of the 14 on track young women were in some kind of preprofessional or specialized program within the larger university or college they attended.[5] Two additional on track young women were majoring in the broader set of categories Steven Brint has called "the practical arts."[6] Their programs (communications and business) did not offer the same exclusivity but did provide vocationally oriented job training and opportunities for career-building internships.[7] Some, like Jordan, entered into these tracks directly from high school, maintaining and further clarifying their career goals. Others entered such a pathway after deviating from their initial aspirations. The remaining young women were enrolled in traditional liberal arts majors but had forged productive ties to faculty, graduate students, and peers.

The preprofessional programs in which these young women were enrolled, such as preteacher, pre-physical therapy, and other such occupationally based college tracks, contained elements crucial to college students' success: personalized advising, opportunities for sharing information between students, and contact with professionals in the field.[8] Much like academic tracking in high school, these programs often included more demanding and specialized coursework than existed outside these tracks.[9] Pathways to the next step (graduate school or employment) were demystified, and the students were offered opportunities to burnish their résumés through volunteering, internships, shadowing career professionals, and applied coursework. Although traditional college majors provide some of this, particularly guidelines on course taking, preprofessional and honors programs offered even more support, and thus delivered more stable and explicit guidance to the young women who were enrolled. Those who majored in the liberal arts could still find sources of support, but they often had to construct them on their own.

Many of these programs—particularly those leading to a lucrative career such as being a pharmacist, physical therapist, or other career professional—were not open to all college students, however, and getting into them required resources. If your parents did not attend college or you had limited financial means, it could be more difficult to fulfill extracurricular requirements like internships, shadowing, and volunteer activities that admissions committees for these programs considered when deciding which students to admit.

For instance, to be admitted into the pharmacy program at MidCity University, Gail, a middle-class White young woman from Kensington, had to show not only top grades in her prepharmacy coursework but also "strong personal attributes" and "pre-pharmacy experiences," as described in the program's information for interested students. Gail began building toward these requirements while still a high school student. She spoke to her guidance counselor regularly about her plans, and in turn her guidance counselor contacted teachers at the school for help setting up shadowing opportunities for Gail. Gail was also proactive, applying online to drugstore pharmacies in her area, and when she heard nothing back, printing out her résumé and going to each store in person until she was hired in an entry-level position. Her research on colleges and discussions with her counselor led her to apply to MidCity University because it offered the opportunity to begin graduate studies early, and she attended a college information session after her junior year to learn more about the graduate program's requirements.

Thus, by the time she entered college Gail was equipped with an understanding of the application process and a résumé and recommendation letters showing her dedication to pharmacy. She added more college extracurricular activities to this over time, including serving as the scholarship chair at her sorority, where she monitored her fellow members' grades and worked with them when they dipped below the required average grade point average. These early experiences prepared her to fulfill the requirements of the pharmacy program, and she was admitted after her sophomore year.

Although the most exclusive preprofessional programs took early planning, some were open to those who pivoted their career interests later. In high school, Jessie, a middle-class White young woman, aspired to be a physical therapist, a career that would require her to get a doctorate in physical therapy degree (DPT). She was well prepared for this role; she had researched her intended career, had spoken to and shadowed physical therapists, and was enrolled in advanced and honors courses and earned mostly As and some Bs. Her parents, a teacher and insurance salesman, helped her look for colleges in her junior and senior years of high school.[10] Ultimately, she decided to apply and was admitted to the small liberal arts college that her parents and several other members of her family had attended.

In 2013, I met Jessie in the lobby of her residence hall. As she explained, she began college intending to follow a health track to a DPT degree, but she received a C in her first biology course:

> JESSIE: After my freshman year I changed my major to education. . . . I am a math and science middle childhood [major]. . . . I realized that I didn't necessarily want to go on to get a doctor degree in life science or anything like that. So, I changed my mind, and I realized that I liked working with children.
>
> INTERVIEWER: In terms of deciding not to go to get your PhD . . . why was that no longer interesting?
>
> JESSIE: My introductory biology class. . . . I got a C in that section of it. So I was just like, "If that's going to be what it is in introductory, I don't know [chuckle] what it's going to be later."

Jessie felt "freaked out" about her low grade in introductory biology because she felt it should have been the easiest course in her intended sequence. She quickly decided she would not thrive in the health sciences and that she needed a new plan. She settled on teaching, explaining that she had considered being a teacher in the past because of a positive experience leading younger children at her church's vacation Bible school. She also felt familiar with the role because her mother was a teacher.

Jessie switched her major to education, although she did not drop her interest in science entirely; she aspired to become a middle school math or science teacher. This required her to take math and science courses in addition to her education courses. She did well in these and was getting all As when I interviewed her in her junior year. Responding to an early low grade seemed prudent to Jessie but also might have belied a lack of confidence or overreliance on signals from "weed out" courses that other students, particularly male students, might ignore.[11] Her pivot to teaching represented a move toward an occupation she had seen her mother take on, albeit one that was lower paid than physical therapy.[12]

Jessie's occupational goals had shifted, but she remained interested in a stable, professional career as a middle school teacher. She was well prepared for this career trajectory, making plans to move out of state for teaching jobs if necessary and planning to return for a master's degree in education after obtaining work experience. This was in large part due to entering a well-developed college program. Within the education program, Jessie had a clear list of required classes and experiential learning requirements, as well as a robust community of other students. She was a member of the middle school teaching association at her college, and through this organization learned career development tips she did not receive in class. She also met regularly with her education program advisor, who guided her in her educational and professional trajectory. In the long term, she thought she might continue her education in order to go into educational administration and leadership.

Four of the on track young women I interviewed pursued more "traditional" arts and sciences majors rather than the practical arts. These young women had to build their own networks of support, aided by systems that were already in place to connect students to advisers and faculty. These ties were also institutional but took more effort for the young women to create and maintain. Denise, a working-class White young woman from Kensington, knew in high school that she wanted to pursue a career in psychology, specifically in the research sector, and she continued to pursue this goal at her large, public not-for-profit university. At college, Denise approached graduate students and faculty, offering to work on research projects that interested her, and they included her in their research. Over one summer, Denise learned how to code and analyze data in the statistical program SAS. She also asked the graduate students for advice on pursuing a PhD and becoming a professor. As she explained, "They kind of guided me. Like, 'This is how I got here, so this is what you need to be doing to get here.'. . . There were a lot of different things that I was, like, 'Oh, I wouldn't have known to do that.'" Through these connections, Denise received advice, valuable learning opportunities, concrete skills, and recommendation letters for graduate school. When I interviewed her in 2014, she had graduated early with a 3.5 grade point average and was living at home, waiting to hear back from her applications to graduate programs in psychology. Young women could make productive connections that facilitated their goals outside of specialized programs, but it took more of their own initiative to do so.

THE TRANSITION TO COLLEGE AND SWITCHING TRACKS

Starting a train is a slow process: the conductor initiates the forward movement of the first car by starting the engine, and one by one, subsequent train cars are pulled forward. The key, at this stage, is the steady initiation of motion by one car at a time, facilitated by the lax connectors between cars. If the connections between the cars are taut, the demand on the front car is too great, and the cars will not budge. Once the train is moving, conductors may adjust the train's speed and oversee track switches initiated by a train dispatcher, but they are at this point ensconced in a larger system of remote control by the tracks below them and the train dispatchers overseeing their progress.

Similarly, college students' trajectories appear to be most at risk at major transition points: the beginning of college, college transfers, and new programs of study. These were the points at which the young women

I interviewed reported that their grades suffered, sometimes to the point of course failure. The on track young women were the best prepared for these tenuous times. They felt comfortable reaching out for help when they needed it. They also received signals from their programs and peers letting them know that such short-term academic struggles were normal, which allowed them to redouble their efforts rather than feeling over-whelmed.[13] This did not mean that they all transitioned smoothly; seven on track young women suffered a period of low grades in their first year.[14] An additional three experienced a decline in grades later in college after maintaining high grades initially. However, they managed these challenges and remained in school, eventually bringing up their grades, finding a home in a college major or preprofessional program, and joining the social and organizational life of their colleges.

Sheryl, for example, was a middle-class Black junior from Kensington at Wave 1 and was enrolled in college prep and honors/AP coursework. She aspired to be an anesthesiologist after an aunt, a nurse, invited her down to Texas to shadow a doctor at her hospital. With this act, Sheryl's aunt recognized her academic credentials and worked to pique her interest in a prestigious and remunerative field. Sheryl was well supported by her immediate and extended family, friends' parents, and other adults in the community. These ties recognized her talents and encouraged her to succeed. After initially considering out-of-state colleges, Sheryl applied and was admitted to State U., her state's flagship public university.

Sheryl enrolled as a premed student at State U. and, like many of her peers, her grades suffered in her first year. She earned a 2.5 grade point average that year and felt "shocked." She had graduated high school with a 3.7 grade point average and had "never seen a two at all in front of a GPA." In her second year, Sheryl began to bring her grades up. She made the dean's list in the fall semester while still enrolled in premed coursework. However, she was unhappy in her major; she didn't feel passionate about the subject matter and was studying all the time. As she explained, she was reluctant to turn away from medicine:

> I was always nervous about what the rest of my family would think, because my grandma has 11 kids—and out of all of the grandkids, I'm the only one who's really doing anything, so I feel like people are always staring at me like, "Okay. She's going to do something good," and I felt like if I switched

to something else people would look at me like I'm not doing anything anymore.

Her father insisted, though, asking Sheryl, "You don't want to do this. Why don't you just switch to something that you want to do?" Eventually she agreed, and she met with the film studies adviser, who helped her change her major to film. Together, they worked out a plan that would keep her from adding extra years to her time in college.

Sheryl was doing well by the time I interviewed her. She continued being on the dean's list at the end of her sophomore year and beginning of her junior year and anticipated being on it again at the end of the year. She felt close to one professor and one graduate student in the film department, the latter of whom was "always there" if she needed help or advice. In addition, she was involved in a student-produced documentary that was being sought by two media companies. When I interviewed her, Sheryl was considering film school, although she also wanted to work to pay off the "tons of loans" she had acquired during college.

Maggie, a middle-class White young woman, ascribed her academic problems to a competing social life and difficulty managing independence. She almost failed out of college during her first semester at a branch campus of State University, then brought her grades up in order to transfer to the main campus.[15] Once she was there, her grades declined again before rebounding. As Maggie described it, the freedom to skip classes contributed to her poor grades in her first semester of college, and large classes with uninterested professors were challenging for her upon transferring to the main campus. She received a 2.5 grade point average in her first semester after transferring and was still trying to bring those grades up when I spoke to her in her second semester. Ultimately, though, Maggie was staying in college and majoring in animal science with a minor in agricultural business. She had shifted her aspiration of becoming a veterinarian or zoologist to working in dairy, particularly in artificial insemination of dairy cows.[16] She became interested in this after working at a dairy farm that her uncle connected her to during the summer after her freshman year.

Not all young women experienced a decline in grades when they attended college. Four experienced smooth transitions to college and high grades, with two of the four experiencing some disruption in grades at a later time. Janice, a biracial young woman from Kensington, attended the same liberal arts college as Jessie. Although she switched majors from her intended concentration in psychology to English and creative writing, this was not prompted by a decline in grades; she graduated with a 3.91 GPA in 2013. Gail, who aspired to be a pharmacist and continued along that track in college, maintained a 3.85 grade point average over her first two years of college. When she was admitted to the graduate portion of her six-year doctor of pharmacy degree in her third year, her GPA slid, reflecting the difficulty of her new coursework. However, she had been warned that this decline in grades was typical in the first year of graduate coursework and was able to rebound. Gail maintained her position in the program and was thriving when I interviewed her in her fourth year, maintaining a GPA of 3.1.

Kathleen also finished her first semester with a grade point average of 3.9, but she saw these grades decline over time due to her struggles with anxiety; her average GPA was a 3.3 when I spoke to her at the end of her junior year. She made use of her school's counseling services, however, and received disability accommodations to take exams in a quiet room and with double time. She was also supported through mentoring programs and student organizations. Not only did Kathleen get help for herself, she also worked to support other Black students at her school. Pointing out that there were no Black professors teaching in the sciences at MidCity, she described how many Black students were dissuaded from continuing in the premed program: "[Black] students don't have someone that pushes them. They don't have someone telling them they can do it. . . . And then all of a sudden, they have one bad grade or they're struggling in a class and there's no one to help them and there's no one telling them they can still do it." Kathleen took it upon herself to encourage her peers to keep going. Although she acknowledged that some students might need a "reality check," others "don't understand that there's a difference between I don't have the ability and I just need a little more help." Kathleen was well positioned to recognize this difference for herself, and she worked to provide encouragement for her peers in similar situations.

Most on track young women experienced a slow start in the transition into college or transition into new college pathways and received low grades for a period of time. Yet they recovered, unlike the young women we will meet in subsequent chapters who, as we will see, often left college or transferred in response to academic troubles. Why? I found that on track young women were well positioned to reach out for help, either from their parents or college communities, in order to recover their footing. Jessie spoke to her family every day, receiving encouragement and advice, as well as to her college adviser. Several reported that they leaned on their parents for support, and in some cases their parents guided them toward new majors. Others, like Gail and Kathleen, had extensive advising support in individual and group settings through their preprofessional programs and college organizations, which helped them not only adjust to new challenges but also recognize lower grades were often a part of the process and that "grades aren't everything" in making a successful career transition. The availability of such institutional support facilitated these young women's ability and inclination to reach out for help, to recognize poor grades as temporary setbacks, and to adjust strategies on the way to a college degree.

BEING ON TRACK IN THE WORKING CLASS

Most of the on track young women were raised in the middle class and went on to a (so far) successful college experience. Their class background offered them the financial resources to navigate college without needing to work long hours or support family members. They were also skilled at seeking support from advisers and faculty, as their experiences in high school gave them confidence that adults in positions of power would help them. However, some working-class young women were also on track when I interviewed them in their early twenties, and their experiences differed from those hailing from the middle class. Middle-class young women in this group were on the express track, as it were; they moved briskly through college and had substantial support behind them. On track working-class young women, on the other hand, often found themselves on the local track, as it were, taking longer to get where they were going. These young women also had to rely to a greater extent on their own agency; more was left to their own control.

Shana was a working-class Black young woman who graduated from Glenbrook in 2010 with a 4.0 grade point average. Her parents both worked in the criminal justice system; her mother was a state highway patrol officer and her father worked as a parole officer. Shana aspired to be a clinical psychologist or school counselor and therefore planned to complete a bachelor's degree and some additional graduate schooling. Her mother took an active role in Shana's planning, researching Shana's career path and the educational requirements and attending college fairs in her stead. Shana, therefore, was well supported in her goals, although she expressed concern about paying for college and said she did not know how to get college loans.

And indeed, Shana initially struggled after graduating high school. Although she applied and was admitted to her father's alma mater, a public university about three hours from Glenbrook, Shana didn't have the money to attend. She deferred for a year and searched for jobs but did not find any, then spent the next 11 months volunteering and caring for her sister's children. About a year after graduation, however, Shana landed a job at the local amusement park and began saving for college. She worked every day for four months, often for twelve hours per day for minimum wage to save money for tuition. That September, she moved to her grandmother's home near the university and began attending college. A junior when I spoke to her, Shana continued to work on campus and pay for college primarily from a combination of loans totaling close to $20,000 so far and her own earnings.

When I interviewed Shana, she was taking course prerequisites in anticipation of applying to the university's well-regarded respiratory therapy program. She was doing well; although her grades initially suffered in her freshman year, she now had a 3.0 grade point average after earning a 3.9 GPA in her last semester. Shana had a respiratory therapy adviser whom she liked and met with often, and she was given a clear set of class requirements. She would receive more support when she enrolled in the respiratory therapy program, which took two years to complete. Shana explained that getting admitted to the program would depend on a combination of her grades, interview performance, and volunteer activities. She was volunteering with a coalition group that combated human sex trafficking and with an animal shelter. She was currently applying for the program and also planned to take a semester off in the spring of her junior year to work full-time and save more money (she was ultimately admitted to and completed the respiratory therapy program).

Shana's specific goals for the future had changed more than once, from interest in psychology and possibly school counseling, to pharmacy when she entered college, to respiratory therapy. Her pathway through these goals and school were also not seamless. She was on track, but a local track; she had gotten to college and was enrolled full-time with a mostly steady progression, but her path into and through college was slowed by financial need. Getting to where she was had taken a great deal of effort on the part of her mother, who took charge of Shana's college planning, and her grandmother, who offered her a home, as well as Shana's own hard work. And by entering into a structured college program geared toward respiratory therapy, Shana would be further supported in her aims.

Working-class young women could get on track, but many struggled in college. None were admitted to preprofessional college programs leading to a high-paying career, such as pharmacy or physical therapy. These kinds of exclusive programs looked for stellar grades, strong recommendation letters, and early evidence of interest in the field, all of which were easier for middle-class young women to acquire. Thus, middle-class students were often more prepared to enter exclusive college programs, particularly those that were highly sought after and resourced. Internal college programs could still be a benefit to working-class young women—Shana pursued respiratory therapy, and Carol, a working-class White young woman, pursued a degree in education to become a special education teacher— but these programs were neither as exclusive nor as highly resourced. In addition, paying for college posed challenges. Some working-class young women had difficulty managing their obligations to family or romantic relationships. Getting into college and pursuing a degree took more active effort for these young women than for those in the middle class. They had more setbacks to manage and fewer resources with which to do so. For the four who managed to stay on track, completing college was an admirable accomplishment against steep odds.

FAMILY SUPPORT AND FAMILY OBLIGATIONS

What role did parents play in their daughters' college pathways? I found that middle-class parents primarily acted as safety nets in times of need. When middle-class young women failed courses, felt uncertain about their goals, encountered problems in their personal lives, and so on, they turned to their families for support; in moments of crisis, they went home.

Working-class families, as we will see, were encouraging but unable to provide much advice or information relevant to their daughters' college experiences. At times, working-class parents also received support from their daughters.

Sarah was a middle-class White and Mexican young woman who attended a large, selective university close to home. She had been an honors student in high school, receiving mostly As and some Bs at Glenbrook and graduating with a 3.7 grade point average. Although Sarah had aspired to become an X-ray technician, her ACT scores were not high enough to gain entry to the university's health college, and she enrolled as an "exploratory" student. She hoped to enter the health college later, but a grade point average of 2.7 in the first two years precluded her from consideration. At the end of her sophomore year, Sarah was at an impasse, and she reached out to her father:

> I was like, "Dad, I don't really know if this is what I want to do anymore." So he was really supportive and he asked around at his work because he works at [a large corporation] and operations management is a really respected degree, so—and I could co-op with that degree and—I guess that's [the] same thing as intern. And so he just really helped me figure something else out because I do like the business aspect, too, because that's around us every single day. And so I was like, "Okay." I went along with that.

Sarah was close to her father and trusted his advice. He had guided her toward radiology in high school and now guided her toward business, which would be an easier program to get into at her college but could lead to steady employment.

Sarah was not alone. Most on track young women either reported receiving advice from their parents or saying that they would turn to their parents for help if they needed it. This assistance was largely in the form of advice and encouragement. Parents did not appear to hover or micromanage their daughters' college pathways. This deviates from Laura Hamilton's findings in *Parenting to a Degree: How Family Matters for College Women's Success*.[17] Hamilton found that many wealthy parents played an active role in their daughters' college lives, which protected their daughters from the pitfalls working-class and even middle-class students encountered. Perhaps because the girls I interviewed did not have exceptionally high-earning parents, I found fewer examples of parents actively helping their children navigate college than Hamilton did.[18] Even the two young women with the highest-earning parents, Jean and Liz, did not report relying on their parents for advice or help in navigating college.

Ultimately, however, parents still played a vital role, both by facilitating informative ties and assisting in college applications while the young women were in high school and by providing advice and support when the young women turned to them for help. Middle-class parents were familiar with how colleges worked and possessed a network of ties they could reach out to when their daughters needed guidance. Sarah's dad spoke to work colleagues to identify alternative pathways for his daughter. Liz obtained a summer job through her father's close friend. These crowdsourced opportunities were not major interventions, but they smoothed these young women's pathways through college and would, in the long term, help them to navigate the transition out of college and into the labor force.

On track young women from the working class were less well situated to receive support from family members than those from the middle class. Their parents were encouraging but often lacked familiarity with college. Shana and Carol were both close to their parents, particularly their fathers, and would call home often. Shana's father had attended college, and she said she would turn to him for "general" advice but would go to a college adviser for school- and career-related questions. As Carol explained, her dad was her sounding board: "I feel the need to always call my dad for like confirmation. 'Is this like a good idea?' [because] I don't really have any like teachers or anything that like I would ask." Neither young woman's parents offered specific information or advice about navigating college, however.

Working-class young women retained the sense of responsibility toward their families and romantic partners that they had felt in high school. Denise had graduated a semester early from college when I interviewed her and was living at home with her mother while waiting to hear back on her applications to graduate programs. Denise's parents were high school graduates. Her mother worked as a secretary while her father worked as a custodian. When Denise was in high school, her mother encouraged her to consider attending a college near home rather than the four-year, selective university two hours away where she ultimately enrolled. Her father, who was divorced from Denise's mother, was supportive of her plan to attend

State U. and helped Denise navigate financial aid and loans. When I spoke to her after she graduated from college, Denise downplayed her mother's hesitation and explained that they were a "huge [State U.] family now." Although her mother was now supportive of Denise's choice, she also relied heavily on support from her daughter. After Denise's sophomore year, and following a fight with Denise's sister, she struggled with feelings of abandonment and began to act "needy." When home, Denise and her boyfriend often took her mother with them on dates and outings at her mother's insistence. Denise also had to call the police in one incident when her mother threatened to commit suicide. As Denise pointed out in frustration, "Most people have someone else their own age to take care of them, or to be a companion all the time. It's not up to me to be that for her because I'm supposed to be going on and having my own life now." This occurred alongside Denise's own struggles from depression and PTSD after her off-campus apartment burned down in a fire, leaving her sleeping at a friend's mother's house until she could secure new housing. Although her father and boyfriend helped her to move her belongings, they could not offer substantial monetary assistance or housing. At a young age, Denise balanced her own struggles and plans for the future alongside her mother's dependency.

In sum, working-class and middle-class young women's parents alike were supportive of their daughters' educational endeavors and career plans. For working-class parents, this primarily took the form of emotional and limited financial support. Middle-class parents also offered emotional support but could and did provide information and advice when their daughters struggled in school or needed something (like a summer job) that their colleges did not provide. Although the majority of middle-class young women did not report asking for substantial help from their parents, they were aware that it was available should they need it.

PAYING FOR COLLEGE

College is expensive, and the costs to attend college, including not only tuition and fees but also books, housing, food, and other living expenses, continue to rise.[19] Very few of the young women I spoke to were exempt from considering these costs when choosing colleges, whether they were working- or middle-class. Only one young woman's tuition was paid for entirely by her parents (Jean). Most reported paying for college and living expenses through a combination of parental support, scholarships, financial aid and loans, and paid work. A few said that their parents were taking out their own loans, known as Parent Plus loans, in addition to their own student loans.[20] Sheryl, who was middle class and Black, reported that her parents had taken out about $55,000 in loans to cover her college costs, while she had loans totaling roughly $20,000. She intended to pay off all of these loans after she got out of college. Janice, a middle-class Black and White young woman, attended a private liberal arts college on scholarship but anticipated she would graduate with approximately $40,000 in loans.[21] We will see how educational loans can become a catch-22 for holding on and navigating rough seas young women in the coming chapters. Among on track young women, however, they seemed to generally serve the function of paying a portion of their college costs so that they could successfully earn a degree. How much of a burden these loans would place on their future financial security was still unclear.

On track young women had enough financial support to avoid working long hours for pay, however. Jessie and Sheryl both worked over school breaks but not while taking classes. Sarah, Kim, and Carol worked part-time during the semesters and more in the summers when they could. For about one-third of the young women, the paid and unpaid jobs they held were mostly, like Jordan's, tied to their planned careers. Maggie, described earlier, worked on a dairy farm during college to learn more about the industry she hoped to enter. Jordan, Gail, and Liz all held internships periodically, and both Kathleen and Denise worked for faculty-run research labs. None of the young women worked more than twenty hours a week while engaged in classes, and most worked fewer than fifteen hours.

Notably, all of the on track working-class young women except Shana avoided working long hours for pay, and even Shana only worked fifteen to twenty hours during the academic semester. Although their parents did not have the money to pay for college, they could help out in smaller ways. Shana reported that her father had recently started helping with tuition after seeing that she was struggling financially. Carol saved money by living at home and attending the lower-cost branch campus of her university for the first two years of college before transferring to the main campus.

Denise's father chipped in with small amounts of money at times to off-set living expenses, and she saved some money by loading up on credits and graduating early. Kim graduated as valedictorian of Glenbrook High School, which facilitated extensive scholarship money from her hometown. She was also able to apply for full financial aid as an independent student after her father passed away in her senior year of high school. In sum, all of the working-class young women either received help from family or creatively managed their college enrollment (or both) to offset their costs.

Paying for college could be a source of family tension. Gail, for example, received scholarships which paid for a large portion of her first year of college but relied on loans to cover the remainder and the full $15,000 bill for each subsequent year. In her six-year program, this meant that she would eventually accrue at least $75,000 in loans. For Gail, this strained her relationship with her father:

> My relationship with my dad has got really bad because of the whole paying for college thing. He basically just said, "I'm not paying for anything," even though he went out and got himself a new car. [He] claimed he had no money . . . and I'm like, "Oh, you don't have any money, but yet you just got yourself a new . . . sports car."

Gail resented her father's unwillingness to pay for her education despite living comfortably. This came to a head when Gail was admitted into the graduate portion of her six-year program. Given the odd timing—Gail was now a graduate student before completing a full bachelor's degree course load—she was ineligible for loans as either an undergraduate or graduate student. To cover her expenses, Gail needed a few thousand dollars to help pay expenses until she requalified for loans. When she turned to her father, Gail explained, he refused and criticized her decision to go into pharmacy even though "my whole life he has told me, 'You need to get into the medical field.'" Although Gail was eventually able to work with the financial aid office to "move money around" among her loans to cover the semester, she distanced herself from her parents, rarely visiting and not speaking to her father unless he initiated conversation.[22]

Most on track young women were headed toward stable careers in which they would be able to pay back their loans. However, a job was not guaranteed, and monthly loan payments can be a burden for young people still in the early phases of their careers. The costs of these payments can put them on a slower track to the middle-class lifestyle they envisioned.[23]

LOOKING AHEAD TO CAREER AND FAMILY
TRANSITIONS IN YOUNG ADULTHOOD

In high school, middle-class girls almost unanimously envisioned completing school, launching a successful career, getting married, and having children by age 30. They anticipated that their lives in adulthood would look like those they were accustomed to, with minor changes. The young women dreamed of stability and middle-class comforts. Some wished to move out of state, but many envisioned raising children close to their own parents, in part due to the childcare their parents might provide. Working-class and poor girls had the same goals—school, work, family, and middle-class stability—but their view of the middle class was from the outside looking in, and their expectations revolved around what they did not want: difficulty paying bills, chaotic home lives, a lack of education. Their goals were more specific regarding the hardships they wished to avoid but less specific about how to achieve these goals.

How did these goals evolve between high school and college for on track middle-class and working-class young women? Now in their early twenties, these young women were getting closer to—yet still distant from—their imagined futures. In the aggregate, their goals remained similar to those they held in adolescence; these young women envisioned adult futures in which they had college degrees, worked, and were close to family (primarily but not exclusively romantic partners and children). As Jordan described it, "I would like to have a house, a husband, and one kid. I would like to have a stable work environment. . . . I would like to be financially stable and just happy." There were adjustments, however. Two young women from this group, Maggie and Denise, who had not envisioned marrying or having children in the future when they were high school students, now hoped to eventually marry and were open to having children. For those who wished to marry or have children, or both, timelines became less fixed than they had anticipated in high school; many did not give exact ages at which they hoped these events would occur. For those who were more specific with their anticipated timelines, the ages at which they aspired to marry and have children remained roughly the same as what they had predicted in high school.

Several on track young women expressed caution about the prospects of both marriage and having children. These young women viewed marriage with some suspicion and wanted to attain financial stability before committing to a partner. Liz, a middle-class White young woman now attending college out of state, explained that she could see marrying for practical reasons, "like taxes," but otherwise did not feel she had to marry. If she did, she said, "I'd like to be stable financially, emotionally, you know, all of that. I'd like to be stable, have a job, have my master's done." Sarah also hoped to settle into a career before starting a family: "I just want to have a nice job. I want to make sure that I can handle myself if I'm alone or if I'm with somebody, make sure that I can provide for myself." Jessie anticipated getting "stabilized" in her career before marrying in her mid-twenties, moving in with her husband, and having children shortly thereafter. When asked why she anticipated this timing, she explained, "I definitely want to be able to provide for myself first before worrying about someone else or anything like that and prove to myself that I don't necessarily have to go straight into a relationship just to be stable." Jessie was cautious about entering into a long-term relationship while in college but imagined a future in which marriage and raising children played a large part. Like many on track young women I interviewed, Jordan, Liz, Sarah, and Jessie valued financial stability for themselves prior to making family commitments.

Other young women emphasized the importance of personal independence, rather than financial stability, before marriage. For instance, Carol said it was "crazy to think" about marriage, explaining:

> I have freedom now, but not a lot because I'm in school. I need to be focused. . . . Once I'm out [I'll work] on building who I am and then I feel like when I'm done, I want to be free to go and be in the world, as that new person. I don't want to—I feel like having a family right out of college. . . . I'd be stuck again.

In Carol's view, entering into family relationships meant being "stuck," as opposed to being free. Some other young women, either while in high school or college (and across class background), expressed similar attitudes. These feelings seemed to be shaped by assumptions about gendered responsibilities within the home. Being a wife and mother was associated with being selfless and focused on caregiving.[24] Some young women wanted time to be "selfish"—that is, think about their own needs and interests—before committing to that obligation.

Finally, marriage was regarded as an emotional risk, particularly for young women who had seen family members' lives disrupted. For Shana, the fighting she observed within her family made the prospect of marriage daunting:

> I used to tell my dad that I would just get artificially inseminated and just have me a little kid. I was watching everybody, all the women in my family, have to deal with their husbands or boyfriends. [It] seemed too time-consuming when you can just go to a sperm bank . . . get artificially inseminated. Then look, you have a baby. You didn't have to deal with the fighting.

Shana's father wanted her to settle down with a man who would "take care of" her, but as Shana reasoned, "[You] can't really have that . . . in this type of economy, you can't really be a stay-at-home mom unless the other person has a really good job." Although she admitted that staying home and teaching her children "sounds nice," she was cautious about her ability to do so and pragmatic about her options. Ultimately, Shana wanted to get her degree, find a stable job, pay back her student loans, and have children in her midthirties.

Similarly, Kim, a working-class White young woman, explained that her boyfriend wanted to marry her but said, "I don't know if I want to get married. . . . Everybody I know gets divorced. And I don't really see the point in getting married if you're going to get divorced." Kim also struggled with feeling "selfish" because she wanted to move out of state and travel, and her boyfriend, who had recently graduated from a public, midsize university near their hometown, was trying to find a job near her and wanted to settle down. Kim was unsure of her postcollege plans and did not want to commit to staying in the local area.

Regardless of exact timeline, most of the college-attending young women I interviewed envisioned getting married and having children after a relatively short "career-building" period. These young women viewed the postcollege and premarriage period as one in which they could focus on themselves and build their finances; their attention was, for the moment, focused on that period. They also assumed that having children would be a career-changing event, and many anticipated stepping down from their careers—for a time—to raise children. When I asked Janice if she would work after having children, she explained, "I wouldn't be opposed to staying at home. . . . I'd probably want to still do stuff, like maybe have a small part-time [job] or like work with a non-profit or like volunteer work." Similarly, Sheryl, who did not anticipate being married but wanted kids in the future, explained, "I definitely think I would have to slow down working. . . . I want to be pretty involved." Thus, although these young women were dedicated to their career paths, they also envisioned not-too-distant futures in which they would step back from those careers in order to raise children. Somewhat surprisingly, few young women considered their future spouse's employment as a factor. Kathleen was an exception, explaining that while she used to want to marry another Black doctor and be a "Black doctor couple," she had decided that marrying a teacher would complement her family goals better: "I feel like my ideal spouse would be a teacher because they get summers off where they could hang out with the kids and then they'd get off at the same time as the kids." For Kathleen, fulfilling her occupational goals would be eased by a less traditional gender arrangement, in which her husband could provide more childcare, allowing for her long hours and time on call.

Regardless of their hopes for the future, on track young women had the advantage of focusing primarily on themselves and their own educational and occupational goals while in college. This was particularly true for those from middle-class families, but even among on track working-class young women, family obligations were often secondary. As we will see in the next two chapters, this was not the case for young women holding on and navigating rough seas.

6 Holding On

INTERVIEWER: Do you think you're generally happy with where your life is right now?

JENNIE: I mean, yeah. This is where I see myself. . . . I'm working. I'm living on my own. You can't really rush things. So I'm pretty happy with where I'm at.

If on track young women were moving forward toward their goals on fixed pathways, holding on young women were working furiously to stay in place. What epitomizes this group of young women was how they struggled to balance multiple domains of life—school, work, and family—while chasing the American Dream. They were not so much holding on to the edge of a cliff as they were holding on across a chasm, straining to hold themselves aloft, trying to complete college while working long hours for pay and caring for others.

Holding on young women graduated high school with a plan for college and work, and they tried to enact these plans but ran up against barriers that set them back. Undeterred and certain that they could prevail through grit, they revised their goals and adjusted their plans to accomplish these new goals. This process of adjustment and persistence, however, often sent them churning through schools and jobs, searching for the right college and degree that would provide them with a ticket to the middle class. Their pursuit of the American Dream both kept them going and encumbered them with debt.

.   .   .   .   .

When Jennie, a poor White young woman from Glenbrook, was in high school, she aspired to complete a four-year college degree, and possibly medical school, to become a photographer or doctor. A college degree would be much more education than was typical for her family members, who had at most completed a GED, but Jennie was determined and earned good grades in her honors classes. When I met Jennie five years later, she was enrolled in college and working toward her bachelor's degree. Getting to this point had taken enormous effort, however, and she still had a long road ahead of her.

Toward the end of high school, Jennie began to stay at friends' homes in order to get out of her mother's house. Although Jennie loved her mother and continued to have a close relationship with her, she left her mother's home because her mom was "a crazy cat lady" with "30, 40 cats. Not even exaggerating." To make ends meet after high school graduation, Jennie moved in with her boyfriend of only a few weeks, delayed college enrollment, and worked fifty hours a week as a pizza chain shift manager, pulling in $900 every two weeks. She returned to school a year later, enrolling at a midsize public university, but once there felt alienated; the college was forty-five minutes away from where she was living, she didn't know anyone, and it seemed large and unwelcoming to her. After one semester, she transferred to Templeton-Glenbrook, a local branch campus of a larger public university, and enrolled in their general education program. At Templeton-Glenbrook, she recognized people she had seen around town and found her fellow students welcoming.

Jennie continued to work while attending college, but juggling school and work was difficult. She left a manager's job requiring more than full-time hours because it interfered with her time at school. After a short stint working at a warehouse, she was hired at another pizza chain as shift manager, working twenty-five to thirty hours a week for $8.50 an hour. When the store manager assigned her to work shifts until 4:00 a.m. on days in which she had morning classes, however, she struggled to keep up. She was able to secure a job as shift manager at a new pizza restaurant that would work with her schedule. When I interviewed Jennie again five years later, she was attending college full-time, living with her boyfriend, and working thirty hours a week at $8.70 an hour.

Even with nearly full-time work, Jennie did not earn enough to pay for college outright. A Pell Grant covered most of her tuition, which was a boon for someone working in fast food with frequently unemployed parents.[1] She covered the remainder of her tuition, fees, and book expenses each semester with a $1,000 loan. To complete her intended degree, however, Jennie would have to take classes at the main campus of Templeton University, where the cost of tuition was more than double what she paid at the branch campus. She was maxed out on her Pell Grant, which meant she was responsible for any additional costs over that amount. Her boyfriend could not help her out either, as he was just beginning to pay off $16,000 of educational loans he had accrued while enrolled in a for-profit art school. After meeting with her college counselor, she learned that she would be charged Templeton-Glenbrook tuition as long as the majority of her classes were at that campus. If Jennie could arrange her schedule so that she would always take more credits at the Glenbrook campus than the main campus, she could successfully finance her college degree.

Jennie's aspirations had shifted considerably since high school; after her experience as a manager, she now planned to go into business and hoped to one day open her own small business. To that end, she planned to apply to the business management program at the community college she attended. Yet her math skills had stymied her thus far. To apply to the business program, Jennie needed to have passed a college math course. However, she was placed in a series of remedial math courses at Templeton-Glenbrook after receiving a low score on the college math placement exam. In order to take (and hopefully pass) the college-level course, she would first need to pass these remedial courses. As I discuss later in this chapter, remedial coursework is often a barrier to degree completion, even for students like Jennie who had done well in advanced courses in high school.

Despite this setback, Jennie was optimistic. She had a 3.4 grade point average in college and only one more math course to complete before entering the business program. In sum, Jennie was holding on. She was managing to pull together enough resources to stay in school, earn a living, and support herself. Juggling school and work was difficult, but with a partner and no child, she made it work.

Yet Jennie was also at risk. Several things outside of her control could propel her into accruing more debt or taking time off from school. Jennie's plans were contingent on taking enough classes at Templeton-Glenbrook to qualify for their lower tuition, but either a mistake in planning or a restriction in the course offerings at her branch campus could leave her paying the main Templeton campus's prices. Colleges sometimes respond to budget shortfalls by reducing course offerings, and courses may be cut last minute if they fail to enroll enough students. She could also lose her job or her Pell Grant, reducing the funds available to her to pay tuition.[2] If she didn't gain admission to the business program due to her difficulties in math, she might find herself completing another series of prerequisites for a different major, extending her schooling even further and placing her aid eligibility at risk. And if her relationship fell apart, as a high proportion of cohabiting relationships do, she would need to move home into an untenable living situation or try to eke out an existence on her own.[3] If she became sick, was injured, or suffered a mental health crisis, she could quickly lose both her work and student statuses. Holding on was difficult and risky, and it meant juggling between bad jobs, sometimes fluctuating living situations, and educational institutions that at times promised more than they could deliver.

One of only two young women from poor families who were in the holding on group and therefore poised to become upwardly mobile relative to her parents, Jennie had a keen ability to think strategically about how to reach her goals. Yet finances were her biggest and most immediate challenge, and so most of this strategic thinking was focused on how to pay for college and sustain herself, rather than preparing for and planning a career. Faced with a difficult living situation and high housing costs, Jennie chose to move in with a boyfriend she had not known for very long. In order to make ends meet, Jennie worked long hours, which in turn made focusing on coursework difficult. An unregulated educational landscape also contributed to the loans her boyfriend owed, which increased the burden on both Jennie and her partner to complete schooling quickly and look for a new job. Yet academic barriers elongated Jennie's pathway to a degree. Given these challenges, it was remarkable that Jennie was holding on.

Holding on young women were caught between their goals for the future—a college education, a good job, family life, and middle-class stability—and the reality of managing and maintaining school, work, and family commitments. In this chapter, I discuss what it meant to be holding on and describe the circumstances that led to, and maintained, these young women's precarious positions. First, I argue that holding on young women were balancing combinations of work, school, and family responsibilities that placed constraints on their ability to get ahead. Work schedules and family duties limited the time these young women had to study and take classes, and elongated paths to college degrees kept them engaged in low-wage work. Second, I show how aspirations for college alongside a complex and expensive educational landscape made getting ahead challenging. Young women were drawn toward postsecondary programs that did not pay off, accruing debt without advancing in their careers. Third, I discuss how, in response to these conflicting demands and significant educational setbacks, these young women shifted their goals for the future, even as they held on to the broad outline of a stable, middle-class future. Fourth, I illustrate how class background shaped the young women's pathways into the holding on group. Particularly for young women from poor and working-class families, holding on was an accomplishment. For those from middle-class families, it could be more of a soft landing following one or more major life disruptions. Finally, I describe how young women in the holding on group put the onus on themselves to succeed, rather than identifying the institutional constraints that have contributed to their difficulties.

MAKING DO IN THE LABOR MARKET, SCHOOL, AND AT HOME

Young women in the holding on group worked long hours while juggling school and home responsibilities. Seven of the fourteen young women in this group worked full-time or more than full-time, while the remainder balanced intensive part-time work (usually twenty-five to thirty hours a week) with school. All but one worked in the service sector and typically made between $9.50 and $13.50 an hour. The low wages forced them to take on more hours than they might otherwise prefer. These jobs also came with few benefits or protections, meaning that they were subject to unpredictable schedules and hours that competed with their school and family obligations, both of which could be significant. Half were currently enrolled in college when I interviewed them and all but two had been enrolled in college for significant lengths of time since high school. And many of these young women balanced family care obligations. Some provided emotional support to family members and others cared for younger siblings or their own children or managed their households. Young women from poor and working-class families, in particular, were viewed as adults who were capable of pitching in to help family members. Ultimately, holding on young women worked hard to creatively navigate the labor market, the educational landscape, and family life.

Madeline, a working-class White young women from Kensington High School, was enrolled in a family studies sequence at a local branch campus when I spoke to her, after leaving the nursing program where she was last enrolled. As Madeline described it, she did not fit the stereotypical image of a young twenty-something: "I don't go out, ever. I don't have very many friends, because I'm always working or doing schoolwork. Always. And I watch my brother in my spare time." Madeline's days were packed. On Mondays and Tuesdays, she took classes in the early afternoon and evenings, ending her last class at 10:00 p.m. She had one class on Wednesday and Thursday afternoons, leaving directly from there to work eight-hour shifts, 4:00 p.m. to midnight, at a local pharmacy. She pulled an additional shift of eight to ten hours on Friday and again on one weekend day a week, for a total of thirty-two hours a week. She also continued to take care of her 8-year-old half brother, Brian. Madeline attended school meetings about Brian's education alongside her mother and cared for him when her mother was at work. When her mother's shifts as a nurse kept her away, Madeline would stay at the house to care for her brother. Afterward, Madeline would drive back to the apartment that she shared with her boyfriend, twenty-five minutes away.

Madeline and Jennie were both examples of young women who were trying to complete a degree while working long hours and managing home and family responsibilities. These competing responsibilities pushed them to make difficult choices. For Jennie, this meant moving in with a boyfriend to escape her mother's house, switching jobs when work interfered with courses, selecting a major that she saw as a ticket to steady work and independence, and balancing coursework across campuses to keep tuition low. Madeline also made choices within a difficult set of circumstances, sacrificing social interactions in order to work and care for family. She also knew she had to complete college and get a job quickly, as her father had made it clear that she and her sister would need to help out with her 16-year-old brother's tuition in the coming years. Madeline saw this as fair; her father had paid for most of her tuition, and now she would help her brother pay for his. This arrangement echoes the reciprocal relationships between working-class and poor parents and their children discussed in part I. Yet, for some holding on young women, these competing priorities slowed their pathways through the transition to adulthood, pushing four-year degrees into six years or more, thereby delaying entry into full-time (and hopefully more stable) work. For others, the need to pursue a degree quickly meant shifting their priorities and choosing a career path with less extensive educational requirements and lower earnings potential.

The jobs that these young women worked often did not offer them many options for schedule control.[4] Managers set schedules, and they had to organize their school and family lives around this work. Amy, who worked forty hours a week while completing her associate's degree, had had her hours cut to just under thirty hours a week shortly before I spoke with her. She also did not have the freedom to set her own hours, explaining, "My life is pure chaos. . . . I work with retail, crazy hours, morning I can work from like 8:00 to 4:00, 7:30 to like 3:30 or work 'til 11:00 at night and have to be in 7:00 a.m." On top of this, Amy picked up extra temporary work at a chiropractor's office for a couple of months before we spoke. Yet despite Amy and her fiancé working full-time, they still lived with his friend in order to make ends meet (a situation she described as "not ideal" and also unlikely to end).

Chelsea, a middle-class Black young woman from Glenbrook, also balanced her obligations as a parent, wife, student, and employee. Chelsea was pushed off course from her goals of pursuing a PhD and working as a therapist by the arrival of a son in her sophomore year of college. Although she had been doing well in her coursework, she felt she needed to complete a degree more quickly and enter a less demanding career after her son was born. She and her boyfriend had broken up shortly after she found out she was pregnant; he was not interested in being a father and questioned whether the child was his. Her parents also stopped paying for college at this point because she was considered an independent student by the federal government and now eligible for Pell Grants. In response to her new circumstances and on the advice of an academic counselor, Chelsea switched majors and completed an associate's degree in early childhood education quickly and was then hired as an assistant teacher at a childcare center. From there, she was soon promoted to teacher and then hired at another center as lead teacher, before being hired at a third center as the assistant director. She now worked 9:00 a.m. to 6:30 p.m. each day at the daycare center. Although this work was demanding—at least as demanding as the career she described as not being "conducive" to being a full-time mother—it allowed her to enroll her son at her workplace where she could see him regularly. She was also back in school, completing her bachelor's degree online through a community college located a short distance away, which meant she often stayed late at work or traveled to her parents' house to watch online lectures until 8:00 or 9:00 p.m.

Other holding on young women reported time-intensive responsibilities in multiple domains. Holly, a working-class White young woman from Glenbrook, attended a nearby public university full-time and a modeling school part-time while working twenty-five hours a week. Although she did not report providing practical support to family members, she frequently visited her grandmother, who had dementia, and struggled with the repercussions of her parents' separation during her first year of college when her father became addicted to oxycodone after an injury. Isabel, a poor Mexican young woman from Glenbrook who did not attend college, worked full-time in a managerial position at a small factory, sold Mary Kay products, and volunteered with her church as an administrator and minister along with her husband. These young women, whether balancing competing demands between all three domains of work, family, and school or intensive demands from two domains, were stretched thin. They were holding on by eking out a living as independent young adults, but their finances were perilous. A "normal unpredictable" event, such as losing a job or relationship or incurring an unexpected expense, could send them into poverty.[5] And, as we will see, not only could a single event have serious repercussions for their livelihoods, but so could a longer slide into debt.

CHASING A COLLEGE DEGREE

College is a meaningful milestone for young people. It is a rite of passage for the middle class and a marker of success for the working class and poor. Middle-class, working-class, and poor alike say that college degrees are the dividing line between good and bad jobs, and by extension, can determine the quality of one's family life and feelings of self-worth. And they are not wrong. Individuals with a college degree stand to earn more than double the lifetime earnings that those without a college degree earn.[6] Having that piece of paper can open up doors that otherwise stay closed. Yet the combination of this imperative to go to college, the complexity of and lack of guidance through the college landscape, and the high cost of tuition make college a risky proposition for many. For those who are not supported by well-resourced colleges and/or college tracks, the pursuit of a college degree can leave them accruing more and more debt as they move between majors and institutions in pursuit of the American Dream.

All but two of the young women in the holding on group attended college for some time, but their paths through postsecondary schooling were not smooth. Half of the holding on young women (N = 7) transferred colleges at least once, and one moved in and out of student status at the same school. One student remained enrolled steadily but switched majors frequently. Four completed an associate's degree or postsecondary certificate (two of whom had also transferred colleges at least once), although only one was currently working in the field in which she received a degree. The remaining three either did not attend college (N = 2) or attended college for a year before dropping out (N = 1).

A number of factors contributed to holding on young women's difficulty in completing college. I first discuss how personal and institutional factors, together, shaped these difficulties. These include the opaqueness of the college landscape, difficulties transitioning to college-level work, a lack of institutional support, and diversionary practices (primarily remedial education and waitlisted program entry) that prevented them from progressing toward a degree. In the following section I discuss how financial costs of college contributed to these young women's difficulties.

Churning through Colleges

Jennifer's path to a college degree was rocky. A working-class Black young woman from Glenbrook, Jennifer aspired to be a psychiatrist when I met her in high school. In Jennifer's senior year, she met a college representative in her home economics class who talked to her about a college in Connecticut. She was motivated to leave Glenbrook and decided immediately that she would enroll there: "I felt like getting away would, you know, solve all those problems. And so that's what led up to that decision.... I just wanted to get away from everything and start over." Jennifer drove to Connecticut in the fall after high school graduation to move in, but she discovered upon arrival that her financial aid did not cover her needs, and she did not have the money to pay the remainder of her bill. She drove home the same day. Later, Jennifer explained that she didn't know the college was a "private" school; she assumed that this explained the financial difficulty she had encountered. In truth, however, the college was a for-profit postsecondary school, one that was soon thereafter under investigation by the federal government for aggressive marketing, high costs, and poor student retention. Jennifer, however, did not know this. She had relied on adults to guide her college decision-making and put her trust in a college representative who came to her school (thus appearing legitimate).

Predatory practices were not the only barrier Jennifer faced. After she returned home, she enrolled at a local not-for-profit public university as a communications major with a business minor. She attended this university for two semesters, getting mostly As and Bs in her first term and then Fs in her second term, when she felt unmotivated and distracted by worry over her aunt's recurrent drinking problems. Jennifer left, and a year later she enrolled at a local community college as a business major. Once again, she attended for two semesters and received good grades in the first semester but failing grades in the second. This time, it was a literal roadblock—the loss of her car—that impeded her progress. Without it, she was unable to get to class.

Jennifer's difficulties completing college were multifaceted. Without help selecting a college, she was lured to an out-of-state college with promises that she could thrive but whose obligations were to shareholders rather than students. Stymied, Jennifer was persistent in pursuing her amended goals. Yet this persistence led to Jennifer churning in and out of college when family problems and economic difficulties—themes we will return to—made her attachment to college tenuous. Her academic performance faltered in response to real barriers to get to and concentrate on school.

Other holding on young women also attended multiple colleges after high school graduation due to academic problems and diversionary practices. Christina, like Jennifer, shuttled in and out of colleges. A middle-class White young woman from Kensington, Christina enrolled at a branch campus of a large university after high school and attended for a year and a half, intending to major in business. She became stuck when attempting to complete remedial math courses, however, and blamed this on her college advisers:

> They would tell me what classes I needed to take and they would be the wrong classes that wouldn't go toward my major. And I failed. . . . And then next semester I took it again with a different professor and I was seeing a tutor three times a week. I did all the extra work. I still failed it. So that put me on academic probation, and I told them I didn't want to take it again because if I failed it again I'm kicked out of school. Well, they said, "You need to take it. You need to take it." So I took it, and I failed it again.

Although Christina described the math course as "wrong," her college advisers had likely not steered her incorrectly. College students must fulfill distribution requirements at most public and private not-for-profit colleges in the United States as a part of the general education curriculum.[7] To do so, some students like Christina (and Jennie, from the opening to this chapter) must first pass a series of remedial courses, usually based on placing below a given cutoff score on a placement test, before enrolling in a course that will fulfill their distribution requirement. This is most common in community colleges and in subjects such as math and English, although even among students at four-year colleges, almost one-third have been referred to remedial courses.[8] Even students who have performed well in advanced coursework in high school, like Jennie, often test below the cutoff and are placed in remedial courses.[9]

Unfortunately, remedial coursework is both costly and an exit point for many students. It is costly because students must pay tuition to take these courses but receive no college credit for them. And it can lead to students dropping out of college when they, like Christina, become frustrated with multiple failures and not making progress toward their goals. This has been criticized as a means of "cooling out" community college students, whereby college staff mask students' remedial status from them and students are "gently led into a long-term process without having any idea of how little progress they are making or how long it will take to attain their goal."[10] On a more practical level, researchers have argued that placement tests can misplace students and that remedial coursework is ineffective.[11] Rather than helping, remedial coursework can divert students away from their goals without evidence that those students would have had the same outcome had they enrolled directly in credit-bearing coursework.

After her third attempt at passing a remedial math course, college counselors told Christina that she would not get into the business major due to her low grade point average. Christina then transferred to Lewis Community College, but she fell behind on her work early in the first semester after becoming ill. She left the school and then tried to enroll at Evansville Nursing College, a for-profit chain of nursing schools, but missed passing the entrance exam by two points. She then took off from college for a year and tried again, now enrolling at a newly built branch campus of a regional community and technical college. The new campus, in Glenbrook, was small and served fewer than 500 students, but Christina liked the cozy atmosphere. She also liked the relatively sparse requirements, saying, "All I have to take is English and math and then a public speaking class, then I just go straight into my degree." It was unclear whether these courses were remedial, but Christina seemed relieved that there were a small number of requirements. Now receiving straight As, Christina planned to obtain her associate's degree in business management.

Some young women were also delayed by being waitlisted by their intended college programs. Waitlists were common among those hoping to enter fields like nursing and radiology. Although some applicants are admitted to these programs immediately, others are provisionally accepted and placed on a waitlist that can take years to get off of. This can occur either when applying to a health school or applying to a health track within a college. Madeline spent a year taking classes at a local branch campus while waitlisted at a nursing college. Cassie, whom we met in chapter 2, was discouraged from pursuing a nursing degree in part because she would have been placed on a two-year waitlist first. Waitlists have been cited in the news as a cause for concern.[12] According to these reports, long waitlists for health-care programs are primarily due to a shortage of faculty to teach courses and a limited number of clinical sites where student health-care professionals can train.

Holding on young women encountered institutional barriers that led them to enroll in multiple colleges, searching for a good fit. Although academic difficulties stemmed from different origins—Jennifer's home distractions and economic need, for example, and Christina's poor academic preparation—both lacked institutional guidance and support in their pathways into and through college, which led to misunderstandings and frustration. Christina, and others we will hear from, would have benefited from academic support to help them transition to college-level work. Jennifer performed well during some semesters, showing the capacity to perform at a high level, but needed better financial assistance. Such assistance would have allowed her to maintain her car, a necessity for commuting to school. It also would have allowed her to move out of her aunt's home, thus separating her from the stress of her aunt's drinking.[13]

Ultimately, it is not enough to say that young people should go to college. Young people know very little about the options available to them or how those options could impact their employment opportunities down the line. Particularly among the working-class young adults I interviewed, but also among some in the middle class, distinctions between institutions in the educational landscape were not always clear. Most understood the difference between private and public colleges, but few understood the distinction between for-profit and not-for-profit. Similarly, most young women understood the difference between an associate's and a bachelor's degree, but the line between certificates and associate's degrees was blurry. Nor did the young women understand accreditation or how this might matter for the link between their degree and employment. This complexity, and the lack of available guideposts for young people, is one of the barriers that stood in the way of following through on their earlier plans and amending new plans once in the transition to adulthood. As a result, many enrolled in colleges that made false promises or did not provide the kind of support they needed to succeed. And as we will see in the next section, these repeated enrollments had a deep financial cost.

The Costs of Chasing a College Degree

Holding on young women desperately wanted a college degree but did not have adequate support or knowledge, which often led to a period (or periods) of trial and error. These periods of trial and error were costly in both time and money. Six months after leaving school, for instance, Jennifer sat with me discussing her current circumstances and plans for the future. Though now $10,000 in debt from school loans and working sixty-five hours a week as a home health aide—a job well-known for paying low wages and requiring back-breaking work—she had not given up on her dream of completing a college degree.[14]

> I've been thinking about going back to school to get certified in business management. And then, hopefully from there . . . I can go back and get an associate['s degree]. And . . . I could just keep building. But I really [want to] go back and get certified. Complete that milestone, you know, instead of just wearing myself out.

Wary of being pushed off her educational goals again, Jennifer hoped to work toward a college degree incrementally. This is a completely logical approach based on her experience. As we have seen, Jennifer could perform well in school, but unexpected roadblocks often foiled her plans. An incremental approach would, in theory, shorten each period in school, thus reducing her odds of dropping out. Yet doing so would also lead to more debt, and there was no guarantee that completing a certificate first would hasten the time spent pursuing an associate's degree, or that this plan would pay off in the labor market.

Other young women were still enrolled in college but would soon be facing large student debt. Chelsea owed about $50,000 in student loans and earned $13.50/hour at her job, which netted less than $30,000 a year. Her husband, a case manager for a homeless shelter, also earned a low salary and was paying off student debt. Despite being more financially settled than anyone else in the holding on group, Chelsea was deeply in debt for a credential in an industry (childcare) that paid less than one could earn as a high school graduate.[15] Tess, a White young woman from a middle-class family, paid her way at a regional public university, first, and later at the local branch campus, almost entirely through loans. These already totaled almost $10,000, and Tess still intended to transfer schools to start either a pre–physical therapy or pre–respiratory therapy program, which would add substantially greater debt. Tess felt that loans were the price of admission to college, explaining, "I figure everyone in college is in debt, so there's really no reason to worry about it now." Holly and Jennie both received some money from Pell Grants and paid the remainder of their costs with loans.

Some young women had already completed their degrees when I met with them but could not find work in their chosen fields. Now burdened with debt, they planned to enroll in school again, accruing more debt. Zakeshia, a middle-class Black young woman from Kensington, enrolled in a for-profit college after high school and completed her certificate in medical billing a year later. She was unable to secure a job in this field, however. She worked instead at a series of service jobs at a fast-food chain, two call centers, and a chain restaurant. She worked for five and a half years at her longest job, at a fast-food restaurant she originally started working for in high school, until a dispute with her manager led him to cut her shifts, leaving her with a reduced income. Her next job was at a call center earning about $8.00/hour, but her managers routinely scheduled her for less than full-time work. Zakeshia moved on to a second call center, earning $10.00/hour, and had been promoted recently to a new department, earning $10.75/hour, although her pay was effectively lower because she lost the ability to earn sales bonuses.

Disappointed by her inability to find work in medical billing, Zakeshia planned to go back to school "for something else like a nursing assistant." Zakeshia was tired of earning an hourly wage and putting in overtime to make ends meet. At the same time, she struggled to maintain financial solvency; she had moved in with her mother after being unable to pay her rent, and her wages were being garnished to pay back the $3,900 she owed to her former landlord. On top of that, she had incurred student loan, medical, and credit card debt in recent years and was considering filing for bankruptcy. Adding more educational loans was risky, but her earnings were too low to pay off her debts, particularly when they fluctuated unexpectedly. Mounting debt and low pay, then, forced Zakeshia into a set of poor options: risk college, which would defer some loans and possibly put her in a position to earn a higher income, but which could also result in accruing more debt without a degree, or stay where she was, earning less than she needed to pay off her existing loans.

Amy, a White young woman of working-class origins, was in a similar spot. She had attended a small private college in her state for one semester and then dropped out; she felt the college had misrepresented itself as more prestigious than it was. The next semester she enrolled in a local college's veterinary technician program. She soon found that she fainted at the sight of blood, however, and decided to pursue an associate's degree in applied business with a major in medical administration instead. Now several months after completing her degree and $20,000 in debt from educational loans, Amy was frustrated by her lack of options, noting that the employers wanted her to have prior experience, even for entry-level jobs:

> I can't get my foot in the door. . . I apply for entry-level positions, but I somehow still don't meet qualifications, and I don't really understand how I'm not meeting the qualifications when I have a degree, but these places are choosing to hire people from a tech school that have a certificate? . . . They hire like, basically straight out of Cantor Tech . . . had I known that I wouldn't have spent $20,000 at an actual college; so kind of bitter towards it.

Amy was now considering deferring her college loans and attending Cantor Technology school for a certificate in medical billing and coding. In the meantime, Amy was working as a pharmacy technician twenty-eight hours a week for $9.50/hour. Although she had previously worked full-time and preferred it, her hours were cut unexpectedly. For both Zakeshia and Amy, completing a degree did not lead to paid work within their field of choice, or even to stable and predictable work. Notably, both of their degrees were in the "practical arts," which are often characterized as being smart choices for getting a job after college.[16] Yet neither could find work in her field, and both planned to return to college for additional credentials.

Holding on young women knew that their best chance to obtain a stable, well-paying job was to complete a college degree, and so they tried—often several times over—to attain this educational marker of success. Yet the cards were stacked against them. Over the past few decades the cost of college has risen (and continues to rise) steeply and much more rapidly than the average family income.[17] And with no clear guideposts through the educational landscape, many fall short of completing a degree. They are not alone; the six-year graduation rate at four-year colleges is only 62%, and at two-year colleges, less than one-third graduate in three years.[18] Those who do not graduate are unlikely to be employed in jobs that pay well. And even when schooling is completed and a degree obtained, there is no guarantee of a "good job." Yet these young people must pay back their debt. The young women I spoke to were aware of this and were working hard to make it. They did their best, within a complex and risky landscape of education and within jobs they had little control over, to hold on.

FORGING NEW PATHS TO NEW SCHOOL, WORK, AND FAMILY GOALS

The young women who comprised the holding on group had high aspirations for themselves in high school, and most had solid plans to fulfill these aspirations. They planned to attend college and often graduate school and to become obstetricians, psychologists, and registered nurses. Some aspired to skilled occupations, such as X-ray technicians and dental hygienists. And they hoped that fulfilling these goals would lead to a stable home life; they wished to own a home, and all but two expected to marry and have children, with most anticipating a short cohabitation beforehand. As Tess described it, they hoped for the "typical American lifestyle," or at least what they imagined the typical American lifestyle to be.

Five years later, these young women's educational and occupational goals and plans had shifted, although the broad outlines of their family plans remained the same. Their college experiences had not lived up to their expectations. Those who had moved away from home—whether across state or city lines—returned to their hometowns.[19] Many encountered academic barriers that prolonged their paths through school or pushed them off those paths entirely. Others completed their degrees but struggled to find work in their chosen fields. Two never enrolled in college at all. Nearly all still aspired to complete a college degree, but many now viewed college as a hurdle to surmount. Like Cortney, a working-class White young woman, some saw a college degree as "a sign of accomplishment. . . . I did something that is socially—that that's what they want you to do, is just to get a degree." Holding on young women still wanted a degree, as both a marker of accomplishment and a pathway to a stable career. Having, in their minds, fallen short of their previous expectations, however, their optimism had dimmed.

In the aggregate, holding on young women's goals for their family lives remained remarkably similar to those they held in high school. Almost all aspired to marry, have children, and be financially stable. Yet while the majority retained roughly the same ideal timing for marriage and child-bearing, about equal numbers now anticipated earlier or later onsets. Those who anticipated forming families at a younger age than they had in high school were already romantically involved and found these relationships to be a source of support and stability, rather than the threat to their careers that their younger selves had anticipated. Chelsea had already had a child and married. Amy had anticipated marrying at age 24 and beginning to have children at age 30 and was now planning her wedding at age 23 and hoped to have a child in the next couple of years. Jennifer had predicted a late timeline in high school (age 35 for marriage and 41 for a child) but now hoped to marry her boyfriend soon and to have children in her thirties.

Other holding on young women worried about finances, and this informed their thoughts on the timing of marriage and childbearing. Holly explained that she wanted to establish a career before marrying and having children. When I asked her what that would look like, she answered, "Definitely being financially stable for myself, being well off, and just having good benefits. Right now I don't have medical insurance, and that stinks so bad. Because my dad is on disability, they took me off of his insurance." Holly wanted to work in a job where she could earn enough to afford insurance—something that would offer her peace of mind and access to medical care if she needed it. Although while in high school she had hoped to marry around age 25 and have children a couple of years later, now she felt unsure about when she would be financially secure enough to marry and anticipated having children in her thirties.

Still other holding on young women said they wished to marry and have children at roughly the same ages they had reported in high school. These young women's educational and occupational plans had changed, but in conflicting ways. They were now anticipating shorter educational timelines than they initially had planned (often because they no longer planned for graduate or professional schooling) while also experiencing real financial pressures. These dual circumstances—one that could speed up family formation and the other that could slow it down—meant that their anticipated family timelines did not change substantially.

All holding on young women had amended their occupational aspirations and plans in some way. A few remained interested in the health field but shifted their sights to a more expedient goal. Zakeshia moved from hoping to be a pediatrician to aspiring to become a nurse. Abby, a working-class White young woman, aspired to either work as an occupational therapist or dental hygienist in high school and had now completed a program to become an occupational therapy assistant. Two now worked or aspired to work in the education field; Chelsea was the assistant director of a childcare center, while Madeline aspired to be a teacher.

By far the most common current aspiration, however, was to work in the business field. In fact, half of the young women now intended to work in business or administration in the future. This shift toward the business field may not be unusual; business is the most popular major among bachelor's degree students in the United States and the third most popular among associate's degree students, while the health field is the second most popular among both groups.[20] According to survey research, business students rank interest as the top reason they choose their major, followed by job opportunities, a good fit with their skills, the desire to have their own business, and earnings.[21] However, this doesn't tell us why this shift to business was so prominent among those in the holding on group. It is striking that this group so decisively shifted toward business while it was rare for both on track and navigating rough seas young women to pursue this goal.[22]

So what inspired these young women to pursue business when they turned away from the health field? Cassie, Jennie, and Jennifer all expressed interest in studying business to become an entrepreneur. Cassie, who majored in organizational leadership within a larger interdisciplinary program, explained that she liked the flexibility her major offered her, and that she was drawn toward business because she had learned she was good at it through working in restaurants. She felt gratified by being recognized by supervisors and receiving promotions at a relatively young age. Jennie explained, "It's going to be a lot of work. But I like the fact of having something that's mine," and Jennifer, similarly, explained, "I always knew that I wanted to be my own boss. I wanted to create something and see it come to pass." This focus on independence was particularly notable among the holding on group. This may be due to the degree to which these young women were already self-sufficient. Most worked full-time or close to full-time (sometimes more), and most were pursuing a college degree, even if intermittently or part-time. Several lived independently from their parents, or at least had done so for some time, and only one had a child. Therefore, they saw themselves as—and often were—self-sufficient but not yet tied to dependent children.

They were also the group of young women who worked the longest hours, making work a central component of their identities, yet they were often in positions where managers could change their schedules, hours, and roles at will. Being their own bosses, or being someone's boss, and earning enough money to start a family appealed to many young women in this group. In addition, an interest in business was, to some extent, a rejection of the academic side of schooling. For young women who worked long hours, college was a chore.[23] In business majors, they found an answer to this dilemma: classes that focused on directly applicable skills and often included work and internship experiences as a part of their requirements. Not only did business degrees offer future independence; they offered a degree of independence within the confines of being a college student.

In the aggregate, majoring in business is a safe bet. However, business is a large field of study that contains more specific majors, including in business management and administration, accounting, finance, general business, and economics. These pathways are stratified. College graduates who major in finance, accounting, and economics report better than average employment following college, while those who major in business management and general business have much higher (and higher than the average college grad) rates of underemployment.[24] Earnings also vary: business majors with a bachelor's degree make an average of $60,000 a year, with those in business economics ($75,000) and actuarial science ($68,000) making the most and those in hospitality management ($50,000) and miscellaneous business and medical administration ($53,000) making the least.[25] Business management majors make up the bulk of all business majors (33%) and earn on the lower end of the scale. Therefore, although choosing a business major can be a wise choice, not all pathways through this major accrue similar rewards.

Most of the young women in the holding on group who aspired to work in business were tracked into the lower end of this distribution by majoring in business management or "miscellaneous" business majors (e.g., applied business, organizational leadership). They also held fairly general goals to "be my own boss" and work in the business field. None reported that they had received professional development or networking assistance through their college programs, unlike on track young women who were enrolled in preprofessional programs. Therefore, although they chose a field that—like health—could be perceived as "safe," it was not without risk.

A SOFT LANDING FOR SOME, CLIMBING A ROCK WALL FOR OTHERS

The holding on group was unique in being diverse by class origin. On track young women hailed mainly from the middle class, with a little under one-third from the working class. The navigating rough seas young women, whom I discuss in the next chapter, grew up predominantly poor and working class. The holding on group, however, was well represented by all class backgrounds. Five had been middle class in high school, seven were in the working class, and two were poor. Their pathways into the holding on group were therefore diverse and instructive; by comparing their pathways and resources received through family members, we can see the role family background plays in shaping not only class replication but also class mobility.

For the middle class, being in the holding on group was a soft landing after life disruptions that sent working-class and poor girls into the rough seas group, as we will see in the next chapter. Chelsea, for example, had a child while in college, pushing her to switch institutions and majors. Zakeshia became embroiled in multiple sources of debt and a brush with the law (misdemeanor charge). Christina failed out of multiple institutions. These roadblocks would have easily pushed working-class and poor girls into rough seas, but those from middle-class origins were able to hold on. Cassie had a soft landing in the holding on group after struggling with alcohol and drug abuse. Although she initially attended a highly regarded in-state public university after high school in the prenursing track, she found college isolating and struggled to cope with the recent loss of her two grandparents. As she explained, "You can't go binge drinking six, seven days a week when you start college. [But] that's what I did.... I was pretty sad when I finished up my senior year of high school, and so I was just ready to rage." After earning a below 2.0 grade point average as a first-year student, Cassie transferred to her local community college, Templeton-Kensington, the next year. She continued to pursue nursing but discovered that between needing to raise her grades and then get on a two-year waitlist, it would take her seven more years of college before she could obtain this degree. Disillusioned, Cassie finished her second year unhappy and directionless.

That summer, Cassie began experimenting with drugs, starting with marijuana and expanding from there: "I had done cocaine. I had done meth. I had done ketamine.... I had taken muscle relaxers, Vicodin, Kpins, Percocets, opiates ... literally everything." According to Cassie, drug use occupied about three months of her life, before she quit cold turkey. She described a near-miss with the police:

> I got pulled over, and I had my car raided and I had a lot of paraphernalia on me, but I was honest with the cop and he said, you can either get out of the car now and give me everything, or we can search your car and I'll charge you for every piece. And so I got out of the car and I handed him everything I had and I was honest and I told him who I was and what I was doing with my life and how I got caught up in a bad situation and this has never happened to me before. And he let me go.... He was like, you're a good kid, and I can tell that. He was like, but you need to get away from this.

Shaken by her encounter, Cassie stopped using hard drugs and decided to take a year off from college to work as a server at a restaurant. She also began living with her boyfriend, an older veteran who had just returned from a tour in Afghanistan. As Cassie described it, their relationship was unhealthy; her boyfriend suffered from PTSD and slept with guns under his pillow. He drank frequently, and would "scream and cry and hoot and holler." Cassie became as much a mother or nursemaid as girlfriend, taking care of his daily living tasks and waiting on him "hand and foot." She slowly began to recognize that his behavior and the degree to which he dominated her emotional and social life was unhealthy, and she pulled herself away from the relationship.

When I interviewed Cassie, she was doing well. She was living at home with her parents, again attending college full-time and majoring in organizational leadership, and working thirty to thirty-five hours a week during the school year. She loved working in the restaurant industry and dreamed of opening her own restaurant one day. She earned a relatively high salary for her position and felt proud of how far she had come. When I asked her where she expected to be at age thirty, she said she anticipated having her master's degree, making six figures, and owning her own home. She was holding on.

Yet holding on, for Cassie, was a soft landing. Drinking, drug use, and destructive relationships left Black and working-class and poor White girls in much more dire straits. Not only was Cassie managing to pursue a degree and work, she had a reliable home life and $35,000 in the bank that she had inherited from her grandfather. This was markedly higher than the average net worth of 22-year-olds in the United States.[26] Thus, Cassie was in a much better financial position than most of her peers. She was also able to cash in on her White, middle-class status within institutional settings. She escaped not only jail time but any serious repercussions after being found with drug paraphernalia in her car because a police officer identified her as a "good kid." Her earnings as a server were substantial for the service industry, and she networked successfully with managers and executive chefs within her workplace to secure references and move to a new and higher-paying job. Thus, while her path to the holding on group was rockier than many, her experience within it was more secure.

For young women from working-class and poor families, however, holding on could be like climbing a rock wall. Cortney was encouraged by her single father and her grandmother to consider pursuing a career in

X-ray technology. A high school senior when I first met her, Cortney was well-informed regarding her intended career and had a plan to pursue it. At the same time, she struggled in her math and science courses, and her father's financial troubles prevented her from taking the ACT in the fall of her senior year.

Five years later, Cortney was living with her boyfriend of two years in a small but well-appointed apartment in her hometown. She had graduated from Kensington High School early and worked briefly at a telemarketing firm before her father secured her a full-time job at a surgery center working as a unit coordinator. The following fall, Cortney enrolled in a surgery technician program at a local branch campus of a larger public university. Although she maintained a grade point average of just over 3.0, Cortney struggled in her chemistry and math courses, and she dropped out after a year. Shortly after that, she tried to enroll in a cosmetology school, but her father refused to fill out the FAFSA paperwork, and she was unable to qualify as an independent student despite living on her own and having continually paid her own way through college.[27] As Cortney described it, when she called FAFSA's hotline to inquire about applying for financial aid as an independent adult, they informed her that she was ineligible and would have to report her father's income (and therefore have that factored into aid and loan packages):

> They asked me, "Are you married?" No. "Do you have kids?" No. "Did you ever serve time in the marines?" No. "In the US Forces, whatever?" No. "Okay, well I'm sorry, you're not going to qualify [for] anything until you're 24." And I'm like, "But I'm paying for everything." I didn't understand that.

Although Cortney did everything she could to qualify as an independent student—she even hurriedly moved into an apartment with her boyfriend in the hopes that this would convince aid officers of her status—she was unable to do so. If she had been treated as an independent adult, she could have received financial aid that would have cut $200 from her monthly tuition. Without this support, she opted not to enroll.

Cortney continued to work and provide for herself in the years after high school. Her job at the surgery center was full-time and paid $13.46 an hour, and she also worked for a tanning salon part-time for $7.75/hour. Between these two jobs Cortney earned less than $30,000 a year, and she was at the whim of scheduling at both jobs, meaning that she occasionally brought in less income per week without warning. She was also paying off college loans and found that between that expense and other bills, she was barely breaking even. When I asked Cortney what she wanted her life to look like at age 30, Cortney explained:

> My American dream is to own a nice condo. And then kids. . . . And I'm making decent money, livable money to pay my rent and to give my kids what they need, some of what they want. . . . When I'm 30, I hope I'm with a partner strongly, maybe [current boyfriend], having a nice condo, having two- to four-year-old kids—and just maintaining. Maintaining a good way. Not paycheck to paycheck. Hopefully a degree in something. . . . And I have a happy, happy life. Happy kids, happy partner, and a nice place to live, and a car that works.

Cortney still dreamed of a stable, financially settled future, one that seemed both around the corner and out of reach. She wanted to complete college and obtain a job that would afford her just a little room to not only pay for her life but have some savings, too. This would allow her to be happy and to pay for her kids' (and presumably her own) needs and some wants.

Cortney was doing relatively well in the early transition to adulthood, yet she didn't have the kind of family background that Cassie did. For her, like others from the working class or poor such as Jennie and Madeline, most of her economic stability was due to her own hard work and persistence, as well as abstaining from the kinds of self-destructive behaviors that Cassie became involved in. Getting to where she was took effort. She worked two jobs just to break even, and she did not have the extra income to pay for college, nor could she qualify for enough financial aid until she could be recognized as an independent adult by the federal government. Thus, despite making reasonable plans for the future while in high school and not falling prey to drug abuse as Cassie had, she was further behind Cassie in her pursuit of the American Dream.

HOLDING ON TO HANG IN

Holding on young women were working very hard just to get by, and when they didn't get ahead, they blamed themselves. As Cortney described:

It's hard to maintain paying rent and wanting to go back to school and also working a full-time job. And you also want to go out and have fun and do stuff, you know. It's hard to try to get all—well, in my case, four things done: part-time job, full-time job, try to get school done, and try to have fun, and try to keep a clean house. I mean, it really is hard. . . . Now it's like, I have got to go home and do the dishes. I have got to go home and do some laundry. It starts to drive you crazy. But, yeah. I just need to work harder, financially-wise and responsibility-wise, to get back to school and finish, so I can make more money hourly. That's the goal.

Like many in the holding on group, Cortney recognized the challenges she faced but placed the responsibility on herself to push past her current circumstances. Zakeshia, too, blamed herself for "messing up" by not looking into employment options before getting her degree in medical billing, and yet the job outlook in this field was strong according to the Bureau of Labor Statistics.[28] It did not occur to her to wonder whether her college had not adequately prepared her for job searching or whether racial bias made it more difficult for her to secure a position.[29]

Holly also felt responsible for pushing herself to succeed, explaining, "I try to stay busy, so I don't get that stressed out. Because then I feel like if I'm not busy, then I'll start to over-think things and get really stressed. I think it's turned out. I wish I [had] graduated by now, but I'm not, so I'm kind of hard on myself about that." Holly blamed herself for not doing better in school despite juggling classes and working nearly full-time alongside her father's oxycodone addiction, her grandmother's progressing dementia, and the death of two friends by suicide. Although she acknowledged that she received very little help from her family and that her academic preparation at Glenbrook had not been sufficient for college, Holly described herself as "lazy" and "not a planner" in interviews.

Holding on young women were firmly committed to self-reliance and a "pull yourself up by the bootstraps" mentality, even when many of their setbacks could be attributed to the high cost of college and college programs that promised more than they could deliver; instability in employment, work hours, and pay; and family problems that took their attention and time. They had made plans to attain a middle-class lifestyle, but knowing the steps to achieving a goal is not sufficient when taking those steps requires financial and social resources. Many of the barriers to a middle-class lifestyle were structural and could be addressed by policies that made college accessible, work equitable, and family lives stable. Yet like Cortney, Zakeshia, and Holly, they assumed that the golden ticket lay in working harder and being smarter. As hard as they worked, however, the holding on group seemed to mostly hang in: bringing in an income but not saving (and often falling further into debt) and working hard but not getting ahead. And this was unlikely to change. Although we do not possess a crystal ball that will predict the pathways that Jennie, Cortney, Jennifer, and the others will take, none had acquired or were close to acquiring credentials that would launch them into a well-paid job, and almost all were in debt to a significant degree. Most of their family members were in similar, or worse, financial shape. And neither colleges nor workplaces provided these young women with enough of a foothold to move past their current circumstances, leaving them working hard just to hold on.

7 Navigating Rough Seas

BRIT: [When I found out I was pregnant] I almost died. My heart dropped, especially since me and Brandon had just broken up like four hours before that. It was pretty crazy, but I'm glad I was pregnant because Brandon was my best friend, too. So, when he hurt me, it was really traumatizing to me. It was really horrible. I almost feel like I might have done really dumb things or something if I hadn't been pregnant; like, went out and partied a lot and just gotten into some bad stuff. So, I'm glad.

Sailing in rough seas is a tricky endeavor. High waves, lost visibility, and lightning all present risks to sailors, and they often have to do the unexpected to ride out the storm: disconnecting power, slowing their speed, changing course to take them farther from their destination, and even stalling the boat in the water.[1] Much like tempest-tossed sailors, young women in the navigating rough seas group found themselves inundated by challenges during their transition to adulthood, which made moving forward toward their goals extremely difficult. These challenges varied but often included family responsibilities and conflict, health problems, lack of workplace protections, and a "lower ed" market focused on selling quick credentials to the working class and poor.[2] What's more, these problems compounded one another. Family responsibilities made short-term educational credentials such as certificates appealing. Health problems interfered with work and the ability to hold onto one's job. Family conflict erupted over or was exacerbated by family responsibilities.

· · · · ·

Brit, a poor White young woman whom we met in chapter 3 when she was planning to become a dental hygienist, was set adrift by a wide array of setbacks in her early transition to adulthood. About six months after graduating early from high school (Brit took an accelerated English course in order to graduate in December of her senior year), Brit's family lost their house when her grandmother, who owned the home, passed away. Brit and her mother moved into Brit's boyfriend's three-bedroom trailer in exchange for helping to pay the bills. Free of school but needing to help her mother pay bills, Brit took a job as an aide in the dementia ward of an assisted living facility, where she worked for about a year. She enjoyed her work with dementia patients but complained that the management understaffed the ward. During this time, Brit was working forty hours a week at odd hours and had trouble taking her birth control regularly. She learned that she was pregnant only a few hours after she broke up with her boyfriend after discovering that he was cheating on her. Her boyfriend subsequently kicked Brit and her mother out of his trailer, and they had to scramble for housing once again, eventually securing rental of a small home in Glenbrook. Around the same time, Brit quit her job over a dispute with her managers.

Brit had not abandoned her goal of becoming a dental hygienist. Shortly after graduating from high school, she enrolled in college in a nearby city to pursue this end, but she was plagued with anxiety over driving to campus and dropped out before ever attending a class.[3] About two years later and while pregnant, she enrolled in a ten-week dental assistant program, for which her father paid the $3,000 tuition. Brit reasoned that training to be a dental assistant would get her part of the way to her occupational goal. However, she swiftly became disenchanted with the program. The teacher was detached and incompetent, often pronouncing words incorrectly and giving the students As even if they did poorly on tests. Brit complained, "It was a waste of my father's money, and I feel bad for even going." Brit's frustration was palpable, and it's not difficult to see why. An A student in high school, Brit knew that her teacher did not understand, or care to understand, the content that she was teaching. Brit, in turn, felt "paranoid" that she wouldn't get a job because she had not learned enough in the class. She completed the program and earned a certificate but felt disillusioned by her experience.

Brit still tried to find a job, but after sending out sixteen résumés and getting no callbacks, she lost hope. Her difficulty may have been due, in part, to her school's accreditation status. Although Brit did not know it, the technology school she attended was unaccredited. The school, of course, did not advertise its status. In fact, its website touted being listed as the "Best Dental School" in the state and its certification as a career college, along with a number of testimonials from successful students, thus making an appealing pitch for students who wanted to start a career in dental health quickly. The lack of accreditation did not disqualify Brit from getting a job as a dental assistant, but it made the road more difficult. Students graduating from unaccredited dental assisting programs were ineligible to take the Dental Assisting National Board's Certified Dental Assistant examination until they had two years of on-the-job experience. But it was hard to find a job to gain the necessary experience without the certification.

Pregnant and unable to find a job, Brit stayed home and helped her mother around the house. As her pregnancy progressed, Brit's blood pressure rose to alarmingly high levels, and her doctor advised rest. She continued to stay home after her son was born because she was breastfeeding, making finding and keeping a job difficult. She received some support from the government in the form of food stamps and Medicaid. When I interviewed her about a year after her son was born, Brit was looking for work again. Her cousin offered to secure her a job at a local factory, which Brit hoped would allow her to move out of the home she shared with her mother, sister, and sisters' two children and move into an apartment her father owned with two of her friends.

Brit was frustrated with her situation and wanted something better. Living at home was difficult; she helped care for her sisters' children, two girls, while her sister was in jail for a week.[4] Now released and under house arrest, her sister was taking Xanax, and Brit continued to help out with the girls. Brit was also frustrated by her experiences with two long-term boyfriends, her son's father and a friend of his, both of whom had cheated on her repeatedly during their relationships. Although Brit wanted marriage and a husband, she didn't trust men. When I asked her what kind of relationship she wanted, she explained:

> Other than the cheating and drinking often, I thought Tony was pretty perfect. He loved my son to death. . . . He did the dishes. He would help with laundry. He took the trash out. . . . He acted like he wanted to work and he wanted to come home and do all the housework [and] that I was only

supposed to worry about taking care of the baby. That was my job. Just take care of the baby. So, I thought he was pretty great.

Brit had been hopeful that Tony would settle down with her. Disillusioned with him and her son's father, Brandon, she still hoped to find someone who was "not a jerk" and have another child. When I asked her what she wanted her life to look like at age 30, Brit imagined living in her father's apartment, having a ten-year-old, and "hopefully by then, I at least have a better job, and I can [pay] rent every month and still have money to afford other things. . . . I don't want to pay my bills and that's all I can pay for. I want to be able to do things, you know, go out to dinner every now and then." Her aspirations were not lofty, but they were very different from her current circumstances.

Brit's vision for the future would be difficult to achieve. She had not held a steady job for any extended period of time, and what little she made when she worked went toward living expenses. There was no extra money for college or a certified job training program. Even full-time work, with only a high school degree and certificate from an unaccredited dental program, was unlikely to move Brit out of poverty. She was weighed down by mutually reinforcing disadvantages: a lack of educational credentials; the concomitant low-wage work she was qualified for; and obligations to her family, including her son, her mother, and her sister and sisters' children. In addition, although she hoped to return to school, enrolling in quick-fix school programs might put her in debt without leading to a job.

The young women navigating rough seas, like Brit, were struggling. They had drifted far from their goals in high school and struggled to find work, to return to school, and to gain an economic foothold. Most of these young women belong to what some have called the "disconnected youth" who are between the ages of 16 and 24 and are neither enrolled in school nor employed.[5] These young people are often portrayed as permanently disconnected from society, an underclass of idle youth. Researchers and policy makers alike express concern about disconnected youth because they are not gaining "useful" skills through school or work, and this can have long-term repercussions on their earnings, reliance on public assistance, health, and criminal involvement.[6] Yet disconnection is neither a permanent nor a complete status. Disconnected youth typically experience multiple periods of unemployment, but often between periods of paid employment.[7] Many move in and out of educational programs. Furthermore, these young people often feel connected to their families and friends, rather than being wholly isolated from social and institutional connections. They are not, therefore, disconnected, although the ties they do have may not be as resource rich as those available to other young adults, or they may be more fraught.[8]

In addition, research and policy attention to disconnected youth have often focused on young men, who have higher rates of unemployment and lower rates of school enrollment than young women.[9] This emphasis likely stems both from statistics that men's educational and labor market outcomes are getting worse over time relative to women's and the tendency to explain away young women's disconnection as due to childbearing or a lack of interest in paid work.[10] Yet it is not at all clear that disconnection is truly a choice rather than a consequence of institutional barriers to school and work. Understanding how—and in what contexts—"disconnected" young women do or do not engage in school and work can help us identify institutional barriers to educational and occupational attainment in the transition to adulthood.

In this chapter, I discuss how young women from different class backgrounds ended up navigating rough seas by examining their pathways after high school and what it really means to be "disconnected" from schooling and work. I show, first, how a lack of support at four-year institutions led some young women out of higher education altogether and led others to seek out short-term programs with high costs and little payoff. Second, I argue that the low-wage jobs these young women could find were unstable and offered few protections, leaving them in economically precarious positions. This was compounded by the fact that most of the navigating rough seas young women had children shortly after high school, and the jobs they held did not offer parental leave, accommodations for pregnant workers, or spaces to pump breastmilk. Third, I describe how these young women were enmeshed in reciprocal relationships with family members, and the economic precarity they and their family members faced often led to conflict. Fourth, I discuss pathways into navigating rough seas and how for some young women, serious setbacks such as struggles with drug use, mental health problems, and abuse led into rough seas. Finally, I discuss how these young women saw their futures as unpredictable and expressed fatalism about how their lives would unfold. Their pathways so far had been rocky in ways they did not anticipate, and they could not see a horizon to reach toward.

FAST EDUCATION, FEW REWARDS

In high school, all of the young women who ended up navigating rough seas planned to attend college. Five aspired to obtain graduate or professional degrees, three aspired to complete a bachelor's degree, four aspired to complete an associate's degree, and one aspired to go to college but was unclear about the specific degree she wanted. Although these young women were, on average, less prepared to attend college than most of their peers, in high school they were still planful with the resources they had available and had aligned their higher education plans to their occupational aspirations.

The most common educational trajectory for these young women was that they enrolled in college after high school—either immediately or within a year of their graduation—but dropped out after a short period. For some, academic troubles and failing courses led to their exit from school. Others found bureaucratic hurdles overwhelming, particularly applying for financial aid. Commitments to work and family also got in the way. And as we will return to later, major life disruptions steered some young women off course. Finally, the three young women who completed a short-term degree, such as a postsecondary certificate, found that work in their field was not readily available; none were yet employed in the field in which they held their degree. Almost none were "disconnected" from higher education institutions. Rather, they were intermittently connected to and often poorly served by these institutions.

Blake, a poor White young woman, was one of only two young women who had already been accepted to college when I interviewed them in the fall of their senior year.[11] An honors student with an above 4.0 grade point average, Blake seemed prepared to pursue her goal to become a neonatal nurse practitioner. Once enrolled at MidCity University, however, Blake struggled. College coursework was much more difficult than what she had encountered at Glenbrook High School, and she became overwhelmed:

> I think I was just so used to being in high school and studying really quick and doing really well. In college it's not like that at all. So I think I kind of got discouraged when I was trying to study for my tests and trying to do really well and trying to put more effort into studying because it was harder and I still wasn't doing good.

Blake was discouraged but also afraid to acknowledge her problems. She didn't want her peers or those in authority to know she was struggling, so she said she "tucked it under the rug." In part, Blake had simply never encountered these problems before; she had earned top grades in high school by studying for tests at the last minute and still doing well. Her college grades surprised her, and she did not know where to turn or how to share her struggles with others. As she explained, "I want people to just think oh, she's doing so good and I don't want them to see like oh, she's not doing so good anymore. I guess I worry too much about what people think about me." Blake wanted to "figure it out on my own" and acknowledged, thinking back, that she should have reached out for help.

Knowing who and how to ask for help is difficult, however. When I asked Blake whether she felt the college had support available for students, she answered, "When I first went to look at the campus, they had told us of all the places you can go to get help. [But] I felt like— I don't know—when I started doing bad I didn't really know who to go to." She was also limited in reaching out to her own networks. In high school, Blake had relied on her friend's parents for help because she saw them as knowing more than her mother did about college. Yet she and her friend, Adriana, had a falling out in her first year of college, leaving Blake without access to the social ties (Adriana's parents) that she had relied upon in high school to help her navigate college admissions. Although she could talk to her mom, she said, her mom would be "in the same boat as me." Blake's mother had only a high school degree, which meant she didn't have firsthand knowledge of how to navigate college. Thus, Blake did not turn to her mother—not because her mother was unsupportive or unwilling to help, but because she knew her mother did not have the resources or knowledge to do so. A mother with a college degree might have advised Blake to go to tutoring or switch majors, or even have coached Blake through grade appeals or requests for a second chance, much like Sarah's father (see chapter 5), who advised Sarah on choosing a new major after she earned low grades in her first two years of college. As research repeatedly finds, middle-class parents martial their substantial resources to extract extra help and favors for their children and coach their children on how to do the same for themselves.[12] Working-class and poor parents, on the other hand, do not have the resources or experience to do the same, and they are more likely to teach their children to follow the rules and re-spect authority. Their children, therefore, are much more likely to attempt to be self-reliant and find answers on their own without asking for help.

It was not until after her second term of school that Blake reached out to a school adviser for help. At that point, her grades had declined too far for admission into the competitive nursing program. Her adviser gave her a schedule of easier classes for the third term so that Blake could improve her overall GPA and stave off an academic suspension. Although Blake's grades did improve, it was not enough, and she was placed on academic suspension, which entailed leaving school for at least a year with no guar-antee of readmission. Blake appealed her suspension but was denied and had to leave school.

Blake was caught unaware by her college experience. It wasn't just that she was academically unprepared; she also did not have the tools to rec-ognize her situation, acknowledge it to others, and ask for help. Although this was her choice, it was a choice facilitated by educational structures. Glenbrook High School, a working-class high school with limited re-sources, focused on maintaining discipline rather than academic success, leaving Blake underprepared for college. Her college provided resources for those who took the initiative but not the support system to guide stu-dents to those resources. In the summer of 2010, Blake left MidCity Uni-versity and returned home, now $10,000 in debt.

This echoes research by Harvard sociologist Anthony Jack, who writes in *The Privileged Poor: How Elite Colleges Are Failing Disadvantaged Students* about how poor, mostly Black and Latino students from pub-lic schools struggle to navigate the unspoken rules and assumptions of elite colleges.[13] Jack shows how, for "doubly disadvantaged" students, the elite university can be an alien environment whose unwritten codes are difficult to decipher. These students are more likely than their peers to go it alone without seeking help. We can see this kind of experience with Blake and other poor young women from Glenbrook. Although Jack's focus was on a different population of students, similar kinds of distinctions emerge for poor students from Glenbrook who make it to residential campuses. They may not have been faced with many peers whose families owned second homes and private jets, but the hidden curriculum of college—that is, the unspoken norms, values, and behaviors expected of students—still eluded them.[14]

Others navigating rough seas enrolled in short-term postsecondary programs after high school. These programs offered what appeared to be a sensible avenue to reduce college costs (due to the short time period to a degree) and acquire a stable job quickly, one that could help them pay off any loans they acquired. Yet these educational institutions often become "educational traps," as sociologist Stefanie DeLuca and colleagues have called them.[15] For-profit schools, in particular, marketed to these young people and made it easier than comparable not-for-profit institutions to enroll in and complete a program.[16] Shauna, a working-class White young woman from Kensington, initially tried to enroll in an associate's degree program at a local not-for-profit university immediately after high school, but "they kept telling me I needed all this paperwork for financial aid. I would bring it, and then they would tell me I needed more. So I just gave up. I was like, 'I'm done.'" Financial aid forms and rules are complicated and can be difficult for working-class and poor families to complete, and even more so for young people, like Shauna, whose families would not or could not help them complete the forms.[17] Obtaining documentation of parents' earnings and assets can be impossible when parents are unable or unwilling to provide such information. For Shauna, the demands of compiling this information became too much, and she decided not to enroll.

A year later, Shauna tried again, this time with a for-profit college and in a medical assisting track. As sociologist Tressie McMillan Cottom has argued, for-profit educational institutions sell the "education gospel" to poor students who wish to improve their chances for upward mobility, pushing them to take on more loans with a promise of a college degree.[18] Moreover, these for-profit schools make financial aid, enrollment, and course taking as easy as possible for students while concealing important differences between traditional, not-for-profit institutions and their own. Namely, dropout rates are high and, for those who finish, the degrees they award are much less likely to lead to stable employment than those from not-for-profit colleges and universities.[19] By doing so, for-profit colleges improve their own bottom line but not their students'. Shauna completed a degree, this time in medical assisting, but for a high price tag of $30,000 in loans at a school she later found out was not accredited.[20] She was unable to find a job as a medical assistant and continued working as an STNA (state tested nursing aide), making $2.50 less an hour than she would have as a medical assistant.

Shauna was worried about the future. She was able to delay payment on her college loans for a year, but they would come due soon at a price tag of $300 a month, a bill she and her husband could not afford. Her husband made a good—but not steady—income as the manager at a fast-food chain, paid based on monthly profits. He had filed for bankruptcy the year before, leaving him with poor credit and some remaining debt to pay off. Now worried about their ability to pay her educational loans, which could not be as easily discharged through bankruptcy, Shauna was considering enrolling in a nursing program to become a registered nurse.[21] This would allow her to defer her college loans but would also increase their debt burden. The school she was considering cost $37,000, but Shauna reasoned that "if medical assisting cost $30,000, then that's a great deal." At this point, Shauna and her husband were deeply in the red, yet unable to secure jobs that would help them pay down their debt. The only solution, in Shauna's mind, was to complete enough education to obtain a higher-paying job. This was a risky proposition, however. She was not guaranteed to finish, as roughly one-half of nursing students do not complete their degrees, and taking out additional loans but not completing her schooling would put her in a far worse position than she was currently in.[22]

Schooling is the golden ticket—not only in the minds of these young women, but according to research. Even considering the rising costs of college, the college wage premium—that is, the relative wages of college graduates vis-à-vis high school graduates—remains high, making a college degree worth the investment.[23] Wages are not the only benefit; college graduates are more likely to be steadily employed and healthy than their less well-educated peers.[24] And as a landmark study tracking the long-term effects of open-access educational policies at the City University of New York found, the benefits pay off across generations, with women's college graduation in one generation predicting greater rates of educational achievement and attainment in their children's generation.[25]

To persist in and reap the rewards of higher education, however, working-class and poor young people need to be able to distinguish between different types of degrees and institutions and to secure financial and academic support once they are enrolled. High schools provide some advising, and many disadvantaged young people apply to and enroll in college with the help of guidance counselors. These institutions, particularly colleges and universities that primarily award bachelor's degrees, are not set up to cater to poor and working-class students, however.[26] These students need flexible schedules to accommodate jobs (or enough financial aid to lessen financial pressures) and academic support and often need childcare assistance as well. Without these structures in place, many drop out.[27] Other poor and working-class young people take time off to work first and enroll in college later. In both cases, they end up searching for a new college pathway on their own. And when earning an income quickly is a priority, quick-fix educational programs present an attractive alternative to more traditional routes. In sum, working-class and poor young women were left with poor options on all sides: low-wage and unstable employment without a degree, a fast degree that was flexible but offered low odds of leading to higher wages (or even graduation), or a traditional degree that did not cater to their life circumstances and thus would take years to complete (if completed at all). Given these options, and little guidance or support, what should they do?

WORKING AT THE MARGINS

Disconnected youth are often portrayed as a fixed monolith: as young people who are neither in school nor "gainfully employed" and thus are at risk for being caught up in criminal enterprises or simply losing out on important job skills. For the young women I interviewed, however, shuttling in and out of work was more common than permanent disconnection from the labor force. Although 8 of the 13 young women I interviewed were not working at the time I spoke to them, they all held jobs at some point after graduating from high school. On average, they held 2.5 jobs over the course of the three to five years after high school graduation, ranging from one to seven jobs total. However, these jobs were often seasonal, temporary, or unstable, and all were low paying, jobs that Arne Kalleberg has described as precarious because they are "uncertain, unpredictable, and risky from the point of view of the worker."[28]

Low-wage work is unstable precisely because businesses can easily replace workers. Blake, for example, worked as an assistant manager at a sandwich chain for almost two years after she left college but became frustrated by the lack of opportunities. Her boss, she learned, only made $1.25 more than she did after working at the job for thirteen years. Her boyfriend's grandmother suggested Blake apply for bank teller jobs, which offered higher pay for high school–educated workers than her job in fast food. She was surprised, but pleased, to find this was an opportunity for her. She began applying for positions and eventually was hired at a bank part-time for $10.50/hour. After almost a year, however, Blake was fired after a bad check cleared her window. The circumstances were unfortunate; the first bad check came to her and she checked it with a supervisor, who approved it. The second came, and Blake assumed it would also be approved, so she cashed it on her own. When both came back bad, Blake—the frontline worker—was fired. She was understandably upset:

> I never would've thought I would've gotten fired. I'm a hard worker. I'm there all the time, on time. Like, when you guys need me to stay late I stay late. If somebody's not there, I come in. I get referrals, I get accounts open, I'm trained in all these areas and this one bad check comes in and then you just throw me away.

Blake's coworkers assured her that these firings were routine, and that they would not be held against her in another position. Her manager offered her a recommendation letter, and she secured a second job a short time later. At the time we spoke, she was still between jobs but would start a new position soon. She would make $10 an hour for full-time work, coming in at $20,800 a year if she remained employed for the year. Still, given Blake's own experience and her coworkers' explanations that such firings were routine, her long-term employment was far from assured.

Other young women also experienced work instability. Lisa, a middle-class White young woman from Kensington, quit her first retail managerial position after her workplace discovered that she was living with one of her employees and initiated an investigation, which Lisa anticipated would result in her firing.[29] Tyra, a middle-class Black young woman from Glenbrook, lost her job working the third shift at a factory producing toiletries when they shifted operations to a new worksite. Brit, a poor White young woman, and Neke, a poor Black young woman, both reported working seasonal jobs, at a Halloween theme park and a distribution center during the Christmas holidays, respectively, which offered only temporary employment.

The low-wage jobs these young women took also did not offer accommodations for pregnancy or parenthood, which ultimately drove many out of the workforce and delayed reentry. Sandra, for example, was a poor White young woman from Glenbrook. Now 22 years old, Sandra was living with her fiancé and two-year-old son and was neither working nor in school. In high school, Sandra had aspired to become a nurse and intended to enroll at a nearby community college once she graduated. Her first year out of high school, however, she worked, first as a cashier and then at a nursing home serving food and drinks to the residents, for $8.00/hour. Sandra worked there for almost two years, and had begun training to become an aide for a raise to $8.50/hour, when she had to quit due to her pregnancy. She was only about five months pregnant but was considered high risk due to two previous miscarriages (one at age 16 and one at age 19). Her doctor advised her not to lift heavy objects, which precluded doing the work of an aide, and she was receiving weekly ultrasounds and injecting heparin shots to prevent blood clots. Some of this may have stemmed from her ongoing health problems; as Sandra described it, she had "sugar problems, blood pressure problems, cholesterol problems." In addition to this she was diagnosed as bipolar. Thus, working was difficult for her. However, had her workplace offered accommodations for her physical health limitations and paid (or even unpaid) family leave, Sandra could have kept her job. Instead, Sandra spent the rest of her pregnancy and the next year and a half at home caring for her son.

When I interviewed her, Sandra had recently spoken to friends who still worked at the nursing home where she previously worked, one of whom was in a managerial position, to inquire about returning. The home's administrator indicated she could return, although she had to delay this in order to heal from a recent knee surgery.[30] Although Sandra spoke eagerly about returning to work and obtaining an STNA license, which would potentially increase her pay to $12.00/hour, she also worried about putting her son in preschool, both because he had not yet spent significant time away from her and because "all this stuff on TV about kids getting killed. I'm just like I don't even want my son to go to school." Her plans, then, were uncertain: "If he can't go, I don't go." She hoped her mother might be able to care for her son, but her mother had her own health problems, including COPD and fibromyalgia. At age 42, her mother was using an oxygen tank full-time. Whether Sandra would be able to return to full-time work or school was therefore unclear.[31]

For Sandra and others, the lack of accommodations around pregnancy and motherhood was a barrier to paid work, leaving young women with a gap in their employment history. Some young women found they had to leave work or educational programs because they were pregnant, either due to the intense physical requirements of manual jobs (like nurse's aides) or contact with harsh chemicals (such as Tyra and Shannon, who both dropped out of cosmetology school when they discovered that they were pregnant). Other young women left paid work to care for young children or because they could not pump breast milk at work, despite laws mandating that breastfeeding mothers be offered time and space to pump milk.[32] Shauna, for instance, left her job as an STNA in an assisted living facility when she was about seven months pregnant, because the work was becoming too physically demanding. When we spoke, she had not yet gone back to work because she was breastfeeding and would have been unable to pump at the facility. She explained that she was trying to wean her son in order to go back to work.

Whether due to pregnancy, other health conditions, childcare needs, a lack of workplace protections, or job loss, young women navigating rough seas could not depend on steady employment. And like those employed in low-wage work from the holding on group, their work hours and schedules were at the whims of their employers, which also made earnings unpredictable. This, in turn, made family ties essential for staying afloat, yet at the same time, the economic precarity they and their family members faced also created contexts in which these ties frayed.

RECEIVING AND GIVING SUPPORT
WITHIN THE FAMILY SAFETY NET

Navigating rough seas young women moved in and out of school and work, sometimes fitting the description of disconnected youth and sometimes not, but their ties to family were a constant part of their lives. Four lived with their parents and sometimes extended family members, six lived with a significant other, one lived with both her parents and boyfriend, one lived by herself with her two children, and one lived with a roommate. None lived alone. Nine had children. These ties offered support and meaning to these young women's lives. Family ties helped some of the young women pay emergency bills or take care of their children, as well as providing housing for some. And in turn, the young women gave emotional and material support and practical help to parents, siblings, partners, and both their own and their family members' children. Known in sociological research as the "family safety net," this kind of support received from kin is vital for young adults broadly.[33] It is particularly important for those with modest educational attainment and income.[34]

Shannon, a biracial (Black and White) young woman of working-class origins from Glenbrook, both received and provided support within her family. In high school, Shannon helped her parents raise her two nieces, who lived with them because Shannon's sister abused drugs. Five years later, her sister was still using, and Shannon continued to provide care while living at her parents' home along with her boyfriend and daughter. Although Shannon had initially left home to attend college on a sports scholarship, she dropped out after her first semester; she felt uncomfortable having to hide her sexuality at the conservative Christian college where she was enrolled. She returned home and continued to pursue a degree, first at a for-profit online college and later at two cosmetology schools; when we spoke, she was enrolled in the second of those schools and anticipated graduating in a little over a year. Her parents supported each of her decisions, taking out parent PLUS loans to cover costs beyond those her financial aid covered and encouraging her to pursue her goals. Once she had their blessing, Shannon explained, "And that right there, I was just like this is—I love it. I knew I'd have fun, and I can still get flexible hours. You know, there's a bunch of cosmetologists out there who have kids, who have families, and they still get to spend time with them, and I'm just like that's what I want to do." In the meantime, her parents supported her (and her boyfriend and child) through direct financial help and housing, and she provided care for her nieces.

Other young women also played important roles as caretakers. Tyra, a middle-class Black young woman from Glenbrook, helped her mother raise her sister after she left high school and took charge of the household so that her mother could work long hours at the hospital. Sandra was a stay-at-home mother and also babysat her sister's baby so that her sister could work. Sandra and her sister lived next door to one another, facilitating this arrangement. Toward the end of high school, Neke took on a part-time job to pay off her own and her twin sister's school fees, which totaled $800. And of course several, like Kimberly and Tiffany, both from working-class White families, cared for their own children. Kimberly juggled a part-time job in food service with caring for her 9-month-old daughter. Tiffany was mother to 5- and 3-year-old boys and pregnant with her third child, raising them and running the household without family help and while her husband often worked twelve- to sixteen-hour days at a local factory.

Despite the support that flowed to and from these young women and their family ties, their relationships were often fraught. Economic instability can create circumstances in which ties fray and begin to break.[35] Higher rates of drug use and violence within their networks likely also contributed to, and in some cases were due to, how closely their networks were intertwined. Young women who were on track or holding on could keep family members at arm's length when they needed to and without abandoning those ties altogether. For young women navigating rough seas, help from family members was essential to getting by, but getting this help often required close quarters and frequent exchanges and therefore could generate more conflict. Take Brit, for example. She and her mother first relied on Brit's boyfriend and boyfriend's mother for housing when they lost their housing after Brit's grandmother's passing. But they were kicked out of the trailer when Brit's relationship with her boyfriend soured. They next found a small house to rent and lent support to Brit's sister and two children, but living with her sister was a burden. Brit was called on to care for her nieces when Brit's sister was arrested and later endured her sister's parole limitations and continuing drug use. Her primary goal, by the time

I spoke to her, was simply to get away from her family members (although by moving into her father's rental unit) in order to lessen her family obligations as well as the chaos that often surrounded them.

In some cases, conflict between young women and their parents arose when the young women got into trouble. Kate was a working-class White young woman with model-high cheekbones, a boyish manner, and a slight drawl. Several run-ins with the law—police found marijuana and open liquor containers in Kate's car multiple times, leading to a suspended license—put Kate on a collision course with her parents. Both parents threw her out of their respective homes at different times: "My dad looked at me and said, you're not my child. . . . I didn't raise a child this hellion." Most recently, Kate had been ordered to go to court to face charges of driving with a suspended license. She asked the judge to send her to jail because she felt like a disgrace to her family and they had "pretty much disowned me," but the judge only issued fines, responding, "Why would I send a pretty girl like you to jail when I'm going to make a whole lot more money if you're staying out?" When I asked her later why she thought she had never been sent to jail after multiple court appearances, Kate attributed it to being female and dressing nicely and to the judge being "some old man." And unspoken, perhaps unrecognized, by Kate, was that she was a White woman in a system that disproportionately incarcerates people of color, particularly Black men and women. White women like Kate (and Cassie from the last chapter) are more likely to receive sympathy from members of the criminal justice system because of the overlapping privilege of being White and the presumed innocence of White women.[36]

Other young women lived with romantic partners, which could be sources of support and strain. Sandra, for instance, lived with her romantic partner, whom she initially referred to as her boyfriend and later said was her "fiancé when I want it to be." She and Brian, her sometimes fiancé, had been a couple since high school, and their relationship was often good; they worked together to parent their son, and Brian had supported Sandra through an early miscarriage, her pregnancy and delivery, and her physical and mental health problems. Yet they also fought, particularly when money was tight and they had to delay paying bills. Although Sandra placed the blame on herself for these arguments, it is not uncommon for couples to fight when finances are insecure.[37] Other couples had more serious disputes. Alice, a poor White young woman from Glenbrook, had a tumultuous relationship with her boyfriend and then husband, ultimately pushing him out of the house after he violently shook their toddler daughter and threw her to the ground.

Poverty creates conditions in which family members must rely on one another for survival and yet also become sources of conflict.[38] For young adults who are trying to make their way in the world, this web of family conflict, obligations, and real assistance makes family both a vital source of support and a barrier to emotional and financial stability. Family members may pitch in to help raise young children, but differences in parenting standards can lead to fights. A sudden loss of income, a dispute with a landlord, or a breakup can force doubling (or tripling) up with family, who may then chafe at being in close quarters. Having more adults in a home can expand both the income pool and the risk that someone will bring drugs, alcohol, or violence into the home. The reciprocal obligations that were a part of these young women's worlds in high school continued and deepened as they moved into young adulthood and served as both vital sources of support and sources of strife.

SERIOUS SETBACKS AND THE JOURNEY FORWARD

How did young women end up navigating rough seas? As we have seen, these young women struggled to make their way through the educational landscape, find secure employment, and manage family obligations and conflict. Colleges and universities were not set up to support them, and quick-fix educational programs did not provide the kinds of credentials they needed to get good jobs. And the work these young women found was unstable and poorly paid. Those from working-class and poor families often helped their parents and siblings with finances and care work. Nine out of thirteen also had a child in the years following (or in one case, before) high school graduation. For these young women, having a child did not drastically change their life circumstances, but it often exacerbated their difficulties. It could mean the difference between holding on and navigating rough seas.

For Shannon, discussed previously, becoming pregnant meant a temporary change in her already unstable trajectory. She had already moved in and out of college programs and short-term, low-wage jobs by the time she was pregnant. Once she was pregnant, she dropped out of her cosmetology program due to the harsh chemicals she was required to work with, and she also stopped working in retail. About a year later she returned to cosmetology school, however, and was close to graduation at the time we talked. For her, having a child was an interruption to her plans but not a permanent one.

For others, like Kimberly, an unplanned pregnancy forced a bigger change in their educational and career plans. Kimberly was enrolled at a community college and pursuing an associate's degree in respiratory therapy when she became pregnant. She earned As and Bs and might have completed this program in other circumstances. After speaking to a college adviser, however, she realized that she needed two more years of preliminary coursework to even apply to the two-year respiratory therapy program. At that point, she felt three more years of schooling was too much. She explained, "I got pregnant, so I wanted something that I could get a job in now." Kimberly enrolled in a for-profit college and earned a certificate in medical billing eleven months later. When I talked to her, she was looking for work while employed part-time at a fast-food chain. Finances were tight, and she was hoping to find full-time work in her chosen field. For young women like Kimberly, having children upended their plans and created additional financial pressures. Kimberly hoped to return to college to become a registered nurse eventually, but for now she was $30,000 in debt with a certificate in a field where, if employed full-time, she could earn about $30,000 per year.

Other young women were pushed into navigating rough seas after multiple serious hardships. Drug and alcohol abuse, mental health problems, and sexual or physical abuse plagued some young women in this group, contributing to, or at least compounding, their precarious circumstances. When we spoke, most depicted themselves as having recovered from such problems after a difficult journey. Whether or not this would ultimately be the case, this language allowed them to frame their experiences in a positive light.

It is also notable that all four self-identified lesbian and bisexual young women were in this group (Shannon, Allison, Lisa, and Kate). Sexual minority youth experience higher rates of discrimination and victimization than heterosexual young people, which increases their levels of stress and number of mental health problems.[39] In particular, research suggests that lesbian and bisexual young women have higher rates of suicidal thoughts and drug use and that bisexual young women also have higher rates of drinking and depression than heterosexual young women, particularly when they do not receive parental support.[40] This is echoed in the transcripts of the young women I interviewed. Allison, Lisa, and Kate all experienced a great deal of conflict with their parents and abused drugs. Allison, Lisa, and Shannon struggled with mental health issues (depression, anxiety, and bipolar disorder).

Allison, a middle-class biracial (Black and White) young woman from Glenbrook whom we met in chapter 3, showed great promise in early high school. She was enrolled in advanced coursework; maintained high grades; and was active in dance, cheerleading, and several school clubs. In her junior year, however, she struggled with depression and voluntarily entered a mental health facility after a suicide attempt. During this time, understandably, her grades slipped and she became less invested in school. When I spoke to Allison in her senior year, her grades were recovering, she was taking courses at the local community college, and she had been dating another young woman for four months. She felt ready to attend college and pursue her goal of becoming a nurse practitioner.

When I spoke to Allison five years later, she was still suffering from mental health problems and had been diagnosed with bipolar disorder and anxiety. After graduating from high school, Allison had enrolled in Powell State College, a local midsize public university, just as her parents moved out of state for her stepfather's job. Alone for the first time while attending a mostly commuter campus, Allison began abusing drugs (primarily her anti-anxiety pills, Ativan and later Klonopin) and alcohol. After receiving a D in an introductory class in her chosen major, Allison dropped out of college. This led to a long period of instability, as Allison lived alternately with various family members, friends, and acquaintances. At one point, she lived with a photographer who had lured her in with promises of a modeling career. Allison received drugs and alcohol from the 60-year-old man, who would then coax her into nude modeling and sexual activity. The way Allison described her experience, this was clearly sexual assault:

I know that I didn't stop anything that happened, but I know that I was completely out of my right mind when things happened. And, yeah, sexual relations happened. So, I know, if I had been in my right mind, I would've said no. . . . It became that he would bring me over, to get me trashed and then that would—that things like that would take place, a lot of the time.

Although disturbing on its own, this was not the only time Allison's safety was endangered in her young adult life.

In the fall of 2010, Allison met the man who would become her husband. As she described their relationship, "there were some ups and downs in our relationship, because he had anger issues and was kind of a little bit violent toward me, but not to the extreme." She described him as shoving her to the floor, threatening to strike her, and preventing her from leaving a room or the house at various times. At one point, she told her mother she was "afraid of what might happen, if I stay," although she explained that it eventually "worked out." The pair moved briefly to her parents' house but left after Allison's stepfather initiated a physical altercation with her and her husband.

When we spoke, Allison reported that she had rededicated herself to Christianity and had helped her husband become saved. She credited her recovery from drug and alcohol abuse to her husband. She was also selling homemade crafts, describing herself as a budding small business owner. Ultimately, when I asked her if she was happy or unhappy with her life, she explained, "I feel very happy, but I know that there's a lot of fear that I think prevents, sometimes, how happy I can be. I still have bad days. . . . But, in general, I am ecstatic with who I'm becoming." Allison depicted her young adult years as a journey that she was traveling through on her way to her authentic self.

Allison was not alone. Several other young women navigating rough seas depicted themselves as on an emotional or spiritual journey, echoing findings by sociologist Jennifer Silva, who has argued that working-class youth have adopted a narrative of "therapeutic selfhood" as a strategy for claiming growth and adult status.[41] As Silva argues, in the current era, working-class youth often cannot attain traditional markers of adulthood through work, family, or consumption. Instead, adulthood is attained through a narrative of personal struggle in which men and women seek to overcome their "demons," such as alcoholism, abuse, mental illness, or betrayal. These narratives offer a sense of trajectory and hope for the future that navigating rough seas young women do not see in other areas of their lives.

LEAVING THE FUTURE TO FATE

"What do you want your life to look like at age 30?" I asked Alice, a lanky young woman with a long, angular face; high cheekbones; blue-green eyes; and a small lip ring. Alice spoke in a drawl with a slight tremor to her voice and an unfocused manner. She responded that she wanted to move away from Glenbrook, and when I asked her where she wanted to go, she took a long drag on her cigarette and responded, "wherever the wind freakin' takes me." It felt, in many ways, like a movie scene: the haze of smoke, her languid manner, and the two young children playing in the background being watched by a couple of young male friends of hers. Yet these were also the very real parameters of Alice's life; from a young age, her family circumstances were unpredictable and chaotic. Even the aspirations she held in high school, to be a writer and child psychologist, stemmed from events she could not control: from having to write to communicate with her mother because her mother's abusive boyfriend did not allow them to speak to one another in his presence, to witnessing a young relative struggling with the emotional repercussions of familial sexual abuse. Later, in high school and in young adulthood, Alice also drifted, first between her parents' homes and then between apartments, short-term jobs, and in and out of an abusive relationship with her boyfriend (later husband).

Alice's desire to let fate (the wind) take control was not unusual for the young women I interviewed who were navigating rough seas. Many alternated between three visions of the future: the hope for a career and middle-class lifestyle, the expectations and (to some extent) known parameters of family life, and the inclination to leave their futures up to fate. These young women still hoped to complete a degree, work, and have a stable family life, yet they did not offer specific time lines for these goals. Instead, most expressed a hope that by age 30 they would have attained more schooling, be engaged in a career, be financially stable (sometimes expressed as owning a home), and be married and have more children. The path to getting there seemed more difficult and murkier now, however, and they had experienced unexpected setbacks that made the future appear (and it was) less controllable than anticipated.

Tiffany, for instance, was married and in a mostly stable financial situation—a rarity for those in the navigating rough seas group—but expressed this mixed view of the future. Thinking about age 30, she said:

> I would like to be almost finished with school. And by the time I'm 30 it'll be easier to do that. . . . They [her children] should all be at school all day by [then]. Other than that, I want to finish something. I want to be able to have my own job because it's nice to be able to say I can do something with my own money. It's not always fun for him being the only income in the house. I want my kids to be healthy and everything to be worked out. I mean, there's probably nothing to be worked out, but you never know. . . . I live life day by day because you never know what life's going to hand you the next day. No idea. So I take every breath in the moment.

On the one hand, Tiffany envisioned a career for herself in surgical nursing. She viewed it as fitting her interests and skills and as giving her the opportunity to bring income into her family. And this vision of her future was sketched around a very concrete picture of her family life. Tiffany quickly calculated her children's ages and life stages as she reflected on her goals for age 30. For Tiffany, this meant that her two young boys would be 12 and 10, and the new baby she was expecting would be about 6, when she turned 30. This offered her new possibilities due to their school schedule, although she recognized that in the next few years, caring for her children would put limitations on her educational and occupational endeavors.

Tiffany also expressed some fatalism, explaining that she lived "day by day" and took "every breath in the moment." For a young woman struggling to manage a household, two young boys, a pregnancy, and depression, Tiffany couldn't do much more than take each day as it came. And this was true for most young women navigating rough seas. In the middle of a storm, sometimes the only way to survive is to ride it out. Others expressed similar feelings of fatalism or of higher powers taking charge. When I asked Allison what she expected her life to look like at age 30, she replied, "I'm so clueless onto exactly what direction God wants for me—even though I might know what I want right now, I know he's going to play and be like, 'Nope, move over here.'" Tyra also connected her future goals to religion, explaining that at age 30 she wanted to "feel like I've accomplished a lot. . . . Just having something to do. Just instead of doing nothing. I know a lot of people who don't do anything, so at least doing something that would make me feel like I'm trying—trying to better myself. And I've been going back to church lately also." When I asked Tyra about her intentions to marry her longtime boyfriend, she left her plans up to fate, explaining that she wanted everything to "flow" right with school and finances and the timing of a marriage and that she would "let it fall into place." Although Tyra had some specific ideas about what she wanted for her work and family futures, she left much up to fate.

As we saw in earlier chapters, these young women were not fatalists in high school. They had ambitions and plans, and many had the good grades to back up their sense of optimism. So why the fatalism now? They had embraced the tenets of the American Dream—that hard work and persistence would lead to mobility—in high school, then saw these expectations fall apart in young adulthood in ways they could neither anticipate nor plan their way out of.[42] The unraveling of their plans owed much to structural impediments, such as poor advising and academic preparation in high school, high costs of college, limited regulatory enforcement of predatory educational institutions, low-wage and unstable work that impacted not only their funds but those of their families, limited workplace protections and childcare options for young mothers, and more. Yet they experienced these barriers as individual setbacks, ones they could neither control nor identify as tied to any larger social pattern.

The problem with believing in the American Dream is that structural impediments and their aftermaths become internalized as personal failures.[43] For those navigating rough seas, these "failures" come unexpectedly and alongside, and sometimes after a lifetime of, other disruptions that are (to them) equally unpredictable and individualized. As sociologist Ranita Ray has observed in her insightful book, *The Making of a Teenage Service Class*, poor young people learn to live alongside uncertainty, still seeking a better life while they "'normalize' these uncertainties by drawing on highly individualistic and often uncontrollable and otherworldly accounts such as 'bad genes,' 'fate,' and 'unknown conspiracies'—accounts that [help] them deal with the unpredictability of life."[44] Alice, Tiffany, Tyra, and Allison, then, continued to make tentative plans and to hope for a better tomorrow, but they balanced this with the understanding that bad things would come their way, seeming to ride in on the wind without warning.

Conclusion

During the transition to adulthood, young women must navigate a complex labor market and educational landscape. Without robust financial assistance in college, many students work to pay tuition, provide for their own living expenses, and sometimes contribute to their families' income, and they do so within a labor market with few protections. Workers without a college degree (and some with a degree) have little say over their schedules and hours and few protections from layoffs. Postsecondary educational institutions are also relatively unregulated, and therefore students must be savvy to correctly identify the kinds of certificates or degrees they need for their intended careers, as well as which institutions are accredited, offer the degrees they need, and do so for a reasonable price. And young women's lives are shaped not only by the free market directly but also by how the free market impacts their families. If their parents and siblings need help caring for a relative, whether a child, romantic partner, or elder, a lack of affordable care options means that it may fall on young adults, particularly young women, to pitch in. When other family members have unpredictable schedules, young adults may be called on to help run the household.

Working-class and poor young women cannot plan for, or out of, these multiple and competing demands. Access to tangible and intangible

157

resources shapes young people's capacity to make plans, enact plans, and recover from plans gone awry. We have seen this play out through these young women's stories, where most young women held reasonable plans to accomplish their occupational aspirations, yet their outcomes were highly stratified. Why do we see this? Class inequality creates situations in which similar goals translate into differential sorting in the labor market. Those with fewer resources are often shunted into low-wage work, while those with more resources move along tracks to a stable career. Planning is one step along this process, but it is not determinative. This book elaborates on two mechanisms of the intergenerational transmission of inequality: how unequal resources sort young people into different pathways, and how these pathways shape their lived experiences in the transition to adulthood in ways that compound inequality.

HOW DO PLANS MATTER?

In beginning this project with a focus on aspirations and plans for the future among young women, I explored a foundational puzzle in sociology: How do individuals make choices within the confines of structure? I found that holding high aspirations, making plans to achieve these aspirations, and having access to tangible and intangible resources were all important components in young women's early adult attainment. Young women who were able to follow through on their early plans, thus putting their aspirations for packaged or repackaged futures within reach, did so when the requirements of the career they aspired to were clear to them, when they were able to bounce back academically from early stumbles, when they were supported by the higher education institutions in which they enrolled, and when they had support from—or at least no obligations to—family. Other young women successfully amended their plans because they recognized early that something was not working, and they were given the support they needed to pivot to a new goal and new schooling plan.[1]

Plans alone were not enough. Some good plans fell apart when finances made it difficult for young women to pay for college, instability at home created more immediate needs than investment in schooling, physical or mental health crises arose, and the college landscape and how this landscape connected to possible careers was unclear to them. Some young women who had less concrete plans in high school still appeared destined to complete college and obtain a good job. In the end, most young women who had strong plans but lacked financial and institutional support ended up in the holding on or rough seas pathways, while being on track took financial and institutional resources, regardless of planning.

Why do we see this? Returning to and elaborating on the concepts of structure and agency, we can see how structure—in the form of both resources (most pressingly here, economic and social capital) and schemas (mental maps used to navigate one's way in the world)—matters in launching young people into adulthood. Not only do both matter, but they build off of and reinforce one another. Applying this to planning for the future, we have seen how for middle-class White girls, knowledgeable adults offered information and career-building opportunities (resources) that informed their ideas about appropriate careers and the importance of planning (schema). As they developed their plans, these young women sought out additional resources by talking to adults they knew inside and outside of school. And they were then able to speak about their plans in a more informed way which, in combination with a middle-class presentation, garnered additional information and resources.

This does not mean that the young women themselves were not displaying agency. Indeed, if agency is "the capacity to transpose and extend schemas to new contexts," then we can see all of the young women in this book as enacting agency as they move through young adulthood.[2] For middle-class White young women, particularly but not exclusively those on track, the *experience* of profiting from resource-rich ties in high school—learning about careers, receiving advice, and accessing opportunities like internships or shadowing professionals—paid dividends in young adulthood. Those young women acquired the skills and awareness to continue to build on and profit from social networks in a new environment. They took these skills and schemas into their approach to advisers and other knowledgeable adults in college and at work, thus continuing to build their social networks.

For middle-class Black girls in high school, their parents (usually mothers) played a more central role in helping them plan than middle-class White parents. This is likely because their mothers had less access to resource-rich ties and because the adults the girls encountered in professional settings did not take the same level of interest in them as reported by White girls in similar encounters. Without as much external support, planning was left to the family. And because this left the middle-class Black girls with fewer role models for their occupational aspirations, they and their parents focused on planning for college. Once they reached institutions of higher education, the middle-class Black young women I spoke to, such as Jordan, took on their mothers' roles, forging connections with peers and faculty where they could and taking on time-consuming but important service and leadership roles. These young women had to work harder than middle-class White young women did to both plan for and achieve their goals. However, like middle-class White young women, they were able to transpose their experiences of planning for the future from high school to college.

Working-class and poor girls, both White and Black, also transposed and extended their schemas from high school; for them, this meant that they had reciprocal relationships with those in their social networks, who were usually financially and emotionally supportive of them but also needed support in return. These obligations were both gendered and classed, as some girls reported performing unpaid care work in the home, such as cleaning and caring for siblings, to help out parents who worked long hours. Others reported providing emotional support to adults they were close to. They continued to apply these learned skills and schemas in young adulthood, sometimes now with partners and children and at other times with siblings, parents, or other relatives. This was particularly true of those navigating rough seas, who have been characterized as "disconnected youth" (i.e., young adults not engaged in work or school) but played vital roles in their families as caretakers in addition to intermittent work and student roles. School and career planning, on the other hand, was a skill they had developed not through connections to others but through their own work of observation and seeking out information wherever they could, often from the institutions themselves. These young women continued to plan for college, identifying routes through which they hoped to obtain a speedy but valuable degree. The challenge for these young women, however, was that the postsecondary educational landscape is one

in which wrong turns (or even all the right ones) can be negatively consequential when you don't have the resources for a course correction. Many
ended up churning through colleges and college programs, acquiring debt
in the process but not a college degree.

Agency is not only conditioned by one's immediate constraints and opportunities, but it is also enacted in response to the logics of the world
in which we live. "Planful competence" looks like it works because better-
resourced young people have better plans (i.e., they knew more of the spe-
cifics of the jobs they wished to hold and pathways to achieve them) *and*
because colleges are structured to reward forms of planning that signal access to resources. Thus, a well-regarded prepharmacy program is likely to
look favorably on applicants who have shadowed a pharmacist or obtained
a part-time job at a pharmacy, but neither of these experiences necessarily
makes it more likely that a student would succeed in the program. Rather,
access to such experiences signals class and race advantage, and class and
race advantages facilitate successfully completing a college program. These
résumé-building experiences can have more or less of an effect on young
people's outcomes, depending on the structure of the education system and
the nature of connections between education and work.[3] The experiences
themselves are also not the only way to plan for the future; working-class
and poor young people can and do show planful competence by researching the careers they wish to hold and the educational pathways needed to
achieve those goals. Their plans may not be as detailed as those expressed
by middle-class young people, but that does not equate to a lack of planfulness. If colleges and college programs were structured to reduce the role of
resources in students' success, then it is possible working-class and poor
young women's plans would do better in facilitating attainment.

WHAT DOES IT MEAN TO TRANSITION TO ADULTHOOD IN AN ERA OF UNCERTAINTY?

We met the subjects of this book while they were high school students
planning for the future amid the most severe economic crisis since the
Great Depression.[4] As high school students in 2008, however, the young
women were not specifically aware of "the Great Recession" as a moment

in time. They were not alone; it is difficult to recognize a historical moment while in the middle of it, and it had not yet been named as such. Yet the recession will likely have an effect on their long- and short-term outcomes; large-scale surveys show that an economic downturn has an impact on cohort educational attainment, employment, and wages.[5] What's more, the Great Recession itself was an acceleration of long-term trends toward inequality and the shift in risk away from employers and onto workers, which had already been felt for years in many of the girls' homes. Many knew what life was like with unemployed or underemployed parents, residential instability, and economic precarity. The Great Recession only expanded and deepened such experiences; it did not fundamentally change the uncertainty these young women faced. Rather, the stories in this book reflect something much more far-reaching: they illustrate how the American ethos of deregulation—an ethos that emphasizes less government oversight at the same time that corporations and universities have embraced the idea that they do not have a shared responsibility to their employees and students—makes the transition to adulthood difficult to navigate for even the most persistent young adults.

Effectively Maintained Inequality in Higher Education

Today's educational landscape does not work well for many young people, and it does not work well for American society. Interest in going to college is near universal because getting a degree is so important for getting a good job and obtaining a stable, middle-class lifestyle. And the labor force needs more educated workers who can take on the kinds of technologically complex jobs available today. Yet colleges and universities have, by necessity, been shifting toward a business model in order to make ends meet, prioritizing wealthy students at the expense of middle-class, working-class, and poor students at more elite institutions while marketing questionable programs and degrees to the working class and poor at less elite institutions.[6] This shift is born of diminishing public support for not-for-profit public colleges, making them dependent on tuition revenue; an increasingly unequal labor market that incentivizes young people to prioritize occupational- and professional-oriented programs; a political ethos that devalues traditional liberal arts education; and a lack of federal regulation of the higher education landscape overall, which has allowed predatory for-profit colleges to make money off desperate students without evidence of effectiveness.[7] On top of this, tuition is rising, and federal support for students is not. This has created an impossible situation for students in which going to college is the only way to get ahead, but doing so comes with a large and risky price tag. As we have seen, many poor and working-class students drop out because they do not have the financial resources to focus on school, and schools themselves do not provide the kind of structural supports needed for these students to thrive.

Most of the young women I interviewed who did not complete college intended to return. Thus, not only did they need to pay back loans from their first institutions, but many took on or intended to take on more debt at new institutions. They are not alone. According to research, the proportion of young adults owing student debt has been rising over time, with 37% of young adult households reporting owing student debt in 2010, when many of the young women in this study first enrolled in college, at a median level of $13,000.[8] And once a young person has accrued debt from educational loans, it cannot be discharged as easily through bankruptcy as other sources of debt.[9] Thus, one of the few options for deferring payment is to reenroll in college. This led some, like Shauna, who owed $30,000 and was facing monthly bills of $300 she could not afford, to consider enrolling in college again to defer loan payments.

The higher education system in the United States, therefore, creates a catch-22 for many. Completing college offers the best chance of attaining a settled, middle-class life. Yet enrolling in college and falling short can have devastating economic consequences with little hope of reprieve, as we saw with too many of the rough seas young women. In the landscape of higher education, "good" choices can still lead to poor outcomes. This doesn't mean that loans shouldn't be deferred; it means that we shouldn't have a system that relies so heavily on loans at all. We are asking young people to borrow against an uncertain future, and they are forced to do so because without it they have an almost certainly poor future.

The stories in this book may indicate to some that we should guide young people toward professionally oriented programs that focus schooling on practical applications, because the most successful girls did this. Yet this ignores the importance of class background among the young women who end up in these programs and the resources directed toward them on the part of the colleges and universities in which they are enrolled. As more young people go to college, we see an increasingly stratified system of higher education, both between and within institutions, and we find once again that class divides who goes where. This stratification maintains and even deepens—due to high debt loads and uncertain occupational paths—inequality. As sociologist Samuel Lucas predicted, the educational system adapts to produce "effectively maintained inequality" by, once an educational level is near-universally attained, segregating students into different tracks within that level.[10] Thus, as a greater proportion of students enter into higher education, colleges and universities create more tracks through which to segregate students by interest and ability. This is further incentivized by the financial needs of these institutions; highly resourced programs help to attract the most sought-after students and boost rankings-related metrics. Within elite college tracks, there really is the kind of system we want to see: strong connections between work and school, opportunities for training, good advising, and clear expectations. In less well-resourced programs and institutions, however, these qualities are advertised but not necessarily present. Instead, many educational institutions are selling credentials to desperate students who do need them, but with little support.

Polarization in the Labor Market

Although preparation for and persistence in higher education is the single best insurance against postgraduation precarious employment, many college graduates end up underemployed or unemployed.[11] It is no surprise, then, that many young women aspire to work in the health field. Jobs in this field offer high wages relative to similarly educated workers, generous benefits, and excellent chances of full employment. Nurses, for example, have seen strong wage growth over the past several decades.[12] College graduates who majored in health also report among the lowest levels of unemployment both immediately after college and in the longer term, and their earnings are among the highest, on a par with architecture and business majors.[13] Thus, careers in the health professions offer a chance at a stable life, reducing the degree of risk that many other workers—even those who are college educated—may face.[14]

Other health-care jobs are not as promising, however. Direct-care workers, for instance, who work in private homes, nursing and assisted living facilities, adult day-care programs, and sometimes hospitals, are poorly paid, receive few if any benefits (including health-care coverage), and are often employed on a part-time basis.[15] One study found that 44% of such workers lived in households earning below 200% of the poverty line, a common threshold used to qualify for public benefits.[16] As we have seen, many young people who start out with an interest in the health professions but do not complete a four-year college degree end up in these jobs. Thus, the health-care industry is a microcosm of the larger labor force, with workforce winners and losers reaping much larger or smaller portions of the pie.

Taken together, the increased risks borne by workers and the division of the labor market into secure and insecure jobs leads to what Arne Kalleberg has described as a polarization in job rewards between "good jobs" that offer greater benefits and security and "bad jobs" that are poorly paid and precarious.[17] We can see these bad jobs in the stories of holding on and rough seas young women who had little control over the scheduling and demands of their work. Those who were young mothers often had to leave the labor market temporarily because of their physical limitations during pregnancy and a lack of parental leave, accommodations for breast pumping, and childcare options. This left many who wished to work unable to do so. Others worked at low-wage jobs, often while attending school. These jobs paid, on average, about $11 an hour, or less than $25,000 per year if they worked forty hours a week all year. They often did not offer full-time hours, however, which also meant that they did not provide benefits such as health care or paid time off. Young women were stuck working as much as they could just to make do.

WHO MOVES UP OR DOWN
THE CLASS LADDER, AND WHY?

Intergenerational mobility—the degree to which children's income varies from that of their parents—is relatively low in the United States.[18] And as recent studies suggest, it may be even more difficult for children to exceed or even match the class status of their parents today than in the past.[19] Thus, upward mobility appears to be a more difficult proposition in recent generations. The findings in this book shed some light on *why* upward mobility has become so difficult and what the transition looks like for those who deviate from their class backgrounds. Young people from working-class and poor backgrounds must not only get to college in order to attain their goal of having a steady, well-paid job, but must get into a good college or even an elite program within a college and complete their degree, all of which require substantial resources.

Although I do not follow the young women in this book throughout adulthood, we have seen how many young women's early transitions to adulthood set them on a path toward upward or downward mobility, or class replication. Class replication appears most common with middle-class young women on track, working-class young women holding on, and poor young women navigating rough seas. These pathways would be difficult to alter significantly. Despite the depiction, by some, of young (or emerging) adulthood as a time of exploration, there is in fact little room for such ambiguity.[20] Relatively small stumbles—enrollment in an educational institution that isn't a good match, poor grades, or demanding work schedules, for example—can disrupt young people's pathways and their chances of completing their degree.[21]

Some young women did appear poised to move up or down the class ladder, however, and their experiences in the transition to adulthood were shaped both by their class destinations and their class origins. That is, these young women carried their class origins into their class destinations, shaping their experiences and resources in the transition to adulthood. Those who grew up in the working class and appeared upwardly mobile showed tremendous persistence in following their goals. They also benefited from some luck and structural opportunities. They were not necessarily more planful than other working-class young women who did not end up on track, but they were academically prepared for college, were well matched with the colleges they attended, and worked fewer hours during the academic year. Yet they also struggled more than their middle-class-origin peers keep moving toward their goals. Financial constraints slowed or diverted their paths at times, as we saw in the case of Shana, and obligations to family created their own sources of tension.

Those who were on a path toward downward mobility usually experienced roadblocks that diverted them from their early plans, including failing out of college, drug use, pregnancy, financial precarity, or a mental health crisis. These roadblocks were mitigated for those from middle-class families, however, often keeping these young women from falling as far as they might have otherwise. A young woman like Cassie, therefore, benefited from both her middle-class background and her White privilege when she inherited a tidy sum from her grandparents, talked her way into mentorships in the restaurant industry, and avoided arrest after being pulled over with drug paraphernalia in her car. Although not quite on track, young women like Cassie managed to hold on in circumstances that would have sent working-class and poor young women into rough seas.

Of course, some middle- and working-class young women experienced other kinds of stumbling blocks that led to downward mobility. Struggles with mental health problems, pregnancy, and substance abuse were prevalent, and self-identified gay and bisexual young women were particularly likely to experience downward mobility. Five young women reported being in or having same-sex relationships either while in high school or after, and four of the five experienced downward mobility. Take, for example, Allison, who dropped out of college after one semester and struggled with addiction, bipolar disorder, and chronic illness. These problems are not unusual among sexual minority youth; research suggests that higher rates of drug abuse and mental health problems among this population stem from lower levels of support and higher levels of physical and sexual victimization compared to heterosexual young people.[22]

Race, as well as class, matters in shaping trajectories through the transition to adulthood. I did not observe different patterns of upward and downward mobility between Black and White young women, but this is not surprising. Recent research finds that although Black Americans have much lower rates of upward mobility than White Americans, this is primarily driven by race differences among men.[23] Black women often experience downward mobility in household income due to marriage patterns, but these disparities do not emerge in young adulthood. However, Black young women are more likely to shoulder large amounts of college debt than White young women, and this has long-term implications for their ability to accrue savings, buy homes, and provide resources for their own children.[24] This research tells us that the Black young women I interviewed will face steeper odds in trying to reach their dreams of packaged and repackaged futures than their White peers, even if we do not yet see differences in educational attainment and work experience.

Whiteness also protected some young women from drastic forms of downward mobility in the wake of run-ins with the law. The White women who were caught with drugs were either let off entirely (Cassie) or given only a fine (Kate). In both cases, agents of the criminal justice system recognized them as "good" young women who had been led astray, rather than as criminals. White privilege, in other words, provided White young women with both resources and second chances while on the road to adulthood. Black young women are often not provided the same opportunities, and this can have consequences for their outcomes in the long term.[25]

HOW DOES GENDER MATTER?

Aspirations and plans in adolescence, and trajectories into the transition to adulthood, are also profoundly gendered. Across social classes, these young women were drawn toward jobs offering intrinsic rewards to "help people." This motivation is likely tied to feelings of competency in this area.[26] As young women are asked to perform helping and caretaking tasks—such as working as a babysitter, caring for a younger sibling, or tending to an ill parent—they build their skills and feelings of competency around caretaking.[27]

Yet gender also operates differently within social classes. Middle-class girls reported that adults in their orbit encouraged two somewhat conflicting considerations. First is that they should establish themselves in careers before marrying and having children.[28] Second is that they should consider "flexible" jobs that would allow them to be mothers. Together, feelings of competency around care work and being pushed toward flexible work nudged adolescent girls toward the caring professions; careers such as nursing, teaching, pharmacy, physical and occupational therapy, and counseling held great appeal. To be sure, these female-dominated but professional occupations offer a good salary and steady employment to young women who achieve the right credentials, but by pursuing these career paths, young women also participated in the creation of social structure. They entered college majors that were dominated by other young women and contributed to those majors' female-ness. They learned additional skills that added to and affirmed their gendered competencies. They followed gendered career paths, making them active participants in the process of occupational gender segregation. And those jobs—or at least those jobs that are both female-dominated and held by middle-class women—seem to offer the flexibility that will make it both possible and convenient for them to be primary caretakers, if and when they have children.[29] Thus, their decisions throughout the transition to adulthood reinscribe gender norms around the kind of work that women do, and why.

Certainly young women could and did make choices to pursue male-dominated or gender-balanced careers. Some aspired to work as medical doctors, for instance. This was more common among Black young women than White young women, which may reflect the tradition of working mothers within Black families in the United States.[30] These processes also do not omit the importance of agency. Both those who follow gendered occupational pathways and those who do not are active agents in their own futures. However, their choices do show how socialization shapes what young women consider and find meaning in as they plan and follow their educational and occupational pathways.

Working-class and poor girls, on the other hand, rarely reported that any adult they knew, directly or indirectly, had cautioned them to consider their family plans when deciding on their career goals.[31] For them, gender shaped their obligations to family at a younger age than middle-class girls; they were often asked to take over household chores and caretaking, thus pulling them away from pursuing their goals.[32] These expectations about care work are both classed and gendered.[33] Women of all class backgrounds expressed feelings of competency around caring and "helping people." Yet middle-class young women were more often protected from the expectation to be caretakers in adolescence and young adulthood, while working-class and poor young women were drafted to help out in ways big and small at a young age. As they grew into adulthood, these roles became a larger part of their lives, particularly when paid work was scarce. Although from the outside many of these young women might be seen as "disconnected youth," they were in fact highly connected and productive members of society.

Additionally, over one-half of the poor women I interviewed had at least one child by the time they were 24 years old. As prior research has shown, having children "early" (in one's teens and early twenties) lowers the odds of attending and completing postsecondary schooling for women.[34] However, the explanations for this association are complex. Although popular accounts often blame poor women for their childbearing decisions, much research finds that poverty and disengagement from school are just as likely to be drivers of early childbearing.[35] Having children can have contradictory impacts on young women's life chances, often improving their available social support and later educational persistence and reducing their risk behaviors.[36] But it adds more responsibilities in a country that offers little support for childcare or workplace protections.[37] The young mothers I spoke to worked hard to create loving, supportive homes for their children and to identify college programs they could complete quickly and workplaces that fit their needs. However, a lack of work-family justice policies placed limitations on their schooling and work engagement while their children were young.

WHAT CAN BE DONE?

This book shows how social class, race, and gender inequality manifests in young women's future plans and early trajectories into young adulthood; how class reproduction and mobility start to take shape during this period; and how the gendered division of paid and unpaid labor is reinscribed through both aspirations and family relationships. So, what can be done to lessen the structural import of social class, race, and gender on young women's life chances? The stories in these pages offer insight for answering this question. Rather than insist individuals pull themselves up by their bootstraps within systems that routinely fail them, we can make changes in the areas of school, work, and family that will improve all young people's chances of attaining a packaged or repackaged future. To do so, we must enact policy changes that lessen the impact of resources on young women's outcomes and increase the efficacy of planning.

Education for All

Creating a system of education that provides equitable opportunities for all is not only a moral good, but a practical one; we should want our schools to promote talent in all its forms. As this book has shown, a primary hindrance to this goal is the cost of higher education. We cannot roll back time and say that young people do not need to attend college. Instead, we need college to be accessible, financially safe, and worth the investment. Three policy prescriptions could alleviate the financial pressure on students and their families.

First, making public, not-for-profit college free, at the very least for the first two years of college, would make college more accessible to the poor and working class and eliminate one incentive for public colleges and universities to prioritize wealthy students and their families.[38] Ideally, this funding would cover tuition, fees, and college students' cost of living while in school.[39] Proposals to make college free have been criticized as a "giveaway" to wealthy students because college students are disproportionately from relatively high-earning families. As we have seen in this book, however, poor and working-class young people are not uninterested in attending college. They want to attend, and many do for short periods, but without substantial assistance, many drop out. Thus, we cannot assume that the current distribution of college students by family income would continue if we make college more accessible to those at the bottom (and middle) of the income distribution. And of course there are benefits to extending support to college students of all backgrounds. Doing so is an investment in the importance of higher education for our society as a whole.

Second, our government must address the student loan crisis both by making educational loans dischargeable via bankruptcy and by offering generous loan forgiveness to current outstanding debt. Total student loan debt stands at about $1.5 trillion in the United States.[40] As we saw, accumulating loans can become a self-perpetuating cycle when young people do not complete a degree or complete a degree that does not lead to a good job and feel they must reenroll and accumulate more debt in order to have any hope of paying off their original loans. The first proposed change would overturn the 2005 classification of educational loans as nondischargeable, which contributed to skyrocketing student loan debt by

creating perverse incentives for lenders to loan large sums to student bor-
rowers regardless of their ability to repay. The second would address the
outstanding debt of those who had already taken on loans for educational
degrees that have not always paid off in the current economy.

Third, government oversight and accreditation processes could do more
to ensure that students are not being taken advantage of by for-profit colleges. These institutions of higher education charge students higher fees
and graduate a far lower proportion of students than equivalent not-for-
profit institutions, yet they are still subsidized through federal student aid.
Poor and working-class students are particularly vulnerable to programs
that offer them speedy and clear pathways to a degree.[41] The overwhelming majority of students who enroll in for-profit programs drop out while
accruing debt.[42] The Obama administration attempted to curtail these
practices, mandating that schools demonstrate graduates' employability
and be transparent about student loan burdens, but these actions were
overturned by the Trump administration.[43] The current administration
should reinstitute and strengthen these regulations to protect vulnerable
students. These changes would help potential students make better decisions in the short term, but in the long term could also encourage for-
profit schools to design educational programs that actually work.

In addition to lessening the costs of college, we can help students plan
better and prepare for the labor market while in high school and college.
As we have seen, effective planning is not a panacea, particularly in the
absence of structural support and resources. However, in combination
with resources, planning can help students identify their career interests
and the steps they need to take to pursue these careers. All high schools
should offer coursework on planning for the future that teaches students
how to match their skills and interests to careers; identify college, vocational education, or job training pathways into those careers; and (when
appropriate) map out the steps required to apply to and enroll in college.
High schools could also collaborate with organizations that facilitate internships for students,[44] as well as direct relationships with employers,[45]
to provide students with access to occupational training. This would require vetting of internship opportunities so that students are not taken
advantage of in such positions.[46] If done well, however, internships can
offer students the opportunity to learn about their intended careers and

sharpen or change their plans before they leave high school. They can also provide students who do not plan to go to college, or do not plan to do so right away, with valuable human capital that can help them navigate the labor market. Providing both planning assistance and practical experiences would be beneficial to all students, and it would take college and career planning out of the hands of families, where wide disparities in resources produce different levels of preparation.

To better serve all students, higher education institutions must consider what college is like for those without family support and work to alleviate the role of family background in completing a college degree. And as others have advocated, college remediation practices need to be overhauled to better serve the needs and goals of the students who qualify.[47] Better guidance and flexibility for students who have responsibilities at home or work, stronger ties to the labor market and employers, and comprehensive academic assistance would help young people from disadvantaged backgrounds succeed both in classes and in making the transition from school to work. Yet these institutions cannot provide additional services without the financial support of state governments; indeed, it is cuts in funding that have led colleges and universities to rely on the money they receive from wealthy parents and alumni. To shift the priorities of these educational institutions, state governments must restore previous levels of funding, thus lessening the centrality of wealthy families in higher education.

The federal government could also do more for low-income students in postsecondary institutions. Proposals to fund more internships through the Federal Work-Study Program hold promise, as these opportunities can make career-building internships accessible to young people who cannot afford to work for free.[48] As education researchers Sandy Baum and Judith Scott-Clayton have proposed, the Pell Grant Program could be restructured to provide not only direct financial assistance to students but also guidance and academic support throughout college.[49] This would have the advantage of targeting students who need support the most and bringing support to them, rather than relying on low-income students to recognize when they need help and find out how to get it. Other reforms to Pell Grants are also warranted; maximum awards cover a shrinking percentage of the cost of tuition at many colleges and universities and do not take into account other costs of being a college student, including living expenses, books, transportation, and technology.[50] Increasing the amount students can qualify for—and making it easier to apply for and retain these funds—would help low-income students devote time to classes and complete a degree.

Supporting Women, Supporting Families

Relative to other Western nations, the United States provides a weak social safety net, particularly for the non-working poor.[51] This places a larger burden on the private safety net, defined as the support individuals and families receive (or can expect to receive) from their social networks.[52] This not only deepens class inequality due to differences in the resources of one's social networks but also, because women take on the primary roles of caretaker and kin keeper, it hinders gender equity. When families must scramble to provide childcare, women often "voluntarily" give up career opportunities for the good of the family.[53] We have seen this in the wake of the coronavirus pandemic, in which women have left the labor force or reduced their hours of paid work in much larger numbers than men in order to care for children.[54] This exit from the labor force has hurt not only family income but also mothers' mental health and romantic relationships.[55]

This burden on women is also unequal across class. As we have seen in this book, young women from working-class and poor backgrounds are called on with more frequency to provide care, even as adolescents. This responsibility only intensifies in young adulthood, leading many to drop out of school and the labor force and end up navigating rough seas. These "disconnected youth" are often depicted as being a problem because they are not engaged in productive work. In truth, however, they provide valuable unpaid care work.[56] This does not mean we should be unconcerned with their educational and occupational outcomes. However, a primary way to improve their long-term chances of securing good jobs and establishing stable family lives is to recognize their deep and enduring connections to others and find ways to alleviate the competing demands placed on them. This means that policies like job training, as former US secretary of education Arne Duncan has proposed for disconnected youth, are insufficient without also providing affordable childcare, strengthening rules surrounding pregnancy discrimination and pumping at work, providing paid family leave and universal health care, and expanding opportunities for family members to be paid to provide care to loved ones.[57] Such policies recognize that not all workers fit the "ideal worker norm" of a devoted employee who works long hours and is unencumbered by family responsibilities,[58] and it makes room for greater participation of all adults in both work and family spheres.

By making work more family friendly, young women would be less likely to be pushed, explicitly or not, toward perceived family-friendly careers. This would allow them to better match their talents and interests to careers they wish to pursue, while retaining their family plans. At the same time, many of the jobs that women perform are devalued in the labor market, precisely because women—and often women of color—have traditionally performed them. Care workers earn less than equivalent workers and enjoy fewer workplace protections.[59] Instituting reforms to make a range of career paths available to women does not mean neglecting those that are already female dominated.

It is not enough to prepare young people for work when the labor force remains deeply divided between (figurative) winners and losers. A large proportion of jobs are precarious, offering low pay and few benefits, less than full-time hours, few job protections, and little autonomy, and some workers will have to fill those jobs, regardless of their educational attainment. And as an increasing proportion of Americans complete postsecondary degrees, a greater number of degree holders will fill these "bad jobs."[60] Thus, labor protection policies are needed to shore up the stability of work in the lowest-paid occupations and replace vanishing middle-income jobs.[61] As Jonathan Morduch and Rachel Schneider argue in *The Financial Diaries*, Americans want and need work that provides stability.[62] To address these issues, public policy must tackle worker protections by eliminating barriers to unionization, increasing the minimum wage, expanding current labor protections and benefits to the gig economy, and decoupling paid work from health-care coverage so that all Americans have access to medical care.

. . . . .

It is important to consider *how* and *by whom* these reforms should be enacted. Some better-resourced high schools now offer classes to help students plan for the future and obtain internships, while others do not. Some colleges do a better job of supporting low-income students, students of color, and first-generation college students than others. Some workplaces offer a greater array of perks, including family-friendly policies, than others. These efforts at reform and support are admirable. However, in many cases they reinforce preexisting class, race, and gender inequalities because of who has access to supportive high schools, colleges, and workplaces. Thus, it is vital that federal policies mandate protections for all students, workers, and families. Congressional oversight of higher education could better protect potential students from accruing debt in college programs that have high dropout rates and lack accreditation. Federal initiatives could fund shadowing and internship programs for high school students. Both steps would alleviate the burden on high schools, particularly underfunded schools where guidance counselors and teachers are already spread thin. Public not-for-profit colleges and universities, too, could be better funded to support all students, thus incentivizing investment in students from all class backgrounds rather than only the wealthy. Similarly, work-family protections—including paid family leave, subsidized childcare, enforcement of rules to provide places for nursing mothers to pump, and protected flex time work options—would better protect all workers if passed at the federal level.

The road to adulthood is filled with potholes, and the purpose of the policies enumerated here is to fill those potholes, smoothing the pathway for young women (and young men) to achieve their goals and become healthy, happy, and productive adults. Take, for example, a policy put in place by the Affordable Care Act of 2010, which allowed young people to stay on their parents' health insurance until age 26. In the years following that policy change, young adults' health-care coverage and use of health-care services increased, while their reports of delaying or forgoing care because of cost and their rate of use of emergency department visits decreased.[63] This strengthening of the safety net for young people improved their daily lives and the health of the workforce. In other words, this simple—but incomplete, for those who are estranged from their parents and those whose parents do not have health care—fix provided measurable gains in the day-to-day lives of young people and our society as a whole.

More of these fixes are needed if we are to prepare our young people to succeed in college, work, and family life. The young women described in these pages held lofty but achievable goals, yet they needed assistance in fulfilling those goals. Those with greater resources, as we saw, were much more likely to be on track to do so. Those who lacked such resources struggled against the tide. Rather than insisting that disadvantaged youth be superheroes who "beat the odds," we can make it easier for working-class and poor young people to thrive in college and beyond. In doing so, we will not only fulfill a moral imperative to reduce inequality, but we will also benefit from the contributions of young people who are buoyed by institutional support systems. This is the future we can work toward—one in which it is possible for all young people to make and achieve the best laid plans.

APPENDIX Methodology

On September 15, 2008, I drove across several states and into the Glenbrook-Kensington area.[1] It was one day after the remnants of a massive storm had wiped out the local power grid and the same day that the breadth of an impending global financial storm took shape. Lehman Brothers declared bankruptcy that day, in what was to be the largest bankruptcy in US history, sending stocks into a tailspin. Over the next few months, as I traveled between the two towns, I listened to the radio with rapidly escalating anxiety; banks failed, the stock market continued to dive, automobile companies were on life support, and the unemployment rate was climbing. I wondered what this meant for me, as a graduate student searching for jobs in a shrinking labor market, and I wondered what this meant for the young women I was meeting, several of whom had family members who had been laid off or were anticipating imminent layoffs. How do you plan for the future when the labor market is being reshuffled in front of your eyes and when the financial resources necessary for college may not be there? Although I did not plan my dissertation with an economic meltdown in mind, it became the backdrop to my time interviewing high school students.

I had come to this area in the East North Central region of the United States after several failed attempts to obtain permission to conduct my research in high schools near me in North Carolina and near my wife, who was then living in Philadelphia. The risk of hosting a researcher can be daunting for school administrators, who worry they will be the target of outsider critiques. Finally, however, through my own social ties—a friend of my mother who had completed consulting work for a high school in the area—I gained access to Glenbrook High School, a large, primarily working-class high school serving the majority of the town's high school–aged students (a Catholic high school nearby served most of the rest). I later received permission to conduct research in Kensington High School with the help of Glenbrook High School's principal.

GLENBROOK

The town of Glenbrook is neither quintessentially urban nor rural, nor would the label of suburban fit it well. When colleagues of mine at the City University of New York read drafts of my book in recent years, they referred to it as rural because, to them, a town of 50,000 people that employs primarily factory workers and has experienced long-term residential displacement seems like the polar opposite of the dense, bustling streets of New York City. Yet to those living in Glenbrook, the tightly clustered neighborhoods, downtown business district, and absence of farmland separates them from rural life. Indeed, the Census Bureau defines Glenbrook and its surrounding area (which the Census includes for purposes of rural-urban classification) as an urbanized area. By population density, this area falls close to the midpoint of urban areas in the United States.

Despite this classification, Glenbrook is the kind of town that elicits elegiac newspaper profiles and memoirs about once-thriving "All American" communities that have hollowed out due to losses in manufacturing.[2] Indeed, Glenbrook has a rich history in manufacturing. Since the late 1800s, when the town incorporated, Carter Steel has been the primary employer in the area, employing workers at all levels from company executives to steel plant laborers. During the 1900s, other manufacturing plants also arrived; car manufacturing factories and paper mills were built in or around the town. At its heart, though, Glenbrook was a "company town" oriented toward Carter Steel.

Today, Carter Steel remains a large employer in Glenbrook, despite a steady decline in the size and prominence of the company. In the early 1990s, the company's headquarters moved to a region with greater access to an educated workforce and technology, thus depopulating Glenbrook of some of its managerial and professional elite. This accelerated economic and population decline in Glenbrook. The better educated and more highly paid workforce left, leaving factory workers and their families in place. The Great Recession, in force when I began my interviews, continued to shrink the manufacturing opportunities in town.

Glenbrook High School (GHS), the sole public high school in Glenbrook, is located off a main thoroughfare in the more middle-class section of town and is situated within walking distance from a regional campus of a larger university, Templeton-Glenbrook University. The high school itself is a low, two-story brick building. Built in the early 1970s, the building's heaviness reflects the brutalist sensibilities of the time. It is situated next to several athletic practice fields for baseball, tennis, and track, as well as a wraparound parking lot for students and faculty. The chain link fence along the driveway leading up to the front entrance is often adorned with homemade posters cheering on the school's sports teams (usually football or basketball), and at the top of the drive, a marquee identifies Glenbrook as "Home of the Wildcats." Off to the side of the high school sits a smaller one-story building, referred to as the Simms building, that houses adult education programs as well as some spillover GHS classrooms. GHS students can be seen moving back and forth between the two buildings between classes.

Inside GHS, about 1,500 students cram through long narrow hallways lined with metal lockers between classes, resulting in what amounts to walking traffic jams at hallway intersections and stairwells. Shouts, laughter, and the sound of lockers opening and closing add to the din. The floors are brown and tan-flecked tile. The ceilings contain rows of fluorescent lights, fit into ceiling panels, some of which are damaged or show signs of water leaks. Teachers and administrators are conspicuously present in the hallways between classes, cautioning students when they skirt rules. During class time, administrators and hall monitors continue to patrol the hallways.

Students at GHS attend seven classes on any given day, with each class lasting about fifty minutes. Academic tracking is divided into two options: "accelerated" and "college-career/tech prep," although classes in the latter track are known among students as "general" courses. Students in the accelerated track take advanced coursework in their freshman and sophomore years, honors in their junior year, and advanced placement (AP) courses in their senior year. Students in college-career/tech prep take general coursework that meet standards for high school graduation and, ideally, college admittance. The school struggles for funding, depending on periodic tax levies to maintain its course offerings. Two years before I arrived at the school, a tax levy failed, and the district ended bussing at the high school, shortened the days to five hours and one fewer classes, and laid off several teachers. Several months later, a new levy passed, and the school resumed normal hours and bussing and rehired most of the teachers. Still, funding is always uncertain, and the school does not offer a lot of academic "extras" to students. An education report card for schools rated GHS a "continuous improvement" school in 2008–2009. Its graduation rate hovers just over 80%, on a par with the national average, and state test scores are lower than state averages in every subject.[3] About one-half of the teachers in the school have a master's degree.

KENSINGTON

Not long after I began interviewing participants at Glenbrook (I describe the selection process in more detail later), I discussed with Glenbrook's principal the possibility of interviewing girls at another high school. I was interested in diversifying my sample, particularly by social class, and he offered to reach out to the principal at Kensington High School. This connection led me to a meeting there, where the principal agreed to provide me access to the school.

Kensington lies twenty miles south of Glenbrook and is similar in population size, although comprised of more middle-class families. The town is situated close to a midsize city and has a more quintessentially suburban appearance than Glenbrook. Incorporated in the mid-twentieth century, Kensington grew exponentially between its founding and 1990, attracting both a thriving working class and middle-class managers and professionals working either in Kensington or nearby urban areas. Similar to Glenbrook, the loss of a manufacturing plant in the late 1980s impacted the town's economic outlook and slowed growth. Still, Kensington's population has continued to grow due to business investments, its location near a larger city, and its high-performing schools.

Kensington High School (KHS) is a large, imposing three-story building built in the mid-1990s. Although the town is slightly less populous than Glenbrook, the high school houses substantially more students.[4] The hallways in KHS are spacious, owing to both their width and the location of the classrooms, which are set back so that students first enter a small recess outside the hallway before entering the classrooms themselves. Although there were often students milling about, particularly in the mornings, sitting in groups in the halls and cafeteria, the noise level struck me as surprisingly low, with little of the yelling and clamor I encountered at Glenbrook. This was aided by the fact that lockers were segregated to the front of the school, not along the hallways. There were noticeably fewer adults in the halls of Kensington. Administrators and other hall monitors were rarely present, and teachers mostly stayed inside their rooms between classes. Kensington hallways were airy and bright, with walls painted in contrasting colors on different floors. In addition, murals hung about the school—some painted directly onto the walls, others hanging in frames.

Academics are also organized differently at KHS than at GHS. Students take four classes during each of two semesters, with block scheduling allowing for longer classroom time. This arrangement means that students take classes in a manner more similar to college students. Students also can start AP coursework much earlier, with some taking at least one AP course in their sophomore year. Tracks are formally similar to Glenbrook's (college-career and accelerated), but in practice there are three tracks: general, college prep, and honors/AP. Kensington was rated an "excellent" school by the state, which is the highest possible rating. Over 95% of students graduate each year, and state test scores are higher than state averages and above 90% in every subject. Nearly two-thirds of the teachers in the school have a master's degree.

SAMPLE SELECTION

I had several goals in mind when selecting my sample. I planned to interview only young women, to better identify social class and race differences within a relatively small sample (I aimed to interview 60 participants and ultimately interviewed 61). I also decided to interview young women who were interested in the health sector. I designed my study in this way with an eye toward limiting variation; if I compared among young women who were interested in the same industry, I could focus more clearly on differences between plans. This design eliminated distractions that can arise in examining different types of goals (e.g., difficulty evaluating advice and resources for becoming an artist or entrepreneur, where career pathways are more varied). The health industry incorporates a wide range of jobs requiring different levels of training and offering different rewards to employees, yet requires specific educational credentials and licensing, ensuring that I could more easily detect whether the young women I interviewed had "realistic" plans.

These jobs were (and are) also highly sought after; the health industry accounted for thirteen of the thirty projected fastest-growing occupations when I designed my study and continues to grow much more rapidly than the average for all other industries.[5] Prior to sample selection, my analysis of the National Study of Youth and Religion, a nationally representative study that includes respondents' verbatim occupational aspirations, revealed that over one-third of junior and senior high school girls aspired to work in a health-related occupation, making it by far the largest occupational sector of interest for young women.

I disseminated a short survey to all junior and senior girls in order to identify my sample at each school. At Glenbrook, surveys were completed in English classes, and at Kensington they were completed in homerooms, according to each principal's recommendation for his school. The survey asked the students their race, class year, occupational aspiration, age, and willingness to participate in an interview, as well as information necessary to contact the students for an interview: name, phone number, email, and mailing address.[6] Students indicated their occupational aspirations by answering an open-ended question (What job or occupation would you like to have when you are 30 years old?), or they could select one or more fields of interest from a list.

I received 150 surveys from junior and senior girls at GHS and 171 at KHS.[7] At each school, I first narrowed my list of eligible students to those who were willing to be interviewed and interested in the health field, broadly construed, including jobs in medicine, psychology, and veterinary science. This included those who indicated a specific or general interest in health professions and those who were interested in more than one occupation, where at least one of their interests was in health. This allowed me to retain those who had less concrete plans for the future, in order to better understand the factors related to developing specific or more general plans. Nearly 60% of all the girls who completed surveys indicated some interest in health (62% of respondents from Glenbrook and 57% of respondents from Kensington), and 83% of the initial sample said they were willing to participate in an interview.

After identifying the 165 students interested in health and willing to participate in the study, I selected potential participants. I did this by sorting students by race, class year, and occupational type (both general versus specific and higher versus lower prestige) and selecting even representation within groups. I did not ask students to indicate their social class status. Many would not know their family's income, and asking about income or other social class–related indicators would likely push some students away from completing the survey. However, I anticipated that selecting a wide range of occupational aspirations would diversify my sample by social class. This appeared to be true based on my final sample. I then met with each student I had selected to give them more information about the study and provide them with a consent form for their parents or themselves (for those who were 18) to sign if they agreed to the interview. Students who were not yet 18 years of age signed an assent form to indicate they agreed to participate. Of the students initially selected at each school, only three later declined to participate or were not given permission by their parents.

INTERVIEWS

I conducted interviews with most participants during school hours, in an extra room at the guidance counselor's offices at GHS and in the library of KHS. A few students chose to complete the interviews after school either on school grounds or at a nearby location, although most took the opportunity to miss a class period or two (this, I found, was a significant incentive to participate for many of the students). The interviews ranged in length, from forty-five minutes to two and a half hours. The average interview lasted about an hour and a half. Students received an incentive of $15 for completing these interviews. Most interviews were audio recorded, except when the parent or student indicated they preferred the interview to not be recorded (nine cases) and in one case of recording malfunction. I took careful notes when interviews were not recorded in order to reconstruct the interviews.[8] Immediately following each interview, I wrote field notes about the meeting, including my impression of the participant's reaction to the interview, demeanor, and general appearance.

In total, I spent four weeks interviewing students at GHS and three weeks interviewing at KHS. During this period, I visited the high schools every day while they were in session. Although most of my time was spent in interviews,

I was able to observe common areas and some classrooms at both schools. These observations offered additional insight into each school's culture, climate, and resources. Casual conversations with teachers and administrators at both sites provided additional context on the educational climate.

Qualitative researchers vary a fair amount in how they think about and plan interview guides. On prior studies I had worked on as a research assistant, I had received detailed interview guides before going out into the field. Another faculty member showed me his guide—a one-page bulleted list of topics—as I was planning my own guide for this study. As someone who is not particularly natural at off-the-cuff conversations, however, I opted for a structured guide, including concrete questions, divided into sections and with possible follow-up questions noted. This was helpful for me to make sure I touched on the topics and questions I wanted to ask and to ensure that I had asked the same general questions of everyone I spoke to. At the same time, I attempted to make the interviews feel as much like a conversation as possible. This meant tracking which topics we had covered and circling back to skipped questions when necessary, while also allowing the conversation to evolve and digress. I enjoyed speaking to the young women I interviewed, and they also expressed enthusiasm for our conversations and readily gave me follow-up contact information for use in the future.

The first round of interviews consisted of five sections: information about their adult social ties, aspirations, life history, adult transition timing, and vignettes. Conversations about social ties and aspirations made up the longest sections of the interviews. In our discussions about aspirations, I asked the girls about their hopes and plans for school, work, and family in the future; any concrete steps they had taken toward college searches and applications; exposure to the careers they wished to pursue (speaking to those in the field, shadowing, etc.); how they had learned about various colleges and career paths; and their thoughts about combining (or not combining) a job with having children. For social ties, I asked the girls for a list of all adults they felt close to or could turn to for advice, then asked about their relationships with each of those ties and each tie's employment and educational attainment. I focused on adults they knew during this conversation, although when the girls nominated siblings or friends (more common among the working class and poor), I asked follow-up questions about them as well. After these initial discussions, I probed for any additional social ties in each of the following domains: family members, friends of their parents, teachers or administrators, neighbors, parents of their friends, and leaders of organizations that they were a part of. These conversations often elicited information about the advice and support they had received in the college- and career-planning process, and at other times these stories came up when discussing aspirations and how they had constructed their plans.

The final three sections were shorter and more directed. The life history calendar mapped out the girls' family compositions, school progress, aspirations, work experiences, friendships, and extracurricular activities from seventh grade to the present. I collected additional information about family structure and residential changes since early childhood when relevant. For some girls, these conversations were brief and straightforward. In other cases, discussing residential and family structure changes elicited longer stories about the hardships they and their family members had endured over time.

In the card sort section, I asked the girls to sort fourteen index cards, each one labeled with an event that young people typically experience in the transition to adulthood. They first selected the events they wanted to experience in their lives and then sorted them according to desired sequence. Additional questions elicited information about how they anticipated balancing their goals for work, education, and family. Finally, at the end of each interview I read participants four vignettes about obstacles hypothetical young women faced in carrying out their plans in early adulthood. In one of these vignettes, a young woman's occupational aspirations conflict with her family plans. In another, a young woman's long-term boyfriend asks her to leave college to marry him. In another, monetary considerations create a barrier to attaining the hypothetical woman's goals, and in the fourth, the parents of a teenager push her toward the pre-med track when she prefers to major in English.[9] I asked the girls to give the vignette characters advice and suggest possible people to speak to, and I asked them whether they had encountered similar experiences and what they had done or would do in those cases. I used these vignettes to prompt their ideas about and knowledge of circumstances that might not be specific to them, or where they might know about a particular avenue of approach but had not taken it. For example, many girls who had not yet looked for financial aid or scholarships for themselves knew to give this advice in response to the vignette about a young woman considering not attending college due to finances.

As noted earlier, I collected contact information in order to follow up with the young women in the future. Most expressed a great deal of enthusiasm for this idea, and all shared contact information with me. In most cases, I collected their addresses, phone numbers, and email addresses, along with contact information for two additional people who would know how to contact them. I asked for information on these contacts because young adulthood is a time of great change and movement, and I did not want to lose track of the girls if they moved and obtained new phone numbers and email addresses.

I followed up with the young women again in 2011, two years before I began a second wave of interviews, to confirm which contact information was still valid and to update information as needed. In this I was generously supported by funds from my NICHD postdoctoral fellowship and the work of Pennsylvania State University's Survey Research Center. Two years later, I applied for and received an internal grant, the University of Missouri Research Board Grant, where I worked at the University of Missouri at Kansas City. This funding allowed me to recontact my sample, conduct a second round of interviews, and pay for a transcription service.[10] This time around, I was also able to offer an incentive of $75 to take part in these interviews. Over the course of the next thirteen months (April 2013 through April 2014), I traveled back and forth between the Glenbrook/Kensington area (as well as making one trip to the southern United States to interview Liz) and my home in Kansas City to conduct interviews. These interviews were primarily conducted in cafés, libraries, and participants' homes. In the summer of 2014, I completed the final five interviews over the phone, as I was moving to a new faculty position at Hunter College in New York City and was not able to continue traveling to the study region. One interview was conducted over email because the young woman was in the military and was unable to set up a phone or in-person interview.

This second round of interviews was more free flowing than when the participants were in high school due to the varied trajectories they took. Some were primarily engaged in college life, and thus we spent a long time talking about their day-to-day lives on campus, classes, experiences with advisers, and extracurricular activities. Others were balancing school and work or working exclusively, and therefore we spoke about workplaces and schedules in addition to college. Still others were home with young children, which introduced a different set of questions. In each interview, I started off the conversation by reminding them about when we last spoke ("In 2008, when you were a junior/senior at Glenbrook/Kensington") and asking what they were now up to. Some young women described their current circumstances while others described their trajectories since high school. In either case, I followed up with questions about their daily lives, schedules, thoughts, and experiences.

Once we finished talking about their current circumstances, I asked them more about their time since high school in the school, work, and family domains. We talked about how they had decided on the colleges in which they enrolled and why they had left or transferred, their experiences in these schools, their academic and extracurricular experiences, and their social lives. I followed up with them about their college application process as well, asking about where and how they had applied to college and who had helped them plan for college (if anyone). We discussed any jobs they had held: how they secured these jobs, what their days were like, how much they were paid, how many hours they worked, and their feelings about the work and their bosses and fellow employees. Finally, we discussed their family and romantic relationships, both at the time and the trajectory from the time I first spoke to them. After this, we spoke about their aspirations for the future and where they hoped to be at age 30. Like when they were in high school, we discussed their aspirations and plans in school, work, and family domains, and how they hoped to get there. I asked, too, about who they turned to, or would turn to, for advice in these domains. Finally, I asked the young women to reflect on their lives: how they felt about where they were at this point in their lives and whether they would change anything about their lives. These interviews ranged from forty minutes in length to more than two and a half hours, for an average of one hour and seventeen minutes.

ANALYSIS

Conducting textual analyses of interview transcripts and field notes was not a straightforward process, particularly because interviews took place over a six-year span and the reading, coding, and thematic interpretation of transcripts took place at four institutions. Over the course of these years and settings, I used two software programs (ATLAS.ti and Dedoose) for coding, as well as a mix of Microsoft Word (to build profiles for each participant), Microsoft Excel (to compare summaries of specific topic areas for each study participant), and highlighters/notations on physical copies of each transcript. When I began my analyses for this book in 2016, I had already conducted coding for journal articles based on the first wave of data and built profiles of each participant using both waves of data with the help of my wonderful graduate research assistant at the University of Missouri-Kansas City, Asia Orr.

In 2016, I began planning for the current book and approached the transcripts anew (albeit continuing to use the profiles Asia and I had established). I worked with my undergraduate research assistant at Hunter College, Alec Cali, to code all Wave 1 and Wave 2 transcripts. I began by generating a list of codes based on my re-reading of the transcripts, and we coded the interview transcripts, adding to the initial code list as themes emerged. Once coding was complete, I used the "effects matrices" approach designed by Miles and Huberman.[11] This involved creating tables to compare one level of coding with another (e.g., a table with different family backgrounds along the top, and categories of social networks and other information sources along the left-hand side). Finally, I drew conclusions based on the patterns found in the data and displayed in the matrices. After drawing initial conclusions, I read back through the transcripts to verify that the findings "made sense" in comparison to individual cases as well as to identify disconfirming evidence. As I began to write this book, discuss it with colleagues, and present preliminary findings, I continually returned to the transcripts and added new fields to the analysis I had completed in order to more fully represent the patterns I found.

FINAL NOTES

It is my hope that I have represented these young women and their plans, resources, barriers, trajectories, and outlooks accurately in this book. I am incredibly grateful for their time and willingness to share their lives with me. A major goal of conducting research is to explain how social structures shape outcomes, and this means grouping participants—or respondents, in the case of survey research—together based on a set of characteristics. This is useful, but it can also flatten the vibrancy of individual histories and how those histories uniquely shape the life course. My goal throughout my interviews and analysis, therefore, was to balance description and explanation. That is, I sought to gather information and produce analyses that would explain how social class origins become social class destinations. At the same time, I also asked young women to tell their stories, and I have reproduced them here as accurately as possible, to show how highly individualistic experiences impacted these young women in big and small ways as they grew into adulthood.

Notes

1. This terminology has been wielded critically toward women who, it is implied, overstep what they should reasonably expect in life or make unpopular trade-offs in their personal and professional lives (Damaske 2011). Indeed, "have it all" is an expression used exclusively for women, not for men, for whom the compatibility of work and family is not questioned. In using the phrase, however, Sidel was interested in how young women aspired toward the future in a new landscape that made the American Dream possible (or at least appear possible) for both men and women.

2. Sidel (1990:9).

3. Sidel (1990:222).

4. Following prior work on high school–aged girls (Bettie 2003), I use *girls* and *young women* interchangeably to discuss my interview subjects. They were between the ages of 16 and 18 when I first interviewed them. In the second part of the book, I refer to them as *young women*, as all were at least age 21 by this time.

5. Hanson (1994); MacLeod (2009); Schoon (2001); Sewell and Shah (1968).

6. Goyette (2008); Reynolds et al. (2006); Schneider and Stevenson (1999).

7. Schneider and Stevenson (1999:7).

8. Research and news articles on this topic focus on both young women and young men (e.g., Clausen 1991; Muir 2014; Porter 2014; Staff et al. 2010).

9. This definition of structure, by Sewell (1992), is sufficiently elastic to encompass both conceptual structures, like language and capitalism, as well as more concrete structures, like institutions (e.g., education, the workplace) and physical spaces (e.g., public parks, prisons).

10. Snyder, de Brey, and Dillow (2016).

11. Author's analysis from publicly available HSLS data. Middle-class young people have at least one parent who completed a bachelor's degree and at least one parent who works in a professional occupation (one that traditionally requires at least a four-year college degree), while working-class young people do not.

12. Among first-generation college students, 47% had not completed a degree eight years later, 17% had completed a certificate, 13% had completed an associate's degree, 20% had completed a bachelor's degree, and 3% had completed a graduate or professional degree. The comparative figures for continuing-generation students are 30% (no degree), 7% (certificate), 8% (associate's), 42% (bachelor's), and 13% (graduate/professional degree) (Redford and Hoyer 2017).

13. Ciocca Eller and DiPrete (2018); Jeffrey (2020).

14. Initial research focused on fathers and sons, but this was expanded to consider mothers' status and daughters' attainment in subsequent years, drawing similar conclusions (Kalmijn 1994; McClendon 1976).

15. Goyette (2008); Reynolds et al. (2006); Schneider and Stevenson (1999).

16. Most research on racial differences in the aspirations-attainment match has focused on White and Black young people, but what we know about educational stratification across racial/ethnic groups suggests that Asian students typically have higher academic achievement and attainment than Whites, while Hispanic/Latinx and indigenous youth have relatively lower levels of achievement and attainment compared to Whites (Kao and Thompson 2003), while Black, Hispanic, and Asian youth report higher aspirations when controlling for family background characteristics compared to Whites (Cooper 2009; Kao and Tienda 1998; Qian and Blair 1999). There is a substantial degree of heterogeneity within Hispanic/Latinx and Asian populations, however, related to their immigration history and family's country of origin (Bohon, Johnson, and Gorman 2006; Kim, Rendon, and Valadez 1998).

17. Occupational goals are less disparate, but there are some indications that Black youths' career aspirations are also high relative to Whites (Howard et al. 2011; MacLeod 2009; Morgan 1996).

18. This belief in the effectiveness of education as a vector of mobility—what Mickelson termed concrete attitudes toward education—was associated with achievement, whereas generalized beliefs about the importance of education were not.

19. Mickelson (1990:59). See also sociologist Prudence Carter's (2006, 2007) study of Black high school students' aspirations and attitudes toward school;

she found differences between three groups of Black young people (cultural mainstreamers, cultural straddlers, and noncompliant believers) in the degree to which their abstract and concrete beliefs about the value of education diverged.

20. Clausen (1991); Kim and Schneider (2005); Reynolds et al. (2006); Schneider and Stevenson (1999); Shanahan, Hofer, and Miech (2003).

21. Schneider and Stevenson (1999).

22. Clausen (1991:811).

23. Although public colleges and universities charge in-state students less for tuition, fees, and room and board than do private colleges and universities, declining state support has led to increasing tuition at public institutions, as well as increasing reliance on out-of-state students paying higher tuition (Barr and Turner 2013; Goldrick-Rab 2016).

24. As Cottom and Tuchman (2015) point out, the term *not-for-profit* is more accurate than *nonprofit* to describe these colleges and universities because there are programs and schools that generate a profit, even if this is not the stated goal of the institution.

25. Armstrong and Hamilton (2013); Hamilton, Roksa, and Nielsen (2018); Long (2002).

26. Because colleges run on funding from multiple sources, including state and federal funds, tuition, and donations, students' tuition does not pay the full cost of their education. Students at less selective postsecondary institutions pay a larger proportion of the cost of their education, however, than do students at more selective institutions (Winston 1999).

27. Belfield, Crosta, and Jenkins (2014).

28. Notably, business credentials are both relatively cheap to offer (Belfield et al. 2014) and highly in demand (Brint et al. 2005).

29. Autor (2010); Oreopoulos and Petronijevic (2013). Sociologist Arne Kalleberg (2013) defines good jobs as jobs that are secure, pay well, and offer benefits, while bad jobs are those that pay poorly, are often contingent or insecure, and do not offer benefits. More college graduates have struggled to find employment in good jobs in the past couple of decades than in the past (Abel, Deitz, and Su 2014; Arum and Roksa 2014).

30. Cottom (2017).

31. Cellini and Darolia (2015); Cellini and Turner (2019); Deming, Goldin, and Katz (2013); Lynch, Engle, and Cruz (2010).

32. Bailey and Dynarski (2011); Jeffrey (2020).

33. Goldrick-Rab (2016).

34. Many students move in and out of postsecondary institutions, and therefore a clear "dropout" rate is difficult to determine. However, data from the National Center for Education Statistics (McFarland et al. 2019) shows that

19% of first-year full-time enrollees at four-year colleges and 38% of equivalent enrollees at two-year colleges do not return to the same institution the following year. In addition, 40% of full-time four-year college enrollees do not complete a degree within six years, and 68% of full-time two-year enrollees do not complete a degree in four years.

35. This is a basic premise of life course theory, which stresses the importance of considering "historical forces" in shaping the life course. As Glen Elder has argued, "All life choices are contingent on the opportunities and constraints of social structure and culture" (Elder 1998:2).

36. Autor, Katz, and Kearney (2006); Dwyer and Wright (2019); Mouw and Kalleberg (2010).

37. Hardy and Marcotte (2020).

38. England (2010); Hochschild (1989).

39. US Bureau of Labor Statistics (2018:data tables).

40. These changes lowered the occupational gender segregation index—a measure of the percentage of working women (or men) who would have to change jobs in order for all occupations' gender distributions to match the over-all labor force gender distribution—from 62% in 1960 to 48.4% in 1990 (Cotter, Hermsen, and Vanneman 2004; England 2010). Notably, this change occurred almost exclusively in middle-class occupations. Working-class occupations maintained nearly the same gender distribution in the last half of the twentieth century.

41. Gottschalk and Danziger (2005).

42. Buchmann, DiPrete, and McDaniel (2008).

43. This commission opposed passage of the Equal Rights Amendment, however.

44. Civil Rights Act of 1964, Pub. L. 88-352, 78 Stat. 241 (1964).

45. This permitted any spouse to ask for and receive a divorce regardless of reason. Other states quickly followed, with all states passing similar laws by the 1980s. This allowed women to leave abusive or unfulfilling marriages more eas-ily, although the economic consequences of these divorces were more severe for women than for men (Hoffman and Duncan 1988).

46. The Equal Credit Opportunity Act, 15 U.S.C. § 1691 et seq.

47. Then law professor Ruth Bader Ginsburg won two landmark cases, *Reed v. Reed*, 404 U.S. 71 (1971) and *Frontiero v. Richardson*, 411 U.S. 677 (1973), as part of her work helming the ACLU's Women's Rights Project. The project's goal was to situate women as "suspect classifications" under the Fourteenth Amendment. The Equal Protection Clause of the Fourteenth Amendment prohibits states from denying any person equal protection of the laws (U.S. Const. amend. XIV, § 1). Over time, the court established different levels of scrutiny for assessing whether state action had violated the amendment: a lower standard requiring

a reasonable argument for discrimination, which amounted to very little oversight, and a higher standard for "suspect classifications" where different application of the law must undergo strict scrutiny. Initially, only race or national origin was included under the strict scrutiny standard. Ginsburg's work pushed gender into a "quasi-suspect" classification where "intermediate scrutiny" was warranted (see Kay 2000; Strauss 2011).

48. Abortion laws began to relax on the state level in many places throughout the 1960s, followed by the Supreme Court striking down abortion bans in the 1973 case *Roe v. Wade*, 410 U.S. 113 (1973). Abortion rights were further solidified later, in 1992's *Planned Parenthood of Southeastern Pa. v. Casey*, 505 U.S. 833 (1992) (Kay 2000).

49. Mann and DiPrete (2013).

50. When occupational desegregation has occurred in the United States, it usually has happened through women moving into male-dominated jobs. Men have been less willing to work in female-dominated occupations (England 2010; Stainback and Tomaskovic-Devey 2012).

51. Although there was a slight uptick in women's employment in the late 1990s, this trend reversed course, and the female employment rate has remained roughly 54% in recent years (US Bureau of Labor Statistics 2018). Notably, this pattern is consistent across race, although differing in overall levels; Black women have higher rates of labor force participation than women of other racial/ethnic groups. Across race, however, women have experienced increasing then stalled or decreasing labor force participation (US Department of Labor, Women's Bureau n.d.). Women of all racial/ethnic backgrounds have continued to catch up to men in earnings, but progress slowed after the 1980s (Bailey and DiPrete 2016).

52. Piketty and Saez (2014).

53. Cherlin (2014); Kalleberg (2013).

54. Autor and Dorn (2013).

55. Cotter, Hermsen, and Vanneman (2001). Care work is poorly paid in large part because it is care work and thus replaces work in the private sphere that has been traditionally performed by women, particularly by women of color (Dwyer 2013; England and Folbre 1999; Glenn 2012).

56. Cowie (2012); Hacker and Pierson (2011).

57. Goldin and Katz (2009).

58. Arum and Roksa (2014); Bartik and Hershbein (2018); Hardy and Marcotte (2020).

59. Piketty and Saez (2014).

60. Cherlin (2014); Ruggles (2015).

61. Mare (1991); Sweeney (2002).

62. Alichi, Kantenga, and Solé (2016); Cooper (2014); Foster and Wolfson (2010); Leigh (2017).

63. See Ashworth and Ransom (2019) and Bartik and Hershbein (2018) for discussion of how the college wage premium has declined both in the aggregate and for disadvantaged groups. See also Hardy and Marcotte (2020), who show that a college degree today no longer provides the same stability and protection from downward mobility that it once did.

64. Hacker (2008).

65. For a discussion of the rise in precarious work and "bad jobs," see Kalleberg (2013). For work on freelancing and the gig economy, see Friedman (2014); Prassl (2018); and Webster (2016).

66. Pugh (2015).

67. Kalleberg and Wachter (2017); Valletta (2018).

68. Settersten (2007:261).

69. Cooper (2014).

70. Silva (2012, 2015).

71. Desmond (2012, 2017); Ray (2017).

72. Ray (2017).

73. Hamilton (2016); Jack (2019).

74. Only one young woman refused to be interviewed in the second wave, due to time conflicts, although two agreed and then did not respond to requests to set up an interview. I was unable to contact the remainder of respondents.

75. Author's analysis of the National Study of Youth and Religion, a nationally representative study of adolescents in the United States. See the methodological appendix for more detail.

76. US Bureau of Labor Statistics (2007, 2021).

77. Names of all persons, institutions, and places in this book are given pseudonyms, to protect anonymity.

78. These numbers were obtained through the American Community Survey (ACS) for 2007–2009, to match the town populations when I first interviewed my participants, in 2008.

79. See Cortés and Pan (2018); Kilbourne et al. (1994); Munasinghe, Reif, and Henriques (2008); Padavic and Reskin (2002). See Gough and Noonan (2013) for a summary of the motherhood wage penalty.

80. Coker (2007); Coker et al. (2016); Collinsworth, Fitzgerald, and Drasgow (2009); Fitzgerald and Cortina (2018); Hlavka (2014); Jina and Thomas (2013).

81. Browne and Misra (2003); Krieger et al. (2006); Ortiz and Roscigno (2009).

82. Barnes (2015); Dow (2016, 2019).

83. Burd-Sharps and Lewis (2018); Hair et al. (2009); Lewis and Gluskin (2018); Wight et al (2010).

84. Clawson and Gerstel (2014) discuss events such as an illness or car breakdown as "normal unpredictability" because we know that they will happen in our lives, but their timing is unpredictable.

85. Ridgeway (2009, 2011).

CHAPTER 1. HIGH SCHOOL GIRLS' PLANS

1. Hartocollis (2017); Porter (2014); Schneider and Stevenson (1999); Vaisey (2010).

2. I also get the question, "Why don't their parents care?," a question based on maddeningly inaccurate assumptions.

3. Clausen (1991); Reynolds et al. (2006); Schneider and Stevenson (1999); Shanahan, Hofer, and Miech (2003).

4. I asked the young women I interviewed to select and put in order a set of cards that listed major life events in the transition to adulthood—events like starting and finishing college, marriage, and buying a house. Events they were not interested in could be removed, and a blank card was included for events I had not considered. After they ordered the cards, I asked the girls to tell me what age they would be, ideally, when each event occurred.

5. As Neugarten and colleagues have argued, "Expectations regarding age-appropriate behavior form an elaborated and pervasive system of norms governing behavior" (Neugarten, Moore, and Lowe 1965:711).

6. Benson and Elder (2011); Burton (2007); Johnson and Mollborn (2009).

7. There was much more variation in when these young women thought they would begin work than in when they anticipated completing major school and family benchmarks. This variability arose because some did not anticipate working at all until school was completed, some did not count part-time work as the beginning of work, and others counted this early work as work.

8. This differs somewhat from the finding in a paper by Cepa and Furstenberg (2020) that socioeconomic status was positively associated with what Americans saw as the "ideal" timing of events such as marriage and childbearing, as well as other markers of adulthood. In other words, those with higher socioeconomic statuses preferred marriage and childbearing occurring at later ages, on average, than did those with lower socioeconomic statuses. However, this work was based on survey questions about the ideal timing of adulthood markers in general, rather than on what young people sought for themselves.

9. Day and Newburger (2002); Carnevale, Rose, and Cheah (2013). See Isen and Stevenson (2010).

10. Marriage is also associated with lower earnings, but this is due primarily to selection effects, and the association has declined over time. For research on marriage, childbearing, and income, see Juhn and McCue (2016); Taniguchi (1999). For research on childbearing and labor force participation, see Brewster and Rindfuss (2000); Kahn, García-Manglano, and Bianchi (2014).

11. In one of few studies that examined future goals holistically, Schneider and Stevenson (1999) argued that young people's educational and occupational goals are "dreamlike," and that occupational aspirations remained unfulfilled because young people did not know the educational credentials necessary for the jobs

they wished to hold in the future. Rather than obtaining information about the qualifications necessary for such jobs, they argue, these young people hold lofty educational aspirations without making plans for how to follow through. As a result, they fall short of their goals, setting themselves up to drift aimlessly into young adulthood.

CHAPTER 2. ANTICIPATING A PACKAGED FUTURE

1. Estimate obtained from the Bureau of Labor Statistics' occupational employment statistics (US Bureau of Labor Statistics 2015b). The mean annual salary for nurse anesthetists as of May 2015 was $160,250, and the median salary was slightly lower, $157,140.

2. The girls nominated 7.2 ties on average, with middle-class girls nominating 8.2 on average and working-class and poor girls nominating 6.5.

3. Newport (2015).

4. For examples of sociological approaches to categorizing class, see Lareau and Conley (2008), Gilbert (2002), and Wright (1997).

5. In categorizing young women by class, I first followed Thompson and Hickey's (2007) schema: upper middle class (parent/s employed in a professional occupation), lower middle class (parent/s employed in a white collar/semiprofessional occupation), working class (parent/s worked in blue or pink collar jobs), and lower class (parent/s worked in very poorly paid jobs or in insecure sectors where unemployment was common). I later combined the upper and lower middle-class groups into one middle-class group and the working and lower classes into working class/poor, based on how similar these combined groups were to one another in preliminary analyses.

6. Bourdieu (1986); Small (2009).

7. *Access* refers to the availability of resource-rich social ties in one's network, whereas *mobilization* refers to the ability to receive information, support, and resources from those ties. Social capital is comprised of both elements: access to resources and the ability to mobilize them (or have them mobilized) on one's behalf (Lin 2001).

8. *U.S. News & World Report* ranks colleges in five categories—most selective, more selective, selective, less selective, and least selective—"based on a formula that accounts for enrollees' test scores and class standing and the school's acceptance rate, the percentage of applicants the school accepts" (Morse and Hines 2021).

9. Mosisa and Hipple (2006).

10. Gerson (2011).

11. As Sarah Damaske (2011) discusses in her book, *For the Family*, many women explain their decision to either work full-time or part-time for pay or

work to raise families based on the needs of the family, even when it is structural constraints that keep them either in or out of the labor market.

12. Buchmann and Dalton (2002); Hauser, Tsai, and Sewell (1983); Sewell, Haller, and Portes (1969); Sewell and Shah (1968).

13. Weak ties can be beneficial in some situations. As Granovetter's (1973) work demonstrates, weak ties can introduce new information vital to obtaining a job. For young people engaged in future planning, however, weak ties appeared less helpful than strong ties, at least for middle-class Black girls. They were more likely to offer one-time advice without sustaining the relationship or connecting the girls to resources like internship opportunities or mentoring.

14. In its 2000 Vision 2020 statement, the American Physical Therapy Association mandated that all physical therapy programs be doctorate level by 2020 (APTA 2013,). However, in 2009, less than one-third of respondents to a survey of physical therapists reported having attained a PhD, a doctorate of physical therapy (DPT), or a transition-DPT degree (offered as an educational option for physical therapists already practicing when the Vision 2020 statement was released). Therefore, the information Jean received was vital to her plans for the future.

15. See Hardie (2015) for an in-depth discussion of sponsored, insulated, and restricted social ties.

16. Hardie (2015).

17. The Kuder assessment tool, developed by a company of the same name (https://www.kuder.com/), is a computer-assisted career planning tool that guides students through a series of questions about their interests within several vocational domains and provides twenty-five potential vocational profiles based on students' responses (Ihle-Helledy, Zytowski, and Fouada 2004). Use of these kinds of tests in schools dates back to the 1950s (Harris-Bowlsbey 2013), although they have evolved in their metrics over time. Several young women I interviewed mentioned Kuder as the genesis of career ambitions.

18. See work by sociologist Steve McDonald (McDonald 2011; McDonald and Day 2010) on how racial and gender homophily in networks can promote differences in access to social capital.

19. Research on family and residential instability has linked this instability to lower child well-being, greater disruptive behaviors, and lower school performance. See Adam and Chase-Lansdale (2002); Fomby and Sennott (2013); Halpern-Meekin and Tach (2008); Heard (2007); Marcynyszyn, Evans, and Eckenrode (2008); Sandstrom and Huerta (2013).

20. Residential instability is most common among the poor, but prior research has not found race differences once income is accounted for; see Astone and McLanahan (1994); Desmond, Gershenson, and Kiviat (2015).

21. These disparities reflect long-standing discriminatory practices and differences in intergenerational inheritance and intragenerational need. See

Hardaway and McLoyd (2009); Oliver and Shapiro (1997); Patillo (2005); Shapiro (2005).

CHAPTER 3. HOPING FOR A REPACKAGED FUTURE

1. My criteria for including young women in the working class was that their parents (1) worked in blue-collar or service jobs and had either completed a high school degree only, attended college but dropped out, or completed a post-secondary certificate or (2) worked in lower-paid white-collar jobs (e.g., secretary, medical billing) and did not attend a postsecondary institution. Poor girls' parents either had not completed a high school degree or had completed a high school degree but were unemployed at the time of the interview or frequently unemployed.

2. I use the term *unemployment* loosely here, as the girls were not always aware of whether their parents were currently looking for work and available to work, which is what qualifies as "unemployed" according to the US Department of Labor (Dunn, Haugen, and Kang 2018).

3. Factory workers can be unionized and paid relatively high wages for their average level of education. However, in this case, one girl's stepfather had only entered her life three years prior and moved in and out of factory work but was employed there at the time of the interview; one was from a family of immigrants who were all working at a small nonunionized manufacturing plant; and one lived with her grandfather, who was a unionized factory worker and therefore earned good pay, but she had only lived with him a short time after bouncing between different family members' homes.

4. Howell (1972).

5. Cherlin (2014); Kalleberg (2013).

6. Cooper (2014).

7. As sociologists Silva and Snellman have described it, college for working-class young people is seen as a "salvation" offering an "escape from their current grim reality" (2018:559).

8. In a slab furnace, large steel slabs are heated to above 1900°F in order to be rolled into smaller, leaner pieces of steel for commercial use.

9. For research on the links between economic hardship and family-level conflict, instability, and child and adult well-being see Conger, Conger, and Martin (2010); Conger et al. (1990); Edin and Kissane (2010); Hardie and Lucas (2010); and McLanahan (2004)

10. Sociologist Kathryn Edin and colleagues have argued that poor women and men value marriage but struggle to meet the "high standards" they see as a necessary requirement for marriage (Edin and Kefalas 2007; Edin and Reed

2005; Gibson-Davis, Edin, and McLanahan 2005). Sociologists Garrett-Peters and Burton (2015), however, have argued that such work relies overly much on how the poor account for their actions, that reluctance to marry among poor women is a response to uncertainty more generally, and that they do make movements to and from committed relationships in ways that reflect this uncertainty. The young women I spoke to were still young and not entering into long-term relationships, for the most part, but their accounts may echo those of older adults who are also grappling with uncertainty.

11. Lareau (2002, 2011) has suggested that middle-class parents cultivate their children's employment-related skills at an early age in part because of their own enjoyment of work, while working-class and poor parents do not enjoy work to the same degree and therefore see childhood as an enjoyable time of life before the onslaught of work and home responsibilities.

12. Hardie (2015).

13. According to Glenbrook High School's program of study guidebook, students need to take fewer than twenty-five credits (in addition to passing state exams) to graduate from high school. More of the required credits are loaded into students' freshman and sophomore years, meaning that students can easily take lighter loads in later years. This is also not unusual; graduation requirements in most states are similar. The Center for American Progress (2018) has pointed out that this leaves a gap between what is required for high school graduation and for admittance into public universities in most states.

14. Gerstel (2000); Bianchi et al. (2000); Yavorsky, Kamp Dush, and Schoppe-Sullivan (2015); Moore (1990); Rosenthal (1985).

15. Stack (1983).

16. Burton (2007).

17. England and Folbre (1999); Glenn (2012).

18. Prior work shows that enrollment in better schools and investment in "shadow education" programs are tied to educational attainment (e.g., Buchmann, Condron, and Roscigno 2010; Palardy 2013; Reardon 2011).

19. Adam and Chase-Lansdale (2002); Crowder and Teachman (2004); Jelleyman and Spencer (2008); Gasper, DeLuca, and Estacion (2012); South, Haynie, and Bose (2007).

20. See Brown (2006); Cavanagh and Huston (2008); Fomby and Cherlin (2007). Notably, most studies of family instability focus on the residential parent's relationship status and changes in romantic partners moving in and out of the home. This is only one form of family instability, however.

21. Desmond and Perkins (2016); Edin and Shaefer (2016).

22. Brand (2015). The risks of incarceration are stratified by both class and race, with poor and working-class Black young men and women at particularly high risk of this status (Western and Pettit 2010).

23. A couple of girls reported living with family members to get into a better high school than the one near their parents, and some lived temporarily with extended family members after getting into trouble at home, as a way to place them away from distractions and temper their behavior.

24. Lee, Tyler, and Wright (2010:503).

25. Students who have been classified as needing special education services receive IEPs, which include documentation of their current performance, annual goals, and planned services. A team consisting of a student's parents, teachers, school staff, and sometimes the student collaboratively develop such plans. Two students I interviewed were enrolled in intervention classes for students with IEPs, but it is possible that other interviewed students also had IEPs, as not all students receiving services are necessarily enrolled in pull-out intervention classes.

26. Fibromyalgia is a chronic condition most commonly experienced by women, involving musculoskeletal pain in addition to fatigue, sleep problems, and mood issues (Mayo Clinic n.d.).

27. Tiffany was still enrolled at Glenbrook when I selected the sample of young women to interview but had transferred to the online program by the time I set up an interview.

28. Domestic violence is of course not limited to the poor and working class. Research does find that class-linked stressors, such as unemployment and neighborhood-level poverty, however, are associated with higher instances of violence in the home (Anderson 2010).

29. There were clear differences in academic preparation, however. Two-thirds of middle-class girls (including all upper-middle-class girls) were enrolled in honors classes compared to slightly over one-fifth of working-class and poor girls. Reported letter grades were more similar, with "As and Bs" being most young women's descriptions of their performance, but this level of work in an honors class, a college preparatory class, or a general education class conveys different skills and likely incurs different payoffs in postsecondary schools.

CHAPTER 4. DREAMS UNFURLED

1. Of the original 61 young women, 41 were reinterviewed. I was unable to reach most of the remaining 20; they had moved or their and their family members' contact information had changed. I was able to find several young women like this through online searches and social media, but others were not as easy to trace. Of the remaining, 1 refused an interview, and 2 more agreed but never followed up after many contacts.

2. As sociologist Jessi Streib (2020) does in her book on class mobility, I think of these early pathways as trajectories toward a class position. These trajectories

are moves toward upward and downward mobility or class stasis, although they may change due to unforeseen circumstances.

3. Research on pathways to and through college finds that early enrollment in four-year institutions promotes degree completion and wage mobility (Bozick and DeLuca 2005; Causey et al. 2020; Elman and O'Rand 2007; Lin and Liu 2019). However, college is not beneficial for all; the college wage premium has flattened in recent years (Ashworth and Ransom 2019) and loans have ballooned, particularly for Black young adults (Addo, Houle, and Simon 2016).

4. Recent research on mobility patterns bears this out (Chetty et al. 2017); rates of absolute upward mobility for those born in 1984 fell by 40 percentage points compared to those born in 1940.

CHAPTER 5. ON TRACK

1. World Bank (n.d.).

2. To preserve anonymity, I have changed the names of some organizations and, for others, given a more general description of their foci than was originally described to me.

3. Cultural capital refers to the kinds of mannerisms, habits, and preferences, or "tastes," that can be used to signal "in-group" status among the elite and that work to shut off access to elite status (see Bourdieu and Passeron 1990; Lamont and Lareau 1988). Food and drink consumption is an important type of cultural capital because social networking opportunities in the business world often take place within informal events such as catered receptions, happy hours, and lunches and dinners.

4. Public accountants usually work for multiple clients, either through their own private practice or through their position at a firm. They handle the kinds of financial reports that must be made available for the public, such as audits and tax reports. They travel often and are under great pressure to produce timely and accurate reports. Private accountants, on the other hand, typically work for a single company and produce internal reports that evaluate the company's performance and expenditures. These jobs typically entail nine-to-five hours and little travel, although their salaries are lower than those of public accountants, on average.

5. Entering preprofessional programs and other vocationally focused majors is not unusual in the United States. Colleges and universities began offering more of these programs (as opposed to more traditional liberal arts majors) in the 1970s. In addition, recessions tend to push more students into such programs, likely in response to an uncertain labor market (Baker and Baldwin 2015; Ferrall 2011; Kimball 2014).

6. Brint (2002).

7. See Moss-Pech (2021) for a discussion of "career conveyor belt internships" that transition directly to postgraduate employment for those in the practical arts.

8. Honors and preprofessional college programs mirror the kind of academic tracking seen in high schools across the country, internally segregating students by perceived ability and occupational interests and allocating resources disproportionately to more prestigious tracks. See Armstrong and Hamilton (2013) and Hamilton, Roksa, and Nielsen (2018) for discussions of how these tracks stratify students within colleges by social class background.

9. Giersch (2018); Lucas (1999).

10. When I interviewed Jessie in Wave 1, her mother had not worked for several years due to a long-term illness, and her father was taking time away from work to care for her mother. Thus, their financial circumstances were more constrained than those of many other middle-class families.

11. As Shelley Correll (2001, 2004) has argued, grades may have a stronger effect on girls' math and science skill self-assessment than on boys', meaning that many boys and young men will continue to rate their skills on math and science high even in the wake of low grades, while girls and young women will not. In turn, this self-assessment may impact young men's and young women's career plans differently, leading young women out of science, technology, engineering, and math (STEM) fields. At the same time, recent research finds mixed evidence of this gendered response to grades, with some studies finding that women are no more responsive to low grades than are young men (Riegle-Crumb, King, and Moore 2016), while others find greater rates of young women switching majors either overall (Astorne-Figari and Speer 2018) or in response to low grades within male-dominated STEM fields (Kugler, Tinsley, and Ukhaneva 2017).

12. The median salary for physical therapists in the United States is $91,010, compared to $62,870 for secondary school teachers (US Bureau of Labor Statistics 2021).

13. As Katherine McClelland points out, "Failing an examination in organic chemistry is likely to have a different meaning to the physician's daughter (who has many other images of success to draw from) than to the son of a day laborer (who has fewer). The lack of resources or of friends and relatives with similar experiences who can be turned to for advice and encouragement continues to be a handicap for individuals from non-privileged social origin" (1990:104)

14. On average, these young women reported GPAs that were half a point lower in college than their high school GPAs. Notably, however, most had spent several semesters pulling their grades up from a first-year low before I interviewed them. Those who mentioned their specific first-year grades, like Sheryl, appeared to have received grades that were closer to a full point lower than their high school grades. In competitive health fields, this often meant they would not be admitted into the program they wished to enter.

15. Branch campuses are hybrid institutions that operate much like community colleges—including open admissions, a focus on certificate and associate's degree programs, lower tuition, and greater flexibility for older and working students—but offer some bachelor's degree programs, either on their own or in conjunction with the university's main campus.

16. Dairy farm profits depend, in part, on their ability to produce more animals. A large proportion of dairy cows are therefore impregnated via artificial insemination (as opposed to "natural service"). Some dairy farmers do this themselves, while others hire out companies that work exclusively on dairy artificial insemination.

17. Hamilton (2016) found that upper- and upper-middle-class parents play "helicopter" roles and manage their daughters' college pathways, or they take a more wait-and-see approach as "paramedics" who solve major roadblocks but let their children handle smaller hurdles, while working- and middle-class parents were more likely to act as "bystanders," trusting that college would work out. Unfortunately, as Hamilton found, the daughters of bystander parents often floundered in college, with many exiting the four-year college route.

18. Hamilton interviewed a number of very wealthy parents for her book, in addition to parents of more modest means, and selected among parents of young women living in the well-known "party dorm." The current study, on the other hand, draws on samples of young women from two high schools and therefore observes how class-based differences in high school play out across the transition to adulthood. Although there was considerable class diversity among these young women, the levels of wealth described in Hamilton's study were not present. Most of the middle-class young women I interviewed were not involved in Greek life and did not have exceptionally high-earning parents. These young women's experiences are important; close to half of all college students in 2012 had parents who earned between $30,000 and $106,000 a year (Baum and Johnson 2015), or between roughly 60% and 200% of the median family income in the United States at the time (Noss 2012). Even at highly selective public universities, students of parents earning multiple hundreds of thousands of dollars a year are not the norm. It is important to understand the experiences of this large swath of undergraduates and how their families do—and sometimes do not—play a role in their success.

19. Goldrick-Rab (2016).

20. Parent PLUS loans are federal loans that parents can take out to help pay their children's college tuitions. These loans account for billions of dollars in aid that parents can easily acquire and that have no caps, but they can be difficult to pay off (Wang, Supiano, and Fuller 2012).

21. Although I asked these young women about the size of their loans, most did not know specific amounts. They knew that a combination of inputs from loans, scholarships, work, and parents paid their total cost of attending college

(including tuition, fees, books, and room and board), but not how much was paid for by each. In addition, scholarship offers varied each year and were most plentiful in their first year of college, so loan amounts fluctuated in response.

22. Most parents appeared supportive of their daughters' college and career plans, but Gail's father was an exception. He was similar to the "total bystanders" in Hamilton's (2016) study of parents who were unconvinced of the usefulness of attending college. Because Gail had extensive support from her college program and live-in boyfriend, however, she was able to compensate for this lack of support from her father.

23. Educational loans are a burden for young people broadly in the United States but are particularly so for Black students who, as Seamster and Charron-Chénier (2017) argue, are the targets of "predatory inclusion" practices that expose them to greater risk (Addo 2014; Hershbein and Hollenbeck 2015; Houle and Addo 2019; Kim and Chatterjee 2019).

24. Damaske (2011, 2021).

CHAPTER 6. HOLDING ON

1. Pell Grants are the US Department of Education's largest grant program. Through this program, the DOE provides need-based grants to low-income students that do not have to be repaid. The amount of the award depends on the student's expected family contribution, credit load, and cost of attendance at their college (Kerr 2019).

2. Students must meet "satisfactory academic progress" to retain their Pell Grants from one semester to the next. Specific requirements for doing so can vary from college to college, but at a minimum, they include keeping a 2.0 grade point average or better, successfully completing a proportion of their attempted courses, and completing a degree program within 150% of the expected time to completion. Approximately one-quarter of students at public two-year colleges are in danger of not meeting the grade point average requirements, and research at one large university system suggests that about 40% of Pell recipients are at risk of losing their grants (Schudde and Scott-Clayton 2016).

3. Guzzo (2014); Lamidi, Manning, and Brown (2019).

4. Kelly and Moen (2007).

5. Clawson and Gerstel (2014).

6. Julian and Kominski (2011).

7. Higher education accrediting bodies require that colleges and universities provide students with a general education background, although the specific courses or content areas students must take to complete these requirements can vary across institutions (Warner and Koeppel 2009).

8. Although community colleges have the highest rates of placement in remediation, an estimated 40% to 60% of all college students, including approximately 30% of four-year college students, are placed in at least one remediation class upon entering college (Fay 2018; Jaggars and Bickerstaff 2018; Jimenez et al. 2016). In one study of over 250,000 community college students, researchers found that 59% of students were referred to remedial math courses and 33% were referred to remedial English courses, and nearly one-fifth of all students placed three levels below college math, requiring extensive noncredit preparation (Bailey, Jeong, and Cho 2010).

9. Several factors likely contributed to Jennie's low score, including inconsistencies in how colleges evaluate scores, lack of advanced warning for remedial testing, and time off in between high school and college. For example, Jaggars and Bickerstaff (2018) point out that colleges use widely different cutoff scores for referring students to remedial coursework. At some institutions, even students with high SAT or ACT test scores have a high probability of referral. In addition, students frequently do not learn about the tests until the day they are to take them, giving them little time to prepare.

10. Deil-Amen and Rosenbaum (2002:264). This has serious financial consequences for students, who pay college tuition for non-credit-bearing courses. Recent estimates suggest that students and families in the United States paid an estimated $1.3 billion for remedial courses in the 2013–2014 academic year (Jimenez et al. 2016).

11. One study found that students who ignore remedial placement and enter straight into credit-bearing classes do better, on average, than those who enter remedial coursework (Bailey et al. 2010). Other studies find that students who score just above the cutoff for remediation and therefore enroll in nonremedial coursework right away are significantly more likely to complete college than those who fall just below the cutoff and are referred to remediation (Bailey et al. 2010; Bailey, Jaggars, and Scott-Clayton 2013; Ngo 2019). Furthermore, research has demonstrated that high school grades do a better job of predicting college students' success in college-level math and English courses in their first year than do placement exams (Scott-Clayton 2012).

12. Davidson (2011); Smith (2016).

13. Recent research has shown that financial assistance coupled with other forms of support is particularly effective. A randomized control study by MDRC and the City University of New York saw graduation rates almost double for low-income developmental education students at two-year colleges within the CUNY system when students received a robust array of support, including free tuition, fees, textbooks, and transportation; specialized advising and career services; and blocked scheduling. In addition to overall effects on completing an associate's degree, program enrollment was associated with increased credits attempted and faster time to a degree (Azurdia and Galkin 2020).

14. Home health aides are paid $13.02/hour on average, amounting to full-time salaries of about $27,000 a year (US Bureau of Labor Statistics 2021). Like Jennifer, most home health aides only have a high school degree and are women of color (Newman 2019; Glenn 2012). These workers also face some of the highest rates of injury due not only to the demands of the job, such as lifting clients and equipment, but also to hazards in the home such as aggressive clients and pets (McCaughey et al. 2012).

15. According to the US Bureau of Labor Statistics (2015a), the median weekly earnings for a high school graduate in 2014 was around $670/week (depending on the quarter). At an estimated 42.5 hours of work a week, Chelsea likely earned about $574/week. If she was paid for her full 9.5 hours a day, she would still earn just under the median earnings for a high school graduate.

16. Brint (2002); Linn (2013).

17. Ma (2020).

18. NCES (2020).

19. This echoes Elizabeth Armstrong and Laura Hamilton's (2013) findings that many lower middle-class young women who began college at the four-year institution they observed ultimately transferred to community colleges near home to complete their degrees.

20. NCES (2020).

21. Kim, Markham, and Cangelosi (2002). Most of these reasons are fairly similar to how all students select their majors (Malgwi, Howe, and Burnaby 2005), although business majors do earn significantly more than other undergraduate majors, even after taking selectivity into account (Eide, Hilmer, and Showalter 2016).

22. Three young women in the on track group were interested in business, but two chose much more specific fields (finance and sports marketing), and one hoped to combine interests in business and nutrition. In the rough seas group, no one mentioned business specifically, although one young woman worked at a bank and hoped to go into human resources, and one sold crafts on the site Etsy and hoped to continue earning money through that work.

23. Prior work suggests that lower-income college students express some ambivalence around their identities as college students (Colyar and Stich 2011; Ostrove and Long 2007), which can be compounded by other time constraints that limit their ability to succeed academically and to participate in extracurricular college activities (Goldrick-Rab 2016; Walpole 2003).

24. Abel and Deitz (2018). There are also varying rates of underemployment among business majors. Underemployment is low for occupation-specific majors like accounting and finance, but high for general business and management. For example, 60% of business management and 55% of general business grads were underemployed in the 2009–2013 period, compared to 37% for finance, 26% for accounting, and 41% for economics. The median underemployment rate for all recent college grads was 44.6%.

25. Carnevele et al. 2013 (using the 2009 ACS).

26. Research by the Federal Reserve found that in 2013, the average net worth of individuals under the age of 35 was just slightly above $10,000 (Bricker et al. 2014). Given rates of student loan debt, it is likely that young people under the age of 25 have a negative net worth.

27. Cortney's father felt that she would receive more help from the government if she only reported her mother's income, as her mother was unemployed. However, Cortney was estranged from her mother and had no way to contact her.

28. Liming and Wolf (2008).

29. It is of course possible Zakeshia did consider the role of race in her difficulties and did not wish to disclose this to a White interviewer. In either case, she placed the lion's share of blame on herself.

CHAPTER 7. NAVIGATING ROUGH SEAS

1. This is known as the "heave to" maneuver, using the sails (partially hauled in) and rudder to stall the boat (Schell 2017).

2. Cottom (2017).

3. Although driving to school may not seem to be a particularly difficulty task, what we know from prior research suggests that young people like Brit, who have experienced poverty and adverse events from a young age, are both more likely to experience anxiety (Mersky, Janczewski, and Nitkowski 2018; Najman et al. 2010) and to have difficulty coping with that anxiety, potentially leading toward disengagement and risk aversion (Evans and Kim 2013; Haushofer and Fehr 2014). This appears to occur because of the way chronic stress impacts the body, elevating allostatic load and cortisol levels.

4. Brit's sister's husband was arrested for selling heroin, and her sister was arrested as an accomplice. Brit explained that her sister's husband tried to prevent her sister from using heroin, but she did so anyway. About six months after I interviewed Brit, her sister died of a heroin overdose.

5. Burd-Sharps and Lewis (2018); Hair et al. (2009); Lewis and Gluskin (2018); Wight et al. (2010). In the United States, 55% of young people ages 18 to 24 are enrolled in school, 56% are working at least part-time, and 14% are neither enrolled in school nor working (author's analysis from the 2017 five-year American Community Survey data).

6. Edelman and Holzer (2014); Burd-Sharps and Lewis (2018).

7. In their study of disconnected youth, sociologists MacDonald and Marsh found that "insecurity, instability and flux were dominant. Individual careers involved numerous, shifting statuses over time. Unemployment was common; the default status to which many returned repeatedly. It was not, however, a permanent condition for any. . . . Moving into and out of jobs was a typical feature

of the interviewees' post-school careers. The same applied to college courses and to training schemes; many were started but fewer were completed" (MacDonald and Marsh 2001:386); see also MacDonald and Marsh (2005).

8. Sociologist Matthew Desmond (2012) argues that the urban poor rely on disposable ties among strangers to get by, precisely because family relationships are so fraught and unstable.

9. Barbaro and Santos (2011); Duncan (2015); Edelman and Holzer (2014); Heinrich and Holzer (2011); Holzer, Edelman, and Offner (2006).

10. Buchmann and DiPrete (2006); Hollister (2011); Şahin, Song, and Hobijn (2010).

11. Gail, a middle-class White young woman who ended up in the on track group, was the other.

12. Calarco (2018); Hamilton (2016); Lareau (2011).

13. Jack (2019) distinguishes between the *privileged poor*, who attended private schools on scholarships and learned to feel at home in these elite environments, and the *doubly disadvantaged*, who attended poor or average high schools and did not possess the social and cultural capital needed to interact comfortably with their peers and faculty.

14. Margolis (2001)

15. DeLuca, Clampet-Lundquist, and Edin (2016); see also Holland and DeLuca (2016).

16. Cottom (2017).

17. Goldrick-Rab (2016).

18. Cottom (2017); see also Belfield (2013); Holland and DeLuca (2016).

19. Cellini and Turner (2019); Deming, Golden, and Katz (2013); Lynch, Engle, and Cruz (2010).

20. In 2012, a Senate report (US Senate Committee on Health, Labor, and Pensions 2012) found that for-profit postsecondary institutions charged, on average, four times the amount that not-for-profit community colleges did for an associate's degree and four and a half times the cost for a certificate. In direct comparisons, the report juxtaposed costs for the same programs within similar regions. For example, it reported that a for-profit college in California charged over $17,000 for a medical assistant certificate program, while a nearby community college charged slightly over $2,000 for the same degree.

21. A change in the law in 2005 made it much more difficult for student loans to be discharged via bankruptcy proceedings (Bankruptcy Abuse Prevention and Consumer Protection Act, 2005).

22. Attrition rates for baccalaureate nursing programs are reported to be about 50%, and slightly less than that for associate's degree programs (Harris, Rosenberg, and O'Rourke 2014).

23. Abel and Deitz (2014); Ashworth and Ransom (2019); Carnevale, Rose, and Cheah (2013).

24. Goldman and Smith (2011); Hout, Levanon, and Cumberworth (2011).

25. Attewell et al. (2009).

26. As Hamilton, Roksa, and Nielsen contend, state budget cuts have forced public colleges and universities to rely more and more on tuition and private donations to stay afloat and therefore, "as privatization continues to develop, cash-strapped public institutions will have little incentive to invest in a functioning mobility pathway: instate families bring less tuition, and students from less affluent backgrounds may not arrive with the high test scores and academic preparation needed to boost universities' academic standing" (2018:126).

27. Bowen, Chingos, and McPherson (2011).

28. Kalleberg (2009:2). Such work is plentiful in the current labor market; since the 1970s, businesses have increasingly taken advantage of a neoliberal policy environment and the deregulation of labor protections to offer jobs that are precarious (Kalleberg 2013). Employment in precarious work is concentrated among workers without a college education (Chancer, Sánchez-Jankowski, and Trost 2018). These jobs are characterized by low wages, unpredictable schedules, and unstable employment, which in turn are associated with lower levels of well-being, health, sleep, and happiness and higher levels of stress (Schneider and Harknett 2019).

29. Lisa's roommate had attempted suicide by swallowing a large number of pills, and after calling an ambulance, Lisa explained to her workplace that her roommate would not be able to make her shift. This revealed her living arrangement to her workplace, resulting in a suspension and investigation.

30. It had taken Sandra quite some time to get scheduled for this surgery (her third) because she was on the state's Medicaid program, which refused to pay for a diagnostic MRI until she completed several physical therapy visits. Although therapy put her through agony and made it more difficult to walk, it was not until after the fourth visit that the doctor determined that she had enough "under her belt" for Medicaid to pay for an MRI. At that point, Medicaid approved the procedure. When we spoke, Sandra had just completed doctor-ordered rest for four weeks and was told she could not begin working for another three weeks.

31. Sandra did enroll in college a year after graduating high school, but halfway through the semester she was contacted by administrative staff, who told her they needed her high school transcripts. At this point, she discovered that she still owed $250 in fees to her high school, which would not release her transcripts until the fees were paid. Unable to pay, Sandra dropped out of college. She explained that she hoped to begin making payments on these fees soon.

32. Although the Patient Protection and Affordable Care Act of 2010 mandated that most workplaces in the United States provide time and space for women to pump, interviews with women who had recently given birth in late 2011 through early 2012 found that only 40% of working women had both space and break time available to them at work to pump, and poor women and those

earning low hourly wages were much less likely to have access to these amenities at work than those who were financially better off (Kozhimannil et al. 2016).

33. Seltzer and Bianchi (2013); see also Edin and Lein's (1997) discussion of the importance of the private safety net, which includes both kin and nonkin ties, for low-income single mothers

34. Allard, Danziger, and Wathen (2012); Stack (1974); Swartz (2009); Wiemers (2014).

35. Mazelis (2017).

36. Researchers have long noted that women are treated with chivalry or paternalism by police officers and the courts and thus receive greater consideration than do men for a range of criminal justice–related outcomes, particularly when they conform to expected gender norms (Farrell, Ward, and Rousseau 2010; Moulds 1978; Visher 1983). However, women's advantages relative to men are predicated on their ability to appear sympathetic to police and court officers, who have historically discriminated against Black and Brown men and women (Brewer and Heitzeg 2008). White Women like Kate and Cassie, therefore, are much more likely to benefit from racial and gender privilege in this context than their non-White peers.

37. Conger et al. (1990); Hardie and Lucas (2010); Schneider, Harknett, and McLanahan (2016).

38. Benson and Fox (2001); Desmond and Valdez (2013); Edin and Shaefer (2016); Robinson (2020); Slabbert (2017).

39. Burton et al. (2013); Williams et al. (2005).

40. Needham and Austin (2010).

41. Silva (2012, 2015).

42. They are not alone. Using responses from the General Social Survey in 1987 and 2010, Reynolds and Xian (2014) found that Americans have consistently expressed belief in the importance of hard work, ambition, and education in getting ahead.

43. Mazelis (2017).

44. Ray (2017:3178).

CONCLUSION: BEYOND PLANFULNESS

1. As sociologist Richard Settersten (2002) has pointed out, an important component of planfulness is the ability to be flexible when plans go awry.

2. Sewell (1992:18).

3. As Sewell has argued, agency is bounded by the social world one inhabits. For example, Sewell argues that "only in a modern capitalist economy can one attempt to make a killing on the futures market" (1992:21).

4. Grusky, Western, and Wimer (2011).

5. This is true for young people graduating from high school or college during a recession, although the impact of graduating from college during a downturn appears to be greater (Hershbein 2012; Oreopoulos, von Wachter, and Heisz 2012).

6. Gumport (2019); Hamilton (2016); Hamilton, Roksa, and Nielsen (2018); Cottom (2017).

7. Brint (2002).

8. Fry (2014). Although media reports of debt sometimes show higher average levels, this is often because relatively rare but extremely high values of debt in the six figures can pull the mean value up. The median, which is not affected by extreme highs and lows, is a better representation of the typical student debt.

9. Bankruptcy Abuse Prevention and Consumer Protection Act, 2005.

10. Lucas (2001).

11. Carnevale, Rose, and Cheah (2013); Abel, Deitz, and Su (2014); Kalleberg (2018).

12. One study found that weekly wages for nurses moved from being on a par with median weekly wages for all workers in 1976 to 1.6 times the median weekly wages of all workers in 2010 (Munnich and Wozniak 2020).

13. Carnevale, Cheah, and Strohl (2013).

14. The experiences of health-care workers during the COVID-19 pandemic have complicated this narrative somewhat. Although rates of employment and wages are strong in the health-care field, reported levels of stress and burnout are also high (Apaydin et al. 2021; Kannampallil et al. 2020).

15. Stone (2004).

16. Scales (2020).

17. Kalleberg (2013).

18. Researchers who study intergenerational mobility use a metric of "earnings elasticity," which measures the degree to which a parent's (often fathers') income predicts a child's (often sons') income. Higher numbers in the 0 to 1 scale indicate a greater degree of class stickiness, and the United States tends to have higher numbers than many other developed nations (see Beller and Hout 2006; Gilbert 2017; Lee and Solon 2009).

19. Chetty et al. (2017); other research finds that across the adult life course, among men, moving up from initially low income levels is rare and moving down the income scale is much more common (Frech and Damaske 2019).

20. Arnett (2007, 2014).

21. Bozick and DeLuca (2005); Causey et al. (2020); Elman and O'Rand (2007); Lin and Liu (2019).

22. Bouris et al. (2015); Lea, de Wit, and Reynolds (2014); Ryan et al. 2009. Bisexual women appear to be particularly at risk (Duncan et al. 2019; Persson, Pfaus, and Ryder 2015).

23. Chetty et al. (2020).

24. Addo, Houle, and Simon (2016); Houle and Addo (2019). Recent research on college savings has found that academically successful Black girls have lower levels of college savings than equivalent White boys and girls and Black boys because they are more likely to come from families with lower household incomes (Quadlin and Conwell 2021).

25. Belknap (2020); Lowery (2019).

26. Research shows that career interests are shaped by a process in which young people make gendered self-assessments of their own competencies (Correll 2001, 2004; Eccles 1987, 1994; Eccles, Jacobs, and Harold 1990; Ridgeway and Correll 2004).

27. As Yasemin Besen-Cassino (2008, 2017) has documented, the concentration of adolescent girls in freelance work such as babysitting also contributes to an emerging and long-lasting wage gap by gender, extending into adulthood.

28. This echoes work by Ellen Lamont that shows parents encourage young women to "deprioritize relationships until they [have] finished their education and established their careers" (2020:25).

29. It is unclear whether female-dominated occupations are actually more likely to offer flexible work arrangements. Recent studies have found that these kinds of perks are most common among the most integrated (i.e., not either male- nor female-dominated) jobs (Deitch and Huffman 2001; Glauber 2011). Although more women than men work part-time, the United States does not offer the same protections for part-time work as other countries, where workers are guaranteed the right to switch to part-time hours (Blau and Kahn 2013).

30. Barnes (2015); Dow (2019); Higginbotham (2001).

31. Prior work has found that working-class and poor women, in contrast to middle-class women, are less likely to think of work and family lives as opposing or in need of "balance" and more likely to weave together these aspects of their lives (Garey 1999). This may explain the differing messages middle-class and working-class and poor young women receive from adults they know.

32. Damaske (2021).

33. Evelyn Nakano Glenn has written about how care work is and has historically been a "status duty" for women generally and a form of gendered servitude for racial minorities in particular, in ways that were both codified into law and cemented by coercion and the internalization of social norms. She argues that "the social organization of care has been rooted in diverse forms of coercion that have induced women to assume responsibility for caring for family members and that have tracked poor, racial minority, and immigrant women into positions entailing caring for others" (2012:5).

34. Basch (2011); Hofferth, Reid, and Mott (2001).

35. Glick et al. (2006); Manlove (1998); Markham et al. (2010).

36. Edin and Kefalas (2007); Hoffman and Maynard (2008). See also Geronimus (2003) for a discussion of how teen childbearing may be advantageous for African American women and their offspring and how condemnation of teen pregnancy therefore harms these young women.

37. Collins (2019).

38. Others have advocated for community college, in particular, to be free (Noonan 2021). This would also expand access, although it might divert some young people who would otherwise thrive at four-year institutions into associate's degrees or require transferring colleges. Transferring from one college setting to another can make it more challenging for students to form mentoring relationships with faculty and other advisers. Providing students with two years of education to take to any public college they wish would allow students to choose the right college education for them.

39. Senator Brian Schatz, for example, has proposed funding students' cost of living at college along with tuition and fees. College students' housing, food, and other cost-of-living expenses can sometimes outstrip what they pay in tuition and fees, and they play an important role in whether students persist in college or drop out (Chabria 2019; Halper 2019).

40. Federal Reserve Bank of New York (2019).

41. Cottom (2017).

42. Belfield (2013); Lynch, Engle, and Cruz (2010).

43. Green (2019).

44. Some particularly effective national programs that support internship programs for underrepresented students are Inroads (https://inroads.org/) and SEO Career (https://www.seo-usa.org/career/).

45. Investment in vocational education could be particularly productive for matching young people with stable jobs. In a review of vocational education and training programs across several industrialized nations, Eichhorst and colleagues (2015) find that these programs can improve employment outcomes for young people.

46. Hora, Wolfgram, and Thompson (2017); Shandra (2018).

47. Fay (2018, 2020); Scott-Clayton, Crosta, and Belfield (2014).

48. Edwards and Hertel-Fernandez (2010).

49. Baum and Scott-Clayton (2013).

50. Goldrick-Rab (2016); Protopsaltis and Parrott (2017).

51. Tach and Edin (2017).

52. Harknett (2006).

53. Damaske (2011).

54. Collins et al. (2021); Kashen, Glynn, and Novello (2020); Petts, Carlson, and Pepin (2021).

55. Calarco, Anderson, et al. (2020); Calarco, Meanwell, et al. (2020).

56. Folbre (2006); Suh and Folbre (2016).

57. Duncan (2015).

58. Williams (2001).

59. England, Budig, and Folbre (2002); Glenn (2012).

60. Kalleberg (2018).

61. Autor and Dorn (2013).

62. Morduch and Schneider (2017).

63. Akosa Antwi, Moriya, and Simon (2015); Hernandez-Boussard et al. (2014); Sommers et al. (2013).

APPENDIX: METHODOLOGY

1. Here and throughout the book, all names of persons, institutions, and places are given pseudonyms to protect anonymity.

2. Similar to the town profiled in *Hollowing Out the Middle: The Rural Brain Drain and What It Means for America* (Carr and Kefalas 2009), Glenbrook had declined in population in recent decades. However, unlike Ellis, the town Carr and Kefalas describe, Glenbrook was not rural, and most of the young women I interviewed stayed in or right around the town in young adulthood.

3. National Center for Education Statistics (2013).

4. This is likely due to both the older population age in Glenbrook and alternative options in the town. Glenbrook high school–aged youth have two alternative options in the immediate area, both private but relatively low-cost religious schools. Kensington youth must go farther outside of their area for private and parochial schooling.

5. US Bureau of Labor Statistics (2007, 2021).

6. At KHS, students also filled in their classes and teachers' names for each period of the day. At Glenbrook, I was able to contact students in their English classes and obtain this information in person.

7. This suggests a sizeable proportion of missing surveys. At Glenbrook, I was able to speak to all the English teachers and confirm that I had received the surveys administered. The low number of surveys was partially due to a high rate of absenteeism at the school, as well as a small number of students not taking English at the school. At Kensington, teachers were asked to deliver their surveys to the school receptionist, where I retrieved them. Some teachers may have declined to administer the surveys, while others may have forgotten to send them to the office. Homeroom was held once a month, so I was unable to go into homeroom classes to confirm whether the surveys had been administered, received, or delivered. At both schools, I was able to confirm through the survey data and interaction with students that the participants represented a range of academic backgrounds and demographic characteristics present at the school.

8. I also took notes during recorded interviews, although not quite as detailed. I was able to reconstruct the interview with a recording malfunction from these notes, due to identifying the problem right after the interview ended.

9. I randomly varied the order of these vignettes in each interview.

10. I contacted sample members through letter, phone, email, and social media, including calling family members whose contact information (and permission to contact) they had granted me. Despite this, I was unable to contact 17 of the 61 original sample members. In some cases, this is because the phone numbers I had for them were no longer in service and other forms of contact were not returned (mailers were typically returned as well for these young women). In other cases, I reached family members but they were either not in contact with the young women or passed on a message that was not returned. Only one young woman directly declined to be interviewed, due to time constraints. Two agreed to be interviewed but did not respond to follow-up scheduling requests.

11. Miles and Hubermann (1994).

References

Abel, Jaison R. and Richard Deitz. 2014. "Do the Benefits of College Still Outweigh the Costs?" *Current Issues in Economics and Finance* 20(3):1–11.

Abel, Jaison R. and Richard Deitz. 2018. "Underemployment in the Early Careers of College Graduates Following the Great Recession." Pp. 149–81 in *Education, Skills, and Technical Change: Implications for Future U.S. GDP Growth*, edited by C. R. Hulten and V. A. Ramey. Chicago: University of Chicago Press.

Abel, Jaison, Richard Deitz, and Yaquin Su. 2014. "Are Recent College Graduates Finding Good Jobs?" *Current Issues in Economics and Finance* 20(1):1–8.

Adam, Emma K. and P. Lindsay Chase-Lansdale. 2002. "Home Sweet Home(s): Parental Separations, Residential Moves, and Adjustment Problems in Low-Income Adolescent Girls." *Developmental Psychology* 38(5):792–805.

Addo, Fenaba R. 2014. "Debt, Cohabitation, and Marriage in Young Adulthood." *Demography* 51(5):1677–1701.

Addo, Fenaba R., Jason N. Houle, and Daniel Simon. 2016. "Young, Black, and (Still) in the Red: Parental Wealth, Race, and Student Loan Debt." *Race and Social Problems* 8(1):64–76.

Akosa Antwi, Yaa, Asako S. Moriya, and Kosali I. Simon. 2015. "Access to Health Insurance and the Use of Inpatient Medical Care: Evidence from the Affordable Care Act Young Adult Mandate." *Journal of Health Economics* 39:171–87.

Alexander, Karl L. and Martha A. Cook. 1979. "The Motivational Relevance of Educational Plans: Questioning the Conventional Wisdom." *Social Psychology Quarterly* 42(3):202–13.

Alichi, Ali, Kory Kantenga, and Juan Solé. 2016. *Income Polarization in the United States*. IMF Working Paper WP/16/121. Washington, DC: International Monetary Fund.

Allard, Scott W., Sandra Danziger, and Maria Wathen. 2012. *Receipt of Public Benefits and Private Support among Low-Income Households with Children after the Great Recession*. Policy Brief 31. Ann Arbor, MI: National Poverty Center.

Allegretto, Sylvia A. and Lawrence Mishel. 2016. *The Teacher Pay Gap Is Wider Than Ever: Teachers' Pay Continues to Fall Further behind Pay of Comparable Workers*. Washington, DC: Economic Policy Institute.

Allegretto, Sylvia A. and Lawrence Mishel. 2018. *The Teacher Pay Penalty Has Hit a New High: Trends in the Teacher Wage and Compensation Gaps through 2017*. Washington, DC: Economic Policy Institute.

American Physical Therapy Association (APTA). 2013. "Vision, Mission, and Strategic Plan." Retrieved May 6, 2019 (http://www.apta.org/vision2020/.

Anderson, Kristin L. 2010. "Conflict, Power, and Violence in Families." *Journal of Marriage and Family* 72(3):726–42.

Apaydin, Eric A., Danielle E. Rose, Elizabeth M. Yano, Paul G. Shekelle, Michael G. McGowan, Tami L. Antonini, Cassandra A. Valdez, Michelle Peacock, Laura Probst, and Susan E. Stockdale. 2021. "Burnout among Primary Care Healthcare Workers during the COVID-19 Pandemic." *Journal of Occupational and Environmental Medicine* 63(8):642–45.

Armstrong, Elizabeth A. and Laura T. Hamilton. 2013. *Paying for the Party: How College Maintains Inequality*. Cambridge, MA: Harvard University Press.

Arnett, Jeffrey Jensen. 2007. "Emerging Adulthood: What Is It, and What Is It Good For?" *Child Development Perspectives* 1(2):68–73.

Arnett, Jeffrey Jensen. 2014. *Emerging Adulthood: The Winding Road from the Late Teens Through the Twenties*. Oxford: Oxford University Press.

Arum, Richard and Josipa Roksa. 2014. *Aspiring Adults Adrift: Tentative Transitions of College Graduates*. Chicago: University of Chicago Press.

Ashworth, Jared and Tyler Ransom. 2019. "Has the College Wage Premium Continued to Rise? Evidence from Multiple U.S. Surveys." *Economics of Education Review* 69:149–54.

Astone, Nan Marie and Sara S. McLanahan. 1994. "Family Structure, Residential Mobility, and School Dropout: A Research Note." *Demography* 31(4):575–84.

Astorne-Figari, Carmen and Jamin D. Speer. 2018. "Drop Out, Switch Majors, or Persist? The Contrasting Gender Gaps." *Economics Letters* 164:82–85.

Attewell, Paul, David E. Lavin, Thurston Domina, and Tania Levey. 2009. *Passing the Torch: Does Higher Education for the Disadvantaged Pay Off across the Generations?* New York: Russell Sage Foundation.

Augustine, Jennifer March. 2016. "Exploring New Life Course Patterns of Mother's Continuing Secondary and College Education." *Population Research and Policy Review* 35(6):727–55.

Autor, David. 2010. *The Polarization of Job Opportunities in the US Labor Market: Implications for Employment and Earnings.* Center for American Progress and The Hamilton Project, 6.

Autor, David H. and David Dorn. 2013. "The Growth of Low-Skill Service Jobs and the Polarization of the US Labor Market." *American Economic Review* 103(5):1553–97.

Autor, David H., Lawrence F. Katz, and Melissa S. Kearney. 2006. "The Polarization of the U.S. Labor Market." *The American Economic Review* 96(2):189–94.

Azurdia, Gilda and Katerina Galkin. 2020. *An Eight-Year Cost Analysis from a Randomized Controlled Trial of CUNY's Accelerated Study in Associate Programs.* Working Paper. New York: MDRC.

Bailey, Martha J. and Thomas A. DiPrete. 2016. "Five Decades of Remarkable but Slowing Change in U.S. Women's Economic and Social Status and Political Participation." *RSF: The Russell Sage Foundation Journal of the Social Sciences* 2(4):1–32.

Bailey, Martha J. and Susan M. Dynarski. 2011. *Gains and Gaps: Changing Inequality in U.S. College Entry and Completion.* Working Paper 17633. Cambridge, MA: National Bureau of Economic Research.

Bailey, Thomas, Shanna Smith Jaggars, and Judith Scott-Clayton. 2013. "Characterizing the Effectiveness of Developmental Education: A Response to Recent Criticism." *Journal of Developmental Education* 36(3):18.

Bailey, Thomas, Dong Wook Jeong, and Sung-Woo Cho. 2010. "Referral, Enrollment, and Completion in Developmental Education Sequences in Community Colleges." *Economics of Education Review* 29(2):255–70.

Baker, Vicki L. and Roger G. Baldwin. 2015. "A Case Study of Liberal Arts Colleges in the 21st Century: Understanding Organizational Change and Evolution in Higher Education." *Innovative Higher Education* 40(3):247–61.

Bankruptcy Abuse Prevention and Consumer Protection Act of 2005, S. 256.

Barbaro, Michael and Fernanda Santos. 2011. "Bloomberg to Use Own Funds in Plan to Aid Minority Youth." *New York Times*, August 3. Retrieved April 8, 2020 (https://www.nytimes.com/2011/08/04/nyregion/new-york-plan-will-aim-to-lift-minority-youth.html).

Barnes, Riché J. Daniel. 2015. *Raising the Race: Black Career Women Redefine Marriage, Motherhood, and Community.* New Brunswick, NJ: Rutgers University Press.

Barr, Andrew and Sarah E. Turner. 2013. "Expanding Enrollments and Contracting State Budgets: The Effect of the Great Recession on Higher Education." *The ANNALS of the American Academy of Political and Social Science*
650(1):168–93.

Bartik, Timothy, and Brad Hershbein. 2018. *Degrees of Poverty: The Relation-
ship between Family Income Background and the Returns to Education.*
SSRN Scholarly Paper. ID 3141213. Rochester, NY: Social Science Research
Network.

Basch, Charles E. 2011. "Teen Pregnancy and the Achievement Gap among
Urban Minority Youth—PubMed—NCBI." *Journal of School Health*
81(10):614–18.

Baum, Sandy, and Martha Johnson. 2015. *Student Debt: Who Borrows Most?
What Lies Ahead*. Washington, D.C.: Urban Institute.

Baum, Sandy and Judith Scott-Clayton. 2013. "Redesigning the Pell Grant
Program for the Twenty-First Century (Discussion Paper No. 2013-04)."
Washington, DC: Brookings Institution, Hamilton Project.

Beckett, Katherine, Kris Nyrop, and Lori Pfingst. 2006. "Race, Drugs, and
Policing: Understanding Disparities in Drug Delivery Arrests." *Criminology*
44(1):105–37.

Belfield, Clive, Peter Crosta, and Davis Jenkins. 2014. "Can Community Colleges
Afford to Improve Completion? Measuring the Cost and Efficiency Consequences of Reform." *Educational Evaluation and Policy Analysis*
36(3):327–45.

Belfield, Clive R. 2013. "Student Loans and Repayment Rates: The Role of
For-Profit Colleges." *Research in Higher Education* 54(1):1–29.

Belknap, Joanne. 2020. *The Invisible Woman: Gender, Crime, and Justice.*
Thousand Oaks, CA: Sage Publications.

Beller, Emily and Michael Hout. 2006. "Intergenerational Social Mobility: The
United States in Comparative Perspective." *The Future of Children*
16(2):19–36.

Benson, Janel E. and Glen H. Elder. 2011. "Young Adult Identities and Their
Pathways: A Developmental and Life Course Model." *Developmental
Psychology* 47(6):1646–57.

Benson, Michael L., and Greer L. Fox. 2001. "Economic Distress, Community
Context and Intimate Violence: An Application and Extension of Social
Disorganization Theory." Final Report (NCJ 193434). Washington, DC:
National Institute of Justice. Retrieved March 23, 2022 (https://nij.ojp.gov
/library/publications/economic-distress-community-context-and-intimate
-violence-application-and-0).

Besen-Cassino, Yasemin. 2008. "The Cost of Being a Girl: Gender Earning
Differentials in the Early Labor Markets." *NWSA Journal* 20(1):146–60.

Besen-Cassino, Yasemin. 2017. *The Cost of Being a Girl: Working Teens and the Origins of the Gender Wage Gap.* 1st edition. Philadelphia: Temple University Press.

Bettie, Julie. 2003. *Women without Class, Race, and Identity.* Berkley: University of California Press.

Bianchi, Suzanne M., Melissa A. Milkie, Liana C. Sayer, and John P. Robinson. 2000. "Is Anyone Doing the Housework? Trends in the Gender Division of Household Labor. *Social Forces* 79(1):191–228.

Blau, Peter M. and Otis Dudley Duncan. 1967. *The American Occupational Structure.* New York: Wiley.

Blau, Francine D. and Lawrence M. Kahn. 2013. "Female Labor Supply: Why Is the United States Falling Behind?" *American Economic Review* 103(3):251–56.

Bohon, Stephanie A., Monica Kirkpatrick Johnson, and Bridget K. Gorman. 2006. "College Aspirations and Expectations among Latino Adolescents in the United States." *Social Problems* 53(2):207–25.

Bourdieu, Pierre. 1977. *Outline of a Theory of Practice.* Cambridge: Cambridge University Press.

Bourdieu, Pierre. 1986. "The Forms of Capital." Pp. 241–58 in *Handbook of Theory and Research for the Sociology of Education,* edited by J. Richardson. Westport, CT: Greenwood Press.

Bourdieu, Pierre and Jean-Claude Passeron. 1990. *Reproduction in Education, Society and Culture, 2nd Edition.* Newbury Park, CA: Sage Publications.

Bourdieu, Pierre and Loïc J. D. Wacquant. 1992. *An Invitation to Reflexive Sociology.* Chicago: University of Chicago Press.

Bouris, Alida, Bethany G. Everett, Ryan D. Heath, Caitlin E. Elsaesser, and Torsten B. Neilands. 2015. "Effects of Victimization and Violence on Suicidal Ideation and Behaviors among Sexual Minority and Heterosexual Adolescents." *LGBT Health* 3(2):153–61.

Bowen, William G., Matthew M. Chingos, and Michael S. McPherson. 2011. *Crossing the Finish Line: Completing College at America's Public Universities.* Reprint edition. Princeton, NJ: Princeton University Press.

Bowles, Samuel and Herbert Gintis. 1977. *Schooling in Capitalist America: Educational Reform and the Contradictions of Economic Life.* New York: Basic Books.

Bozick, Robert, Karl Alexander, Doris Entwisle, Susan Dauber, and Kerri Kerr. 2010. "Framing the Future: Revisiting the Place of Educational Expectations in Status Attainment." *Social Forces* 88(5):2027–52.

Bozick, Robert and Stefanie DeLuca. 2005. "Better Late Than Never? Delayed Enrollment in the High School to College Transition." *Social Forces* 84(1):531–54.

Brand, Jennie E. 2015. "The Far-Reaching Impact of Job Loss and Unemployment." *Annual Review of Sociology* 41(1):359–75.

Brand, Jennie E. and Yu Xie. 2010. "Who Benefits Most from College? Evidence for Negative Selection in Heterogeneous Economic Returns to Higher Education." *American Sociological Review* 75(2):273–302.

Brewer, Nathan, Kristie A. Thomas, and Julia Higdon. 2018. "Intimate Partner Violence, Health, Sexuality, and Academic Performance among a National Sample of Undergraduates." *Journal of American College Health* 66(7):683–92.

Brewer, Rose M. and Nancy A. Heitzeg. 2008. "The Racialization of Crime and Punishment: Criminal Justice, Color-Blind Racism, and the Political Economy of the Prison Industrial Complex." *American Behavioral Scientist* 51(5):625–44.

Brewster, Karin L. and Ronald R. Rindfuss. 2000. "Fertility and Women's Employment in Industrialized Nations." *Annual Review of Sociology* 26(1):271–96.

Bricker, Jesse, Lisa J. Dettling, Alice Henriques, Joanne W. Hsu, Kevin B. Moore, John Sabelhaus, Jeffrey Thompson, and Richard A. Windle. 2014. "Changes in US family finances from 2010 to 2013: Evidence from the Survey of Consumer Finances." *Federal Reserve Bulletin* 100(4):1–41. Retrieved November 2, 2019 (https://www.federalreserve.gov/pubs/bulletin/2014/pdf /scf14.pdf).

Brint, Steven, Mark Riddle, Lori Turk-Bicakci, and Charles S. Levy. 2005. "From the Liberal to the Practical Arts in American Colleges and Universities: Organizational Analysis and Curricular Change." *The Journal of Higher Education* 76(2):151–80.

Brint, Steven G. 2002. *The Future of the City of Intellect: The Changing American University*. Stanford, CA: Stanford University Press.

Brown, Susan L. 2006. "Family Structure Transitions and Adolescent Well-Being." *Demography* 43(3):447–61.

Browne, Irene, and Joya Misra. 2003. "The Intersection of Gender and Race in the Labor Market." *Annual Review of Sociology* 29(1):487–513.

Buchmann, Claudia, Dennis J. Condron, and Vincent J. Roscigno. 2010. "Shadow Education, American Style: Test Preparation, the SAT and College Enrollment." *Social Forces* 89(2):435–61.

Buchmann, Claudia and Ben Dalton. 2002. "Interpersonal Influences and Educational Aspirations in 12 Countries: The Importance of Institutional Context." *Sociology of Education* 75(2):99–122.

Buchmann, Claudia and Thomas A. DiPrete. 2006. "The Growing Female Advantage in College Completion: The Role of Family Background and Academic Achievement." *American Sociological Review* 71(4):515–41.

Buchmann, Claudia, Thomas A. Diprete, and Anne McDaniel. 2008. "Gender Inequalities in Education." *Annual Review of Sociology* 34:319–37.

Budig, Michelle J. 2002. "Male Advantage and the Gender Composition of Jobs: Who Rides the Glass Escalator?" *Social Problems* 49(2):258–77.

Burd-Sharps, Sarah and Kristen Lewis. 2017. "Promising Gains, Persistent Gaps: Youth Disconnection in America." New York: Measure of America. Retrieved August 15, 2019 (https://ssrc-static.s3.amazonaws.com/moa /Promising%20Gains%20Final.pdf).

Burd-Sharps, Sarah and Kristen Lewis. 2018. "More Than a Million Reasons for Hope: Youth Disconnection in America Today." New York: Measure of America. Retrieved August 15, 2019 (https://ssrc-static.s3.amazonaws.com /moa/dy18.full.report.pdf).

Burton, Chad M., Michael P. Marshal, Deena J. Chisolm, Gina S. Sucato, and Mark S. Friedman. 2013. "Sexual Minority-Related Victimization as a Mediator of Mental Health Disparities in Sexual Minority Youth: A Longitudinal Analysis." *Journal of Youth and Adolescence* 42(3):394–402.

Burton, Linda. 2007. "Childhood Adultification in Economically Disadvantaged Families: A Conceptual Model." *Family Relations* 56(4):329–45.

Calarco, Jessica McCrory. 2018. *Negotiating Opportunities: How the Middle Class Secures Advantages in School.* Oxford: Oxford University Press.

Calarco, Jessica McCrory, Elizabeth Anderson, Emily Meanwell, and Amelia Knopf. 2020. "'Let's Not Pretend It's Fun': How COVID-19-Related School and Childcare Closures Are Damaging Mothers' Well-Being." SocArXiv.

Calarco, Jessica McCrory, Emily Meanwell, Elizabeth Anderson, and Amelia Knopf. 2020. "'My Husband Thinks I'm Crazy': COVID-19-Related Conflict in Couples with Young Children." SocArXiv.

Carnevale, Anthony P., Ban Cheah, and Jeff Strohl. 2013. "Hard Times: College Majors, Unemployment and Earnings: Not All College Degrees Are Created Equal." Georgetown University Center on Education and the Workforce. Retrieved March 28, 2022 (https://repository.library.georgetown.edu/handle /10822/559308).

Carnevale, Anthony P., Stephen J. Rose, and Ban Cheah. 2013. "The College Payoff: Education, Occupations, Lifetime Earnings." Georgetown University Center on Education and the Workforce. Retrieved March 14, 2020 (https:// repository.library.georgetown.edu/handle/10822/559300).

Carr, Patrick J., and Maria J. Kefalas. 2009. *Hollowing Out the Middle: The Rural Brain Drain and What It Means for America.* Boston: Beacon Press.

Carter, Prudence L. 2006. "Straddling Boundaries: Identity, Culture, and School." *Sociology of Education* 79(4):304–28.

Carter, Prudence L. 2007. *Keepin' It Real: School Success Beyond Black and White.* New York: Oxford University Press.

Cater, Åsa K., Laura E. Miller, Kathryn H. Howell, and Sandra A. Graham-Bermann. 2015. "Childhood Exposure to Intimate Partner Violence and

Adult Mental Health Problems: Relationships with Gender and Age of Exposure." *Journal of Family Violence* 30(7):875–86.

Causey, J., F. Huie, R. Lang, M. Ryu, and D. Shapiro. 2020. *Completing College 2020: A National View of Student Completion Rates for 2014 Entering Cohort.* Signature Report No. 19. Herndon, VA: National Student Clearinghouse Research Center.

Cavanagh, Shannon E. and Aletha C. Huston. 2008. "The Timing of Family Instability and Children's Social Development." *Journal of Marriage and Family* 70(5):1258–70.

Cellini, Stephanie Riegg and Rajeev Darolia. 2015. "College Costs and Financial Constraints: Student Borrowing at For-Profit Institutions." Pp. 137–74 in *Student Loans and the Dynamics of Debt,* edited by B. Hershbein and K. M. Hollenbeck. Kalamazoo, MI: W. E. Upjohn Institute.

Cellini, Stephanie Riegg and Nicholas Turner. 2019. "Gainfully Employed? Assessing the Employment and Earnings of For-Profit College Students Using Administrative Data." *Journal of Human Resources* 54(2):342–70.

Center for American Progress. 2018. "Are High School Diplomas Really a Ticket to College and Work?" April 2. Retrieved February 24, 2022 (https://www .americanprogress.org/issues/education-k-12/reports/2018/04/02/447717 /high-school-diplomas/).

Cepa, Kennan and Frank F. Furstenberg. 2020. "Reaching Adulthood: Persistent Beliefs about the Importance and Timing of Adult Milestones." *Journal of Family Issues* 42(1):27–57.

Chabria, Anita. 2019. "Community Colleges Can Cost More than Universities, Leaving Neediest Students Homeless." *Los Angeles Times,* May 7, 2019.

Chancer, Lynn S., Martín Sánchez-Jankowski, and Christine Trost. 2018. *Youth, Jobs, and the Future: Problems and Prospects.* Oxford: Oxford University Press.

Cherlin, Andrew J. 2004. "The Deinstitutionalization of American Marriage." *Journal of Marriage and Family* 66(4):848–61.

Cherlin, Andrew J. 2014. *Labor's Love Lost: The Rise and Fall of the Working-Class Family in America.* New York: Russell Sage Foundation.

Chetty, Raj, David Grusky, Maximilian Hell, Nathaniel Hendren, Robert Manduca, and Jimmy Narang. 2017. "The Fading American Dream: Trends in Absolute Income Mobility since 1940." *Science* 356(6336):398–406.

Chetty, Raj, Nathaniel Hendren, Maggie R. Jones, and Sonya R. Porter. 2020. "Race and Economic Opportunity in the United States: An Intergenerational Perspective." *The Quarterly Journal of Economics* 135(2):711–83.

Ciocca Eller, Christina, and Thomas A. DiPrete. 2018. "The Paradox of Persistence: Explaining the Black-White Gap in Bachelor's Degree Completion." *American Sociological Review* 83(6):1171–1214.

Civil Rights Act of 1964. Pub. L. 88-352, 78 Stat. 241 (1964).

Clausen, John S. 1991. "Adolescent Competence and the Shaping of the Life Course." *American Journal of Sociology* 96(4):805–42.

Clawson, Dan and Naomi Gerstel. 2014. *Unequal Time: Gender, Class, and Family in Employment Schedules.* New York: Russell Sage Foundation.

Coker, Ann L. 2007. "Does Physical Intimate Partner Violence Affect Sexual Health? A Systematic Review." *Trauma, Violence, & Abuse* 8(2):149–77.

Coker, Ann L., Diane R. Follingstad, Heather M. Bush, and Bonnie S. Fisher. 2016. "Are Interpersonal Violence Rates Higher among Young Women in College Compared with Those Never Attending College?" *Journal of Interpersonal Violence* 31(8):1413–29.

Collins, Caitlyn. 2019. *Making Motherhood Work: How Women Manage Careers and Caregiving.* Princeton, NJ: Princeton University Press.

Collins, Caitlyn, Liana Christin Landivar, Leah Ruppanner, and William J. Scarborough. 2021. "COVID-19 and the Gender Gap in Work Hours." *Gender, Work & Organization* 28(S1):101–12.

Collinsworth, Linda L., Louise F. Fitzgerald, and Fritz Drasgow. 2009. "In Harm's Way: Factors Related to Psychological Distress Following Sexual Harassment." *Psychology of Women Quarterly* 33(4):475–90.

Colyar, Julia E. and Amy E. Stich. 2011. "Discourses of Remediation: Low-Income Students and Academic Identities." *American Behavioral Scientist* 55(2):121–41.

Conger, Rand D., Katherine J. Conger, and Monica J. Martin. 2010. "Socioeconomic Status, Family Processes, and Individual Development." *Journal of Marriage and Family* 72(3):685–704.

Conger, Rand D., Glen H. Elder, Jr., Frederick O. Lorenz, Katherine J. Conger, Ronald L. Simons, Les B. Whitbeck, Shirley Huck, and Janet N. Melby. 1990. "Linking Economic Hardship to Marital Quality and Instability." *Journal of Marriage and Family* 52(3):643–56.

Conti, Gabriella, James Heckman, and Sergio Urzua. 2010. "The Education-Health Gradient." *The American Economic Review* 100(2):234–38.

Cooper, Marianne. 2014. *Cut Adrift: Families in Insecure Times.* 1st edition. Berkeley: University of California Press.

Cooper, Michelle Asha. 2009. "Dreams Deferred? The Relationship Between Early and Later Postsecondary Educational Aspirations among Racial/Ethnic Groups." *Educational Policy* 23(4):615–50.

Correll, Shelley J. 2001. "Gender and the Career Choice Process: The Role of Biased Self-Assessments." *American Journal of Sociology* 106(6):1691–1730.

Correll, Shelley J. 2004. "Constraints into Preferences: Gender, Status, and Emerging Career Aspirations." *American Sociological Review* 69(1):93–113.

Cortés, Patricia and Jessica Pan. 2018. "When Time Binds: Substitutes for Household Production, Returns to Working Long Hours, and the Skilled Gender Wage Gap." *Journal of Labor Economics* 37(2):351–98.

Cotter, David A., Joan M. Hermsen, and Reeve Vanneman. 2001. "Women's Work and Working Women: The Demand for Female Labor." *Gender & Society* 15(3):429–52.

Cotter, David A., Joan M. Hermsen, and Reeve Vanneman. 2004. *Gender Inequality at Work*. New York: Russell Sage Foundation.

Cottom, Tressie McMillan. 2017. *Lower Ed: The Troubling Rise of For-Profit Colleges in the New Economy*. New York: The New Press.

Cottom, Tressie McMillan and Gaye Tuchman. 2015. "Rationalization of Higher Education." Pp. 1–17 in *Emerging Trends in the Social and Behavioral Sciences*, edited by R. A. Scott and S. M. Kosslyn. New York: Wiley.

Cowie, Jefferson R. 2012. *Stayin' Alive: The 1970s and the Last Days of the Working Class*. New York: The New Press.Crimmins, Eileen M., Richard A. Easterlin, and Yasuhiko Saito. 1991. "Preference Changes Among American Youth: Family, Work, and Goods Aspirations, 1976–86." *Population and Development Review* 17(1):115–33.

Crowder, Kyle and Jay Teachman. 2004. "Do Residential Conditions Explain the Relationship Between Living Arrangements and Adolescent Behavior?" *Journal of Marriage and Family* 66(3):721–38.

Damaske, Sarah. 2011. *For the Family? How Class and Gender Shape Women's Work*. New York: Oxford University Press.

Damaske, Sarah. 2021. *The Tolls of Uncertainty: How Privilege and the Guilt Gap Shape Unemployment in America*. Princeton, NJ: Princeton University Press.

Danziger, Sheldon H. and Peter Gottschalk, eds. 1994. *Uneven Tides: Rising Inequality in America*. New York: Russell Sage Foundation.

Davidson, Kate. 2011. "Health Care Students Face Long Wait Lists (Part 1)." *Michigan Radio NPR*, March 2 Retrieved May 26, 2020 (https://www.michiganradio.org/post/health-care-students-face-long-wait-lists-part-1).

Day, Jennifer Cheeseman and Eric C. Newburger. 2002. "The Big Payoff: Educational Attainment and Synthetic Estimates of Work-Life Earnings. Special Studies. Current Population Reports." Retrieved May 6, 2019 (http://eric.ed.gov/?id=ED467533).

Deil-Amen, Regina and James E. Rosenbaum. 2002. "The Unintended Consequences of Stigma-Free Remediation." *Sociology of Education* 75(3):249–68.

Deitch, Cynthia H. and Matt L. Huffman. 2001. "Family-Responsive Benefits and the Two-Tiered Labor Market." Pp. 103–30 in *Working Families: The Transformation of the American Home*, edited by R. Hertz and N. L. Marshall. Berkeley: University of California Press.

DeLuca, Stefanie, Susan Clampet-Lundquist, and Kathryn Edin. 2016. *Coming of Age in the Other America*. 1st edition. New York: Russell Sage Foundation.

Deming, David, Claudia Goldin, and Lawrence Katz. 2013. "For-Profit Colleges." *The Future of Children* 23(1):137–63.

Desmond, Matthew. 2012. "Disposable Ties and the Urban Poor." *American Journal of Sociology* 117(5):1295–1335.

Desmond, Matthew. 2017. *Evicted: Poverty and Profit in the American City.* Reprint edition. New York: Crown.

Desmond, Matthew, Carl Gershenson, and Barbara Kiviat. 2015. "Forced Relocation and Residential Instability among Urban Renters." *Social Service Review* 89(2):227–62.

Desmond, Matthew and Kristin L. Perkins. 2016. "Housing and Household Instability." *Urban Affairs Review* 52(3):421–36.

Desmond, Matthew, and Nicol Valdez. 2013. "Unpolicing the Urban Poor: Consequences of Third-Party Policing for Inner-City Women." *American Sociological Review* 78(1):117–41.

Dow, Dawn Marie. 2016. "Integrated Motherhood: Beyond Hegemonic Ideologies of Motherhood." *Journal of Marriage and Family* 78(1):180–96.

Dow, Dawn Marie. 2019. *Mothering While Black: Boundaries and Burdens of Middle-Class Parenthood.* Oakland: University of California Press.

Duncan, Arne. 2015. "Reconnecting Young People with a Bright Future." *Medium*, August 5. Retrieved December 8, 2019 (https://medium.com /@arneduncan/reconnecting-young-people-with-a-bright-future-fdadb 500702f).

Duncan, Dustin T., Sophia Zweig, H. Rhodes Hambrick, and Joseph J. Palamar. 2019. "Sexual Orientation Disparities in Prescription Opioid Misuse among U.S. Adults." *American Journal of Preventive Medicine* 56(1):17–26.

Dunn, Megan, Steven E. Haugen, and Janie-Lynn Kang. 2018. *"The Current Population Survey—Tracking Unemployment in the United States for Over 75 Years.* Washington, DC: US Bureau of Labor Statistics.

Dwyer, Rachel E. 2013. "The Care Economy? Gender, Economic Restructuring, and Job Polarization in the U.S. Labor Market." *American Sociological Review* 78(3):390–416.

Dwyer, Rachel E. and Erik Olin Wright. 2019. "Low-Wage Job Growth, Polarization, and the Limits and Opportunities of the Service Economy." *RSF: The Russell Sage Foundation Journal of the Social Sciences* 5(4):56–76.

Eccles, Jacquelynne S. 1987. "Gender Roles and Women's Achievement-Related Decisions." *Psychology of Women Quarterly* 11(2):135–72.

Eccles, Jacquelynne S. 1994. "Understanding Women's Educational and Occupational Choices." *Psychology of Women Quarterly* 18(4):585–609.

Eccles, Jacquelynne S., Janis E. Jacobs, and Rena D. Harold. 1990. "Gender Role Stereotypes, Expectancy Effects, and Parents' Socialization of Gender Differences." *Journal of Social Issues* 46(2):183–201.

Edelman, Peter B. and Harry J. Holzer. 2014. "Connecting the Disconnected: Improving Education and Employment Outcomes among Disadvantaged Youth." Pp. 81–107 in *What Works for Workers? Public Policies and*

Innovative Strategies for Low-Wage Workers, edited by S. Luce, J. Luff, J. A. McCartin, and R. Milkman. New York: Russell Sage Foundation.

Edin, Kathryn and Maria Kefalas. 2007. *Promises I Can Keep: Why Poor Women Put Motherhood before Marriage*. Berkeley: University of California Press.

Edin, Kathryn and Rebecca Joyce Kissane. 2010. "Poverty and the American Family: A Decade in Review." *Journal of Marriage and Family* 72(3):460–79.

Edin, Kathryn and Laura Lein. 1997. "Work, Welfare, and Single Mothers' Economic Survival Strategies." *American Sociological Review* 62(2):253–66.

Edin, Kathryn and Joanna M. Reed. 2005. "Why Don't They Just Get Married? Barriers to Marriage among the Disadvantaged." *The Future of Children* 15(2):117–37.

Edin, Kathryn and H. Luke Shaefer. 2016. *$2.00 a Day: Living on Almost Nothing in America*. Reprint edition. New York: Mariner Books.

Edwards, Kathryn Anne and Alex Hertel-Fernandez. 2010. *Paving the Way through Paid Internships: A Proposal to Expand Educational and Economic Opportunities for Low-Income College Students*. Economic Policy Institute. Retrieved March 28, 2021 (https://vtechworks.lib.vt.edu/handle/10919 /90852).

Eichhorst, Werner, Núria Rodríguez-Planas, Ricarda Schmidl, and Klaus F. Zimmermann. 2015. "A Road Map to Vocational Education and Training in Industrialized Countries." *ILR Review* 68(2):314–37.

Eide, Eric R., Michael J. Hilmer, and Mark H. Showalter. 2016. "Is It Where You Go or What You Study? The Relative Influence of College Selectivity and College Major on Earnings." *Contemporary Economic Policy* 34(1):37–46.

Elder, Glen H. 1998. "The Life Course as Developmental Theory." *Child Development* 69(1):1–12.

Elman, Cheryl and Angela M. O'Rand. 2007. "The Effects of Social Origins, Life Events, and Institutional Sorting on Adults' School Transitions." *Social Science Research* 36(3):1276–99.

England, Paula. 2010. "The Gender Revolution: Uneven and Stalled." *Gender & Society* 24(2):149–66.

England, Paula and Nancy Folbre. 1999. "The Cost of Caring." *The ANNALS of the American Academy of Political and Social Science* 561(1):39–51.

England, Paula, Michelle Budig, and Nancy Folbre. 2002. "Wages of Virtue: The Relative Pay of Care Work." *Social Problems* 49(4):455–73.

Equal Credit Opportunity Act, 15 U.S.C. § 1691 et seq.

Evans, Gary W. and Pilyoung Kim. 2013. "Childhood Poverty, Chronic Stress, Self-Regulation, and Coping." *Child Development Perspectives* 7(1):43–48.

Farrell, Amy, Geoff Ward, and Danielle Rousseau. 2010. "Intersections of Gender and Race in Federal Sentencing: Examining Court Contexts and the Effects of Representative Court Authorities." *Journal of Gender, Race and Justice* 14:85–125.

Fay, Maggie P. 2018. "Faculty & Student Experiences across Redesigned Developmental Math Course Models." Graduate NYC: College Readiness & Success. Retrieved September 11, 2019 (https://www.cuny.edu/wp-content /uploads/sites/4/page-assets/about/administration/offices/oira/policy /seminars/Fay_GNYC-Remediation-Report-2018.pdf).

Fay, Maggie P. 2020. "Varsity Blues Wasn't the Only Way Poor People Are Denied Access to Higher Education." *Inside Higher Ed*, October 26.

Federal Reserve Bank of New York. 2019. "Quarterly Report of Household Debt and Credit." Retrieved March 29, 2021 (https://www.newyorkfed.org /medialibrary/interactives/householdcredit/data/pdf/hhdc_2019q3.pdf).

Ferrall, Victor E., Jr. 2011. *Liberal Arts at the Brink*. Cambridge, MA: Harvard University Press.

Fitzgerald, Louise F. and Lilia M. Cortina. 2018. "Sexual Harassment in Work Organizations: A View from the 21st Century." Pp. 215–34 in *APA Handbook of the Psychology of Women: Perspectives on Women's Private and Public Lives*, Vol. 2, *APA Handbooks in Psychology*®. Washington, DC: American Psychological Association.

Folbre, Nancy. 2006. "Measuring Care: Gender, Empowerment, and the Care Economy." *Journal of Human Development* 7(2):183–99.

Fomby, Paula and Andrew J. Cherlin. 2007. "Family Instability and Child Well-Being." *American Sociological Review* 72(2):181–204.

Fomby, Paula and Christie A. Sennott. 2013. "Family Structure Instability and Mobility: The Consequences for Adolescents' Problem Behavior." *Social Science Research* 42(1):186–201.

Foster, James E. and Michael C. Wolfson. 2010. "Polarization and the Decline of the Middle Class: Canada and the U.S." *The Journal of Economic Inequality* 8(2):247–73.

Frech, Adrianne and Sarah Damaske. 2019. "Men's Income Trajectories and Physical and Mental Health at Midlife." *American Journal of Sociology* 124(5):1372–1412.

Friedman, Gerald. 2014. "Workers without Employers: Shadow Corporations and the Rise of the Gig Economy." *Review of Keynesian Economics* 2(2):171–88.

Fry, Richard. 2014. "Young Adults, Student Debt and Economic Well-being." Washington, DC: Pew Research Center's Social and Demographic Trends Project. Retrieved February 12, 2020 (https://www.pewsocialtrends.org/2014 /05/14/section-1-student-debt-and-overall-economic-well-being/).

Furstenberg, Frank F. 2008. "The Intersections of Social Class and the Transition to Adulthood." *New Directions for Child and Adolescent Development* 2008(119):1–10.

Fussell, Elizabeth and Anne H. Gauthier. 2005. "American Women's Transition to Adulthood in Comparative Perspective." Pp. 76–109 in *On the Frontier of Adulthood: Theory, Research, and Public Policy*, edited by

R. A. Settersten Jr., F. F. Furstenberg, and R. G. Rumbaut. Chicago: University of Chicago Press.

Garey, Anita Ilta. 1999. *Weaving Work and Motherhood*. Philadelphia: Temple University Press.

Garrett-Peters, Raymond and Linda M. Burton. 2015. "Reframing Marriage and Marital Delay among Low-Income Mothers: An Interactionist Perspective." *Journal of Family Theory & Review* 7(3):242–64.

Gasper, Joseph, Stefanie DeLuca, and Angela Estacion. 2012. "Switching Schools: Revisiting the Relationship Between School Mobility and High School Dropout." *American Educational Research Journal* 49(3):487–519.

Gaston, Shytierra. 2019. "Enforcing Race: A Neighborhood-Level Explanation of Black–White Differences in Drug Arrests." *Crime & Delinquency* 65(4):499–526.

Gauchat, Gordon, Maura Kelly, and Michael Wallace. 2012. "Occupational Gender Segregation, Globalization, and Gender Earnings Inequality in U.S. Metropolitan Areas." *Gender & Society* 26(5):718–47.

Geronimus, Arline T. 2003. "Damned If You Do: Culture, Identity, Privilege, and Teenage Childbearing in the United States." *Social Science & Medicine* 57(5):881–93.

Gerson, Kathleen. 2011. *The Unfinished Revolution: Coming of Age in a New Era of Gender, Work, and Family*. 1st edition. New York: Oxford University Press.

Gerstel, Naomi. 2000. "The Third Shift: Gender and Care Work Outside the Home." *Qualitative Sociology* 23(4):467–83.

Gibson-Davis, Christina M., Kathryn Edin, and Sara McLanahan. 2005. "High Hopes but Even Higher Expectations: The Retreat from Marriage among Low-Income Couples." *Journal of Marriage and Family* 67(5):1301–12.

Giddens, Anthony. 1993. *New Rules of Sociological Method: A Positive Critique of Interpretative Sociologies*. 2nd edition. Cambridge, UK: Polity.

Giersch, Jason. 2018. "Academic Tracking, High-Stakes Tests, and Preparing Students for College: How Inequality Persists within Schools." *Educational Policy* 32(7):907–35.

Gilbert, Dennis. 2002. *The American Class Structure in an Age of Growing Inequality, 6th Edition*. Belmont, CA: Wadsworth Publishing Company.

Gilbert, Dennis L. 2017. *The American Class Structure in an Age of Growing Inequality*. Thousand Oaks, CA: Sage Publications.

Glauber, Rebecca. 2011. "Limited Access: Gender, Occupational Composition, and Flexible Work Scheduling." *The Sociological Quarterly* 52(3):472–94.

Glenn, Evelyn Nakano. 2012. *Forced to Care: Coercion and Caregiving in America*. Cambridge, MA: Harvard University Press.

Glick, Jennifer E., Stacey D. Ruf, Michael J. White, and Frances Goldscheider. 2006. "Educational Engagement and Early Family Formation: Differences by Ethnicity and Generation." *Social Forces* 84(3):1391–1415.

Goldin, Claudia Dale and Lawrence F. Katz. 2009. *The Race between Education and Technology*. Cambridge, MA: Harvard University Press.

Goldman, Dana and James P. Smith. 2011. "The Increasing Value of Education to Health." *Social Science & Medicine (1982)* 72(10):1728–37.

Goldrick-Rab, Sara. 2016. *Paying the Price: College Costs, Financial Aid, and the Betrayal of the American Dream*. Chicago: University of Chicago Press.

Goldrick-Rab, Sara and Nancy Kendall. 2014. *Redefining College Affordability: Securing America's Future with a Free Two Year College Option*. Indianapolis, IN: Lumina Foundation.

Goodman, Lisa A., Mary P. Koss, and Nancy Felipe Russo. 1993. "Violence against Women: Physical and Mental Health Effects. Part I: Research Findings." *Applied and Preventive Psychology* 2(2):79–89.

Gottschalk, Peter and Sheldon Danziger. 2005. "Inequality of Wage Rates, Earnings and Family Income in the United States, 1975–2002." *Review of Income and Wealth* 51(2):231–54.

Gough, Margaret, and Mary Noonan. 2013. "A Review of the Motherhood Wage Penalty in the United States." *Sociology Compass* 7(4):328–42.

Goyette, Kimberly A. 2008. "College for Some to College for All: Social Background, Occupational Expectations, and Educational Expectations over Time." *Social Science Research* 37(2):461–84.

Granovetter, Mark S. 1973. "The Strength of Weak Ties." *American Journal of Sociology* 78(6):1360–80.

Green, Erica L. 2019. "DeVos Repeals Obama-Era Rule Cracking Down on For-Profit Colleges." *New York Times*, June 28.

Grusky, David B., Bruce Western, and Christopher Wimer. 2011. *The Great Recession*. New York: Russell Sage Foundation.

Gumport, Patricia J. 2019. *Academic Fault Lines: The Rise of Industry Logic in Public Higher Education*. Baltimore, MD: Johns Hopkins University Press.

Guzzo, Karen Benjamin. 2014. "Trends in Cohabitation Outcomes: Compositional Changes and Engagement among Never-Married Young Adults." *Journal of Marriage and Family* 76(4):826–42.

Hacker, Jacob S. 2008. *The Great Risk Shift: The New Economic Insecurity and the Decline of the American Dream*. Revised, updated edition. Oxford: Oxford University Press.

Hacker, Jacob S. and Paul Pierson. 2011. *Winner-Take-All Politics: How Washington Made the Rich Richer—and Turned Its Back on the Middle Class*. New York: Simon & Schuster.

Hair, Elizabeth C., Kristin A. Moore, Thomson J. Ling, Cameron McPhee-Baker, Brett V. Brown, and Harriet J. Scarupa. 2009. *Youth Who Are Disconnected and Those Who Then Reconnect: Assessing the Influence of Family, Programs, Peers and Communities*. Publication #2009-37. Washington, DC: Child Trends.

Halper, Evan. 2019. "2020 Candidates Are Talking about 'Free College': Here's What They're Not Telling You." *Los Angeles Times*. June 7, 2019.

Halpern-Meekin, Sarah and Laura Tach. 2008. "Heterogeneity in Two-Parent Families and Adolescent Well-Being." *Journal of Marriage and Family* 70(2):435–51.

Hamilton, Laura, Josipa Roksa, and Kelly Nielsen. 2018. "Providing a 'Leg Up': Parental Involvement and Opportunity Hoarding in College." *Sociology of Education* 91(2):111–31.

Hamilton, Laura T. 2016. *Parenting to a Degree: How Family Matters for College Women's Success*. Chicago: University of Chicago Press.

Hansmann, Henry. 1981. "The Rationale for Exempting Nonprofit Organizations from Corporate Income Taxation." *The Yale Law Journal* 91(1):54–100.

Hanson, Sandra L. 1994. "Lost Talent: Unrealized Educational Aspirations and Expectations among U.S. Youths." *Sociology of Education* 67(3):159–83.

Hardaway, Cecily R. and Vonnie C. McLoyd. 2009. "Escaping Poverty and Securing Middle-class Status: How Race and Socioeconomic Status Shape Mobility Prospects for African Americans during the Transition to Adulthood." *Journal of Youth Adolescence* 38:242–56.

Hardie, Jessica Halliday. 2015. "The Best Laid Plans: Social Capital in the Development of Girls' Educational and Occupational Plans." *Social Problems* 62(2):241–65.

Hardie, Jessica Halliday and Amy Lucas. 2010. "Economic Factors and Relationship Quality Among Young Couples: Comparing Cohabitation and Marriage." *Journal of Marriage and Family* 72(5):1141–54.

Hardy, Bradley L. and Dave E. Marcotte. 2020. *Education and the Dynamics of Middle-Class Status*. Washington, DC: The Brookings Institution.

Harknett, Kristen. 2006. "The Relationship between Private Safety Nets and Economic Outcomes among Single Mothers." *Journal of Marriage and Family* 68(1):172–91.

Harris, Robin C., Lisa Rosenberg, and Marilyn E. Grace O'Rourke. 2014. "Addressing the Challenges of Nursing Student Attrition." *Journal of Nursing Education* 53(1):31–37.

Harris-Bowlsbey, JoAnn. 2013. "Computer-Assisted Career Guidance Systems: A Part of NCDA History." *The Career Development Quarterly* 61(2):181–85.

Hartocollis, Anemona. 2017. "College Is the Goal. Will These Three Teenagers Get There?" *New York Times*, March 16.

Hauser, Robert M., Shu-Ling Tsai, and William H. Sewell. 1983. "A Model of Stratification with Response Error in Social and Psychological Variables." *Sociology of Education* 56(1):20–46.

Haushofer, Johannes and Ernst Fehr. 2014. "On the Psychology of Poverty." *Science* 344(6186):862–67.

Heard, Holly E. 2007. "Fathers, Mothers, and Family Structure: Family Trajec-tories, Parent Gender, and Adolescent Schooling." *Journal of Marriage and Family* 69(2):435–50.

Hearn, James C. and Andrew S. Belasco. 2015. "Commitment to the Core: A Longitudinal Analysis of Humanities Degree Production in Four-Year Colleges." *The Journal of Higher Education* 86(3):387–416.

Heathcote, Jonathan, Fabrizio Perri, and Giovanni L. Violante. 2010. "Unequal We Stand: An Empirical Analysis of Economic Inequality in the United States, 1967–2006." *Review of Economic Dynamics* 13(1):15–51.

Heinrich, Carolyn J. and Harry J. Holzer. 2011. "Improving Education and Employment for Disadvantaged Young Men: Proven and Promising Strate-gies." *The ANNALS of the American Academy of Political and Social Science* 635(1):163–91.

Hemez, Paul. 2018. "Young Adulthood: Sequencing of Union Experiences Relative to First Birth." Family Profiles, FP-18-24. Bowling Green, OH: National Center for Family & Marriage Research.

Hernandez-Boussard, Tina, Carson S. Burns, N. Ewen Wang, Laurence C. Baker, and Benjamin A. Goldstein. 2014. "The Affordable Care Act Reduces Emergency Department Use by Young Adults: Evidence from Three States." *Health Affairs* 33(9):1648–54.

Hershbein, Brad J. 2012. "Graduating High School in a Recession: Work, Education, and Home Production." *The B.E. Journal of Economic Analysis & Policy* 12(1).

Hershbein, Brad and Kevin M. Hollenbeck. 2015. *Student Loans and the Dynamics of Debt*. Kalamazoo, MI: W. E. Upjohn Institute.

Higginbotham, Elizabeth. 2001. *Too Much to Ask: Black Women in the Era of Integration*. New edition. Chapel Hill: University of North Carolina Press.

Hlavka, Heather R. 2014. "Normalizing Sexual Violence: Young Women Account for Harassment and Abuse." *Gender & Society* 28(3):337–58.

Hochschild, Arlie. 1989. *The Second Shift: Working Parents and the Revolution at Home*. First edition. New York: Viking Adult.

Hochschild, Jennifer L. 1996. *Facing Up to the American Dream*. Reprint edition. Princeton, NJ: Princeton University Press.

Hofferth, Sandra L., Lori Reid, and Frank L. Mott. 2001. "The Effects of Early Childbearing on Schooling over Time." *Family Planning Perspectives* 33(6):259–67.

Hoffman, Saul D. and Greg J. Duncan. 1988. "What Are the Economic Conse-quences of Divorce?" *Demography* 25(4):641–45.

Hoffman, Saul D. and Rebecca A. Maynard. 2008. *Kids Having Kids: Economic Costs & Social Consequences of Teen Pregnancy*. Washington, DC: Urban Institute.

Holland, Megan M. and Stefanie DeLuca. 2016. "'Why Wait Years to Become Something?' Low-Income African American Youth and the Costly Career Search in For-Profit Trade Schools." *Sociology of Education* 89(4):261–78.

Hollister, Matissa. 2011. "Employment Stability in the U.S. Labor Market: Rhetoric versus Reality." *Annual Review of Sociology* 37(1):305–24.

Hollister, Matissa N. and Kristin E. Smith. 2014. "Unmasking the Conflicting Trends in Job Tenure by Gender in the United States, 1983–2008." *American Sociological Review* 79(1):159–81.

Holzer, Harry, Peter Edelman, and Paul Offner. 2006. *Reconnecting Disadvantaged Young Men*. Washington, DC: Urban Institute Press.

Hora, Matthew T., Matthew Wolfgram, and Samantha Thompson. 2017. *What Do We Know about the Impact of Internships on Student Outcomes? Results from a Preliminary Review of the Scholarly and Practitioner Literatures.* Research Brief #2. Madison, WI: Center for Research on College-Workforce Transitions.

Houle, Jason N. and Fenaba R. Addo. 2019. "Racial Disparities in Student Debt and the Reproduction of the Fragile Black Middle Class." *Sociology of Race and Ethnicity* 5(4):562–77.

Hout, Michael. 2012. "Social and Economic Returns to College Education in the United States." *Annual Review of Sociology* 38(1):379–400.

Hout, Michael, Asaf Levanon, and Erin Cumberworth. 2011. "Job Loss and Unemployment." Pp. 59–81 in *The Great Recession*, edited by D. B. Grusky, B. Western, and C. Wimer. New York: Russell Sage Foundation.

Howard, Kimberly A. S., Aaron H. Carlstrom, Andrew D. Katz, Aaronson Y. Chew, G. Christopher Ray, Lia Laine, and David Caulum. 2011. "Career Aspirations of Youth: Untangling Race/Ethnicity, SES, and Gender." *Journal of Vocational Behavior* 79(1):98–109.

Howell, Joseph T. 1972. *Hard Living on Clay Street: Portraits of Blue Collar Families*. Prospect Heights, IL: Waveland Press.

Hoxby, Caroline M. 2009. "The Changing Selectivity of American Colleges." *Journal of Economic Perspectives* 23(4):95–118.

Ihle-Helledy, Kristin, Donald G. Zytowski, and Nadya A. Fouada. 2004. "Kuder Career Search: Test-Retest Reliability and Consequential Validity." *Journal of Career Assessment* 12(3):285–97.

Isen, Adam and Betsey Stevenson. 2010. *Women's Education and Family Behavior: Trends in Marriage, Divorce and Fertility*. Cambridge, MA: National Bureau of Economic Research. Retrieved November 16, 2016 (http://www.nber.org/papers/w15725).

Jack, Anthony Abraham. 2019. *The Privileged Poor: How Elite Colleges Are Failing Disadvantaged Students*. Cambridge, MA: Harvard University Press.

Jackson, Pamela Braboy and Quincy Thomas Stewart. 2003. "A Research Agenda for the Black Middle Class: Work Stress, Survival Strategies, and Mental Health." *Journal of Health and Social Behavior* 44(3):442–55.

Jaggars, Shanna Smith and Susan Bickerstaff. 2018. "Developmental Education: The Evolution of Research and Reform." Pp. 469–503 in *Higher Education: Handbook of Theory and Research*, published under the Sponsorship of the Association for Institutional Research (AIR) and the Association for the Study of Higher Education (ASHE), Higher Education: Handbook of Theory and Research, edited by M. B. Paulsen. Cham, Switzerland: Springer International Publishing.

Jeffrey, Wesley. 2020. "Crossing the Finish Line? A Review of College Completion Inequality in the United States by Race and Class." *Sociology Compass* 14(5):e12787.

Jelleyman, T. and N. Spencer. 2008. "Residential Mobility in Childhood and Health Outcomes: A Systematic Review." *Journal of Epidemiology & Community Health* 62(7):584–92.

Jimenez, Laura, Scott Sargrad, Jessica Morales, and Maggie Thompson. 2016. *Remedial Education: The Cost of Catching Up.* Washington, DC: Center for American Progress.

Jina, Ruxana and Leena S. Thomas. 2013. "Health Consequences of Sexual Violence against Women." *Best Practice & Research Clinical Obstetrics & Gynaecology* 27(1):15–26.

Johnson, Monica Kirkpatrick and Stefanie Mollborn. 2009. "Growing up Faster, Feeling Older: Hardship in Childhood and Adolescence." *Social Psychology Quarterly* 72(1):39–60.

Johnson, Monica Kirkpatrick and Jeylan T. Mortimer. 2011. "Origins and Outcomes of Judgments about Work." *Social Forces* 89(4):1239–60.

Johnson, Monica Kirkpatrick and John R. Reynolds. 2013. "Educational Expectation Trajectories and Attainment in the Transition to Adulthood." *Social Science Research* 42:818–35.

Johnson, David S., Timothy M. Smeeding, and Barbara Boyle Torrey. 2005. "Economic Inequality through the Prisms of Income and Consumption." *Monthly Labor Review* 128:11.

Juhn, Chinhui and Kristin McCue. 2016. "Evolution of the Marriage Earnings Gap for Women." *The American Economic Review* 106(5):252–56.

Julian, Tiffany and Robert Kominski. 2011. *Education and Synthetic Work-Life Earnings Estimates. American Community Survey Reports.* ACS-14. Washington, DC: US Census Bureau.

Kahn, Joan R., Javier García-Manglano, and Suzanne M. Bianchi. 2014. "The Motherhood Penalty at Midlife: Long-Term Effects of Children on Women's Careers." *Journal of Marriage and Family* 76(1):56–72.

Kalleberg, Arne L. 2009. "Precarious Work, Insecure Workers: Employment Relations in Transition." *American Sociological Review* 74(1):1–22.

Kalleberg, Arne L. 2013. *Good Jobs, Bad Jobs: The Rise of Polarized and Precarious Employment Systems in the United States 1970s to 2000s*. New York: Russell Sage Foundation.

Kalleberg, Arne L. 2018. "Precarious Work and Young Workers in the United States." Pp. 35–52 in *Youth, Jobs, and the Future: Problems and Prospects*, edited by L. S. Chancer, M. Sánchez-Jankowski, and C. Trost. Oxford: Oxford University Press.

Kalleberg, Arne L. and Till M. Von Wachter. 2017. "The U.S. Labor Market During and After the Great Recession: Continuities and Transformations." *RSF: The Russell Sage Foundation Journal of the Social Sciences* 3(3):1–19.

Kalmijn, Matthijs. 1994. "Mother's Occupational Status and Children's Schooling." *American Sociological Review* 59(2):257–75.

Kannampallil, Thomas G., Charles W. Goss, Bradley A. Evanoff, Jaime R. Strickland, Rebecca P. McAlister, and Jennifer Duncan. 2020. "Exposure to COVID-19 Patients Increases Physician Trainee Stress and Burnout." *PLOS ONE* 15(8):e0237301.

Kao, Grace and Jennifer S. Thompson. 2003. "Racial and Ethnic Stratification in Educational Achievement and Attainment." *Annual Review of Sociology* 29:417–42.

Kao, Grace and Marta Tienda. 1998. "Educational Aspirations of Minority Youth." *American Journal of Education* 106(3):349–84. https://doi.org/10.1086/444188.

Kashen, Julie, Sarah Jane Glynn, and Amanda Novello. 2020. *How COVID-19 Sent Women's Workforce Progress Backward*. Washington, DC: Center for American Progress.

Kawachi, Ichiro, Norman Daniels, and Dean E. Robinson. 2005. "Health Disparities by Race and Class: Why Both Matter." *Health Affairs* 24(2):343–52.

Kay, Herma. 2000. "From the Second Sex to the Joint Venture: An Overview of Women's Rights and Family Law in the United States during the Twentieth Century." *California Law Review* 88(6):2017.

Kelly, Erin L. and Phyllis Moen. 2007. "Rethinking the ClockWork of Work: Why Schedule Control May Pay Off at Work and at Home." *Advances in Developing Human Resources* 9(4):487–506.

Kerr, Emma. 2019. "Everything You Need to Know about the Pell Grant/Paying for College/US News." *US News & World Report*, March 28.

Kilbourne, Barbara Stanek, Paula England, George Farkas, Kurt Beron, and Dorothea Weir. 1994. "Returns to Skill, Compensating Differentials, and Gender Bias: Effects of Occupational Characteristics on the Wages of White Women and Men." *American Journal of Sociology* 100(3):689–719.

Kim, David, F. Scott Markham, and Joseph D. Cangelosi. 2002. "Why Students Pursue the Business Degree: A Comparison of Business Majors Across Universities." *Journal of Education for Business* 78(1):28–32.

Kim, Doo Hwan and Barbara Schneider. 2005. "Social Capital in Action: Alignment of Parental Support in Adolescents' Transition to Postsecondary Education." *Social Forces* 84(2):1181–1206.

Kim, Heather, Laura Rendon, and James Valadez. 1998. "Student Characteristics, School Characteristics, and Educational Aspirations of Six Asian American Ethnic Groups." *Journal of Multicultural Counseling and Development* 26(3):166–76.

Kim, Jinhee and Swarn Chatterjee. 2019. "Student Loans, Health, and Life Satisfaction of US Households: Evidence from a Panel Study." *Journal of Family and Economic Issues* 40(1):36–50.

Kimball, Bruce A. 2014. "Revising the Declension Narrative: Liberal Arts Colleges, Universities, and Honors Programs, 1870s-2010s." *Harvard Educational Review* 84(2):243–64.

Kozhimannil, Katy B., Judy Jou, Dwenda K. Gjerdingen, and Patricia M. McGovern. 2016. "Access to Workplace Accommodations to Support Breastfeeding after Passage of the Affordable Care Act." *Women's Health Issues* 26(1):6–13.

Krieger, Nancy, Pamela D. Waterman, Cathy Hartman, Lisa M. Bates, Anne M. Stoddard, Margaret M. Quinn, Glorian Sorensen, and Elizabeth M. Barbeau. 2006. "Social Hazards on the Job: Workplace Abuse, Sexual Harassment, and Racial Discrimination—A Study of Black, Latino, and White Low-Income Women and Men Workers in the United States." *International Journal of Health Services* 36(1):51–85.

Kugler, Adriana D., Catherine H. Tinsley, and Olga Ukhaneva. 2017. *Choice of Majors: Are Women Really Different from Men?* Working Paper #23735. Cambridge, MA: National Bureau of Economic Research.

Kuo, Janet Chen-Lan and R. Kelly Raley. 2016. "Diverging Patterns of Union Transition among Cohabitors by Race/Ethnicity and Education: Trends and Marital Intentions in the United States." *Demography* 53(4):921–35.

Lamidi, Esther O., Wendy D. Manning, and Susan L. Brown. 2019. "Change in the Stability of First Premarital Cohabitation among Women in the United States, 1983–2013." *Demography; Silver Spring* 56(2):427–50.

Lamont, Ellen. 2020. *The Mating Game: How Gender Still Shapes How We Date.* 1st edition. Oakland: University of California Press.

Lamont, Michele and Annette Lareau. 1988. "Cultural Capital: Allusions, Gaps and Glissandos in Recent Theoretical Developments." *Sociological Theory* 6(2):153–68.

Lareau, Annette. 2002. "Invisible Inequality: Social Class and Childrearing in Black Families and White Families." *American Sociological Review* 67(5):747–76.

Lareau, Annette. 2011. *Unequal Childhoods: Class, Race, and Family Life, 2nd Edition with an Update a Decade Later.* Berkeley: University of California Press.

Lareau, Annette and Dalton Conley. 2008. *Social Class: How Does it Work?* New York: Russell Sage Foundation.

Lea, Toby, John de Wit, and Robert Reynolds. 2014. "Minority Stress in Lesbian, Gay, and Bisexual Young Adults in Australia: Associations with Psychological Distress, Suicidality, and Substance Use." *Archives of Sexual Behavior* 43(8):1571–78.

Lee, Barrett A., Kimberly A. Tyler, and James D. Wright. 2010. "The New Homelessness Revisited." *Annual Review of Sociology* 36(1):501–21.

Lee, Chul-In and Gary Solon. 2009. "Trends in Intergenerational Income Mobility." *The Review of Economics and Statistics* 91(4):766–72.

Leigh, Nancey Green. 2017. *Stemming Middle-Class Decline : The Challenges to Economic Development.* New York: Routledge.

Lewis, Kristen and Rebecca Gluskin. 2018. *Two Futures: The Economic Case for Keeping Youth on Track.* New York: Measure of America.

Liming, Drew and Michael Wolf. 2008. "Job Outlook, by Education, 2006–16." *Occupational Outlook Quarterly* 52(2):2–29.

Lin, Nan. 2001. *Social Structure: A Theory of Social Structure and Action.* New York: Cambridge University Press.

Lin, Yuxin and Vivian Yuen Ting Liu. 2019. *Timing Matters: How Delaying College Enrollment Affects Earnings Trajectories.* CCRC Working Paper No. 105. New York: Community College Research Center.

Linn, Allison. 2013. "For a Job after Graduation, Major in These, Not Those." *CNBC*, May 30. Retrieved February 7, 2021 (https://www.cnbc.com/id/100777334).

Long, Bridget Terry. 2002. *Attracting the Best: The Use of Honors Programs to Compete for Students.* No. ED465355. Chicago: ERIC Reproduction Service.

Lowery, Patrick G. 2019. "Plea Bargains among Serious and Violent Girls: An Intersectional Approach Exploring Race in the Juvenile Court." *Feminist Criminology* 14(1):115–39.

Lucas, Samuel R. 1999. *Tracking Inequality: Stratification and Mobility in American High Schools.* New York: Teachers College Press.

Lucas, Samuel R. 2001. "Effectively Maintained Inequality: Education Transitions, Track Mobility, and Social Background Effects." *American Journal of Sociology* 106(6):1642–90.

Lynch, Mamie, Jennifer Engle, and Jose L. Cruz. 2010. *Subprime Opportunity: The Unfulfilled Promise of For-Profit Colleges and Universities.* Washington, DC: Education Trust.

Ma, Jennifer. 2020. "Trends in College Pricing and Student Aid 2020." The College Board. Retrieved February 7, 2021 (https://research.collegeboard.org/pdf/trends-college-pricing-student-aid-2020.pdf).

MacDonald, R., and J. Marsh. 2005. *Disconnected Youth? Growing up in Britain's Poor Neighbourhoods*. Houndmills, UK: Palgrave Macmillan.

MacDonald, Robert and Jane Marsh. 2001. "Disconnected Youth?" *Journal of Youth Studies* 4(4): 373–91.

MacLeod, Jay. 2009. *Ain't No Makin' It: Aspirations and Attainment in a Low-Income Neighborhood, 3rd Edition*. Boulder, CO: Westview Press.

Malgwi, Charles A., Martha A. Howe, and Priscilla A. Burnaby. 2005. "Influences on Students' Choice of College Major." *Journal of Education for Business* 80(5):275–82.

Mandel, Hadas and Moshe Semyonov. 2014. "Gender Pay Gap and Employment Sector: Sources of Earnings Disparities in the United States, 1970–2010." *Demography* 51(5):1597–1618.

Manlove, Jennifer. 1998. "The Influence of High School Dropout and School Disengagement on the Risk of School-Age Pregnancy." *Journal of Research on Adolescence* 8(2):187–220.

Mann, Allison and Thomas A. DiPrete. 2013. "Trends in Gender Segregation in the Choice of Science and Engineering Majors." *Social Science Research* 42(6):1519–41.

Marcynyszyn, Lyscha A., Gary W. Evans, and John Eckenrode. 2008. "Family Instability during Early and Middle Adolescence." *Journal of Applied Developmental Psychology* 29(5):380–92.

Mare, Robert D. 1991. "Five Decades of Educational Assortative Mating." *American Sociological Review* 56(1):15–32.

Margolis, Eric. 2001. *The Hidden Curriculum in Higher Education*. New York: Routledge.

Marini, Margaret Mooney, Pi-Ling Fan, Erica Finley, and Ann M. Beutel. 1996. "Gender and Job Values." *Sociology of Education* 69(1):49–65.

Markham, Christine M., Donna Lormand, Kari M. Gloppen, Melissa F. Peskin, Belinda Flores, Barbara Low, and Lawrence Duane House. 2010. "Connectedness as a Predictor of Sexual and Reproductive Health Outcomes for Youth." *Journal of Adolescent Health* 46(3, Supplement):S23–41.

Mayo Clinic. N.d. "Fibromyalgia." Retrieved February 24, 2022 (http://www.mayoclinic.org/diseases-conditions/fibromyalgia/home/ovc-20317786).

Mazelis, Joan Maya. 2017. *Surviving Poverty: Creating Sustainable Ties among the Poor*. Reprint edition. New York: New York University Press.

McCaughey, Deirdre, Gwen McGhan, Jungyoon Kim, Diane Brannon, Hannes Leroy, and Rita Jablonski. 2012. "Workforce Implications of Injury among Home Health Workers: Evidence from the National Home Health Aide Survey." *The Gerontologist* 52(4):493–505.

McDonald, Steve. 2011. "What's in the 'Old Boys' Network? Accessing Social Capital in Gendered and Racialized Networks." *Social Networks* 33(4):317–30.

McDonald, Steve and Jacob C. Day. 2010. "Race, Gender, and the Invisible Hand of Social Capital." *Sociology Compass* 4(7):532–43.

McClelland, Katherine. 1990. "Cumulative Disadvantage among the Highly Ambitious." *Sociology of Education* 63(2):102–21.

McClendon, Mckee J. 1976. "The Occupational Status Attainment Processes of Males and Females." *American Sociological Review* 41(1):52–64.

McFarland, J., B. Hussar, J. Zhang, X. Wang, K. Wang, S. Hein, M. Diliberti, E. Forrest Cataldi, F. Bullock Mann, and A. Barmer. 2019. *The Condition of Education 2019* (NCES 2019-144). US Department of Education. Washington, DC: National Center for Education Statistics. Retrieved May 14, 2020 (https://nces.ed.gov/pubs2019/2019144.pdf).

McLanahan, Sara. 2004. "Diverging Destinies: How Children Are Faring under the Second Demographic Transition." *Demography* 41(4):607–27.

Mersky, Joshua P., Colleen E. Janczewski, and Jenna C. Nitkowski. 2018. "Poor Mental Health among Low-Income Women in the U.S.: The Roles of Adverse Childhood and Adult Experiences." *Social Science & Medicine* 206:14–21.

Meyer, Madonna Harrington, ed. 2002. *Care Work: Gender, Labor, and the Welfare State.* New York: Routledge.

Mickelson, Roslyn Arlin. 1990. "The Attitude-Achievement Paradox Among Black Adolescents." *Sociology of Education* 63(1):44–61.

Miles, Matthew B., and A. Michael Huberman. 1994. *Qualitative Data Analysis: An Expanded Sourcebook, 2nd Edition.* Thousand Oaks, CA: SAGE Publications.

Mitchell, Ojmarrh and Michael S. Caudy. 2017. "Race Differences in Drug Offending and Drug Distribution Arrests." *Crime & Delinquency* 63(2):91–112.

Moore, Gwen. 1990. "Structural Determinants of Men's and Women's Personal Networks." *American Sociological Review* 55(5): 726–35.

Morduch, Jonathan and Rachel Schneider. 2017. *The Financial Diaries: How American Families Cope in a World of Uncertainty.* Princeton, NJ: Princeton University Press.

Morgan, Stephen L. 1996. "Trends in Black-White Differences in Educational Expectations: 1980-92." *Sociology of Education* 69(4):308–19.

Morse, Robert, and Kenneth Himes. 2021. "How to Use the 2022 U.S. News Best Colleges Directory." *U.S. News & World Report*, September 12. Retrieved February 23, 2022 (https://www.usnews.com/education/best -colleges/articles/how-to-use-the-directory).

Mosisa, Abraham and Steven Hipple. 2006. "Trends in Labor Force Participation in the United States." *Monthly Labor Review* 129:35.

Moss-Pech, Corey. 2021. "The Career Conveyor Belt: How Internships Lead to Unequal Labor Market Outcomes among College Graduates." *Qualitative Sociology* 44(1):77–102.

Moulds, Elizabeth F. 1978. "Chivalry and Paternalism: Disparities of Treatment in the Criminal Justice System." *The Western Political Quarterly* 31(3):416–30.

Mouw, Ted and Arne L. Kalleberg. 2010. "Occupations and the Structure of Wage Inequality in the United States, 1980s to 2000s." *American Sociological Review* 75(3):402–31.

Muir, Hugh. 2014. "Why It's Critical That We Boost the Aspirations of Black Children." *The Guardian*, June 30.

Mulligan, Casey B. 2009. "What Explains the 'Mancession'?" *Economix Blog*. Retrieved June 6, 2020 (https://economix.blogs.nytimes.com/2009/09/30 /what-explains-the-mancession/).

Munasinghe, Lalith, Tania Reif, and Alice Henriques. 2008. "Gender Gap in Wage Returns to Job Tenure and Experience." *Labour Economics* 15(6):1296–1316.

Munnich, Elizabeth and Abigail Wozniak. 2020. "What Explains the Rising Share of US Men in Registered Nursing?" *ILR Review* 73(1):91–123.

Najman, Jake M., Mohammad R. Hayatbakhsh, Alexandra Clavarino, William Bor, Michael J. O'Callaghan, and Gail M. Williams. 2010. "Family Poverty over the Early Life Course and Recurrent Adolescent and Young Adult Anxiety and Depression: A Longitudinal Study." *American Journal of Public Health* 100(9):1719–23.

National Center for Education Statistics (NCES). 2013. "Public School Graduates and Dropouts from the Common Core of Data: School Year 2009–10." NCES 2013-309rev. Retrieved January 10, 2020 (https://nces.ed.gov/pubs 2013/2013309rev.pdf).

National Center for Education Statistics (NCES). 2020. "The Condition of Education." Retrieved May 20, 2020 (https://nces.ed.gov/programs/coe /indicator_cta.asp).

Needham, Belinda L. and Erika L. Austin. 2010. "Sexual Orientation, Parental Support, and Health During the Transition to Young Adulthood." *Journal of Youth and Adolescence* 39(10):1189–98.

Neugarten, Bernice L., Joan W. Moore, and John C. Lowe. 1965. "Age Norms, Age Constraints, and Adult Socialization." *American Journal of Sociology* 70(6):710–17.

Newman, Andy. 2019. "On the Job, 24 Hours a Day, 27 Days a Month." *New York Times*, September 2.

Newport, Frank. 2015. "Fewer Americans Identify as Middle-class in Recent Years." Retrieved May 6, 2019 (http://www.gallup.com/poll/182918/fewer -americans-identify-middle-class-recent-years.aspx).

Ngo, Federick. 2019. "Fractions in College: How Basic Math Remediation Impacts Community College Students." *Research in Higher Education* 60(4):485–520.

Noonan, David. 2021. "Can Free Community College Unite a Divided U.S.?" *Scientific American*, January 6. Retrieved February 3, 2021 (https://www.scientificamerican.com/article/can-free-community-college-unite-a-divided-u-s/).

Noss, Amanda. 2012. *Household Income for States: 2010 and 2011*. Washington, DC: US Department of Commerce, Economics and Statistics Administration, US Census Bureau.

Oliver, Melvin L. and Thomas M. Shapiro. 1997. *Black Wealth/White Wealth: A New Perspective on Racial Inequality*. New York: Routledge.

Oreopoulos, Philip and Uros Petronijevic. 2013. *Making College Worth It: A Review of Research on the Returns to Higher Education*. Working Paper 19053. Cambridge, MA: National Bureau of Economic Research.

Oreopoulos, Philip, Till von Wachter, and Andrew Heisz. 2012. "The Short- and Long-Term Career Effects of Graduating in a Recession." *American Economic Journal: Applied Economics* 4(1):1–29.

Ortiz, Susan Y. and Vincent J. Roscigno. 2009. "Discrimination, Women, and Work: Processes and Variations by Race and Class." *The Sociological Quarterly* 50(2):336–59.

Ostrove, Joan M. and Susan M. Long. 2007. "Social Class and Belonging: Implications for College Adjustment." *The Review of Higher Education* 30(4):363–89.

Padavic, Irene and Barbara F. Reskin. 2002. *Women and Men at Work*. 2nd edition. Thousand Oaks: Sage Publications.

Palardy, Gregory J. 2013. "High School Socioeconomic Segregation and Student Attainment." *American Educational Research Journal* 50(4):714–54.

Patient Protection and Affordable Care Act, 42 U.S.C. § 18001 et seq. (2010).

Patillo, Mary. 2005. "Black Middle-Class Neighborhoods." *Annual Review of Sociology* 31:305–29.

Persson, Tonje J., James G. Pfaus, and Andrew G. Ryder. 2015. "Explaining Mental Health Disparities for Non-Monosexual Women: Abuse History and Risky Sex, or the Burdens of Non-Disclosure?" *Social Science & Medicine* 128:366–73.

Petts, Richard J., Daniel L. Carlson, and Joanna R. Pepin. 2021. "A Gendered Pandemic: Childcare, Homeschooling, and Parents' Employment during COVID-19." *Gender, Work & Organization* 28(S2):515–34.

Piketty, Thomas and Emmanuel Saez. 2014. "Inequality in the Long Run." *Science* 344(6186):838–43.

Porter, Eduardo. 2014. "One Key to Success: A Belief in a Future." *New York Times*, June 11.

Prassl, Jeremias. 2018. *Humans as a Service: The Promise and Perils of Work in the Gig Economy*. Oxford, Oxford University Press.

Protopsaltis, Spiros and Sharon Parrott. 2017. "Pell Grants—A Key Tool for
     Expanding College Access and Economic Opportunity—Need Strengthening,
     Not Cuts." Washington, DC: Center on Budget and Policy Priorities. Retrieved
     December 17, 2020 (https://www.cbpp.org/sites/default/files/atoms/files/7-27
     -17bud.pdf).
Pugh, Allison J. 2015. *The Tumbleweed Society: Working and Caring in an Age
     of Insecurity*. 1st edition. New York: Oxford University Press.
Qian, Zhenchao and Sampson Lee Blair. 1999. "Racial/Ethnic Differences in
     Educational Aspirations of High School Seniors." *Sociological Perspectives*
     42(4):605–25.
Quadlin, Natasha and Jordan A. Conwell. 2021. "Race, Gender, and Parental
     College Savings: Assessing Economic and Academic Factors." *Sociology of
     Education* 94(1):20–42.
Raley, Sara and Suzanne Bianchi. 2006. "Sons, Daughters, and Family Processes:
     Does Gender of Children Matter?" *Annual Review of Sociology* 32:401–21.
Ray, Ranita. 2017. *The Making of a Teenage Service Class*. Oakland: University
     of California Press.
Reardon, Sean F. 2011. "The Widening Academic Achievement Gap between the
     Rich and the Poor: New Evidence and Possible Explanations." Pp. 91–116 in
     *Whither Opportunity? Rising Inequality, Schools, and Children's Life
     Chances*, edited by G. J. Duncan and R. J. Murnane. New York: Russell Sage
     Foundation.
Redford, Jeremy and Kathleen Mulvaney Hoyer. 2017. "First-Generation and
     Continuing-Generation College Students: A Comparison of High School and
     Postsecondary Experiences." National Center for Education Statistics Report
     # NCES 2018-009.
Reynolds, Jeremy and He Xian. 2014. "Perceptions of Meritocracy in the Land
     of Opportunity." *Research in Social Stratification and Mobility* 36:121–37.
Reynolds, John, Michael Stewart, Ryan MacDonald, and Lacey Sischo. 2006.
     "Have Adolescents Become Too Ambitious? High School Seniors' Educa-
     tional and Occupational Plans, 1976 to 2000." *Social Problems* 53(2):186–206.
Reynolds, John R. and Stephanie Woodham Burge. 2008. "Educational Expec-
     tations and the Rise in Women's Post-Secondary Attainments." *Social
     Science Research* 37(2):485–99.
Ridgeway, Cecilia L. 2009. "Framed before We Know It: How Gender Shapes
     Social Relations." *Gender & Society* 23(2):145–60.
Ridgeway, Cecilia L. 2011. *Framed by Gender: How Gender Inequality Persists
     in the Modern World*. New York: Oxford University Press.
Ridgeway, Cecilia L. and Shelley J. Correll. 2004. "Unpacking the Gender
     System A Theoretical Perspective on Gender Beliefs and Social Relations."
     Gender & Society 18(4):510–31.

Riegle-Crumb, Catherine, Barbara King, and Chelsea Moore. 2016. "Do They Stay or Do They Go? The Switching Decisions of Individuals Who Enter Gender Atypical College Majors." *Sex Roles* 74(9):436–49.

Rindfuss, Ronald R. 1991. "The Young Adult Years: Diversity, Structural Change, and Fertility." *Demography* 28(4):493–512.

Robinson, Brandon Andrew. 2020. *Coming Out to the Streets: LGBTQ Youth Experiencing Homelessness*. First edition. Oakland: University of California Press.

Roksa, Josipa. 2011. "Differentiation and Work: Inequality in Degree Attainment in U.S. Higher Education." *Higher Education* 61(3):293–308.

Rosenthal, Carolyn J. 1985. "Kinkeeping in the Familial Division of Labor." *Journal of Marriage and Family* 47(4):965–74.

Ross, Catherine E. and Chia-ling Wu. 1995. "The Links between Education and Health." *American Sociological Review* 60(5):719–45.

Ruggles, Steven. 2015. "Patriarchy, Power, and Pay: The Transformation of American Families, 1800–2015." *Demography* 52(6):1797–1823.

Russo, Nancy Felipe and Angela Pirlott. 2006. "Gender-Based Violence: Concepts, Methods, and Findings." *Annals of the New York Academy of Sciences* 1087:178–205.

Ryan, Caitlin, David Huebner, Rafael M. Diaz, and Jorge Sanchez. 2009. "Family Rejection as a Predictor of Negative Health Outcomes in White and Latino Lesbian, Gay, and Bisexual Young Adults." *Pediatrics* 123(1):346–52.

Şahin, Ayşegül, Joseph Song, and Bart Hobijn. 2010. *The Unemployment Gender Gap During the 2007 Recession*. SSRN Scholarly Paper. ID 1582525. Rochester, NY: Social Science Research Network.

Sandstrom, Heather and Sandra Huerta. 2013. *The Negative Effects of Instability on Child Development: A Research Synthesis*. Washington, DC: Urban Institute.

Scales, Kezia. 2020. "It's Time to Care: A Detailed Profile of America's Direct Care Workforce." Retrieved March 4, 2020 (file:///Users/jessica/Downloads/Its-Time-to-Care-2020-PHI.pdf: PHI).

Schell, Andy. 2017. "Cruising Tips: Heave To." *Sail Magazine*, August 2. Retrieved August 18, 2019 (https://www.sailmagazine.com/cruising/cruising-tips-heaving-to).

Schneider, Barbara and David Stevenson. 1999. *The Ambitious Generation: America's Teenagers, Motivated but Directionless*. New Haven, CT: Yale University Press.

Schneider, Daniel and Kristen Harknett. 2019. "Consequences of Routine Work-Schedule Instability for Worker Health and Well-Being." *American Sociological Review* 84(1):82–114.

Schneider, Daniel, Kristen Harknett, and Sara McLanahan. 2016. "Intimate Partner Violence in the Great Recession." *Demography* 53(2):471–505.

Schoon, Ingrid. 2001. "Teenage Job Aspirations and Career Attainment in Adulthood: A 17-Year Follow-up Study of Teenagers Who Aspired to Become Scientists, Health Professionals, or Engineers." *International Journal of Behavioral Development* 25(2):124–32.

Schudde, Lauren and Judith Scott-Clayton. 2016. "Pell Grants as Performance-Based Scholarships? An Examination of Satisfactory Academic Progress Requirements in the Nation's Largest Need-Based Aid Program." *Research in Higher Education* 57(8):943–67.

Scott-Clayton, Judith. 2012. "Do High-Stakes Placement Exams Predict College Success?" CCRC Working Paper No. 41. New York: Community College Research Center.

Scott-Clayton, Judith, Peter M. Crosta, and Clive R. Belfield. 2014. "Improving the Targeting of Treatment: Evidence from College Remediation." *Educational Evaluation and Policy Analysis* 36(3):371–93.

Seamster, Louise and Raphaël Charron-Chénier. 2017. "Predatory Inclusion and Education Debt: Rethinking the Racial Wealth Gap." *Social Currents* 4(3):199–207.

Seltzer, Judith A. and Suzanne M. Bianchi. 2013. "Demographic Change and Parent-Child Relationships in Adulthood." *Annual Review of Sociology* 39:275–90.

Settersten, Richard A. 2002. "Socialization and the Life Course: New Frontiers in Theory and Research." *Advances in Life Course Research* 7:13–40.

Settersten, Richard A. 2007. "Passages to Adulthood: Linking Demographic Change and Human Development." *European Journal of Population/Revue Européenne de Démographie* 23(3):251–72.

Sewell, William H. 1992. "A Theory of Structure: Duality, Agency, and Transformation." *American Journal of Sociology* 98(1):1–29.

Sewell, William H., Archibald O. Haller, and Alejandro Portes. 1969. "The Educational and Early Occupational Attainment Process." *American Sociological Review* 34(1):82–92.

Sewell, William H. and Vimal P. Shah. 1968. "Social Class, Parental Encouragement, and Educational Aspirations." *The American Journal of Sociology* 73(5):559–72.

Shanahan, Michael J., Scott M. Hofer, and Richard A. Miech. 2003. "Planful Competence, the Life Course, and Aging: Retrospect and Prospect." Pp. 189–211 in *Personal Control in Social and Life Course Contexts, Societal Impact on Aging*. New York: Springer Publishing.

Shandra, Carrie. 2018. "The New Bottom Rung? Internship Vacancies, Courses, and Implications." Paper presented at the National Symposium on College

Internship Research, September 28, Center for Research on College-Workforce Transition.

Shapiro, Thomas M. 2005. *The Hidden Cost of Being African American: How Wealth Perpetuates Inequality*. 1st edition. New York: Oxford University Press.

Sidel, Ruth. 1990. *On Her Own: Growing up in the Shadow of the American Dream*. New York: Viking.

Silva, Jennifer M. 2012. "Constructing Adulthood in an Age of Uncertainty." *American Sociological Review* 77(4):505–22.

Silva, Jennifer M. 2015. *Coming Up Short: Working-Class Adulthood in an Age of Uncertainty*. Oxford: Oxford University Press.

Silva, Jennifer M. and Kaisa Snellman. 2018. "Salvation or Safety Net? Meanings of 'College' among Working- and Middle-Class Young Adults in Narratives of the Future." *Social Forces* 97(2):559–82.

Slabbert, Ilze. 2017. "Domestic Violence and Poverty: Some Women's Experiences." *Research on Social Work Practice* 27(2):223–30.

Small, Mario Luis. 2009. *Unanticipated Gains: Origins of Network Inequality in Everyday Life*. Oxford: Oxford University Press.

Smith, Ashley. 2016. "Wanted: Nursing Instructors." *Inside Higher Ed*, January 27 Retrieved May 26, 2020 (https://www.insidehighered.com/news/2016/01/27/colleges-contend-few-nursing-instructors-and-wait-lists).

Smock, Pamela J., Wendy D. Manning, and Meredith Porter. 2005. "'Everything's There Except Money': How Money Shapes Decisions to Marry among Cohabitors." *Journal of Marriage and Family* 67(3):680–96.

Snyder, Thomas D., Cristobal de Brey, and Sally A. Dillow. 2016. "Digest of Education Statistics." National Center for Education Statistics.

Sommers, Benjamin D., Thomas Buchmueller, Sandra L. Decker, Colleen Carey, and Richard Kronick. 2013. "The Affordable Care Act Has Led to Significant Gains in Health Insurance and Access to Care for Young Adults." *Health Affairs* 32(1):165–74.

South, Scott J., Dana L. Haynie, and Sunita Bose. 2007. "Student Mobility and School Dropout." *Social Science Research* 1(36):68–94.

Stack, Carol B. 1974. *All Our Kin: Strategies for Survival in a Black Community*. New York: Harper & Row.

Staff, Jeremy, Angel Harris, Ricardo Sabates, and Laine Briddell. 2010. "Uncertainty in Early Occupational Aspirations: Role Exploration or Aimlessness?" *Social Forces* 89(2):659–83.

Stainback, Kevin and Donald Tomaskovic-Devey. 2012. *Documenting Desegregation: Racial and Gender Segregation in Private Sector Employment since the Civil Rights Act*. New York: Russell Sage Foundation.

Stevens, Mitchell L. 2009. *Creating a Class: College Admissions and the Education of Elites*. Cambridge, MA: Harvard University Press.

Stone, Robyn I. 2004. "The Direct Care Worker: The Third Rail of Home Care Policy." *Annual Review of Public Health* 25(1):521–37.

Strauss, Marcy. 2011. "Reevaluating Suspect Classifications." *Seattle University Law Review* 35:135.

Streib, Jessi. 2020. *Privilege Lost: Who Leaves the Upper Middle Class and How They Fall.* New York: Oxford University Press.

Suh, Jooyeoun and Nancy Folbre. 2016. "Valuing Unpaid Child Care in the U.S.: A Prototype Satellite Account Using the American Time Use Survey." *Review of Income and Wealth* 62(4):668–84.

Sullivan, Teresa A., Elizabeth Warren, and Jay Westbrook. 2001. *The Fragile Middle Class: Americans in Debt.* New Haven, CT: Yale University Press.

Swartz, Teresa. 2009. "Intergenerational Family Relations in Adulthood: Patterns, Variations, and Implications in the Contemporary United States." *Annual Review of Sociology* 35:191–212.

Sweeney, Megan M. 2002. "Two Decades of Family Change: The Shifting Economic Foundations of Marriage." *American Sociological Review* 67(1):132–47.

Tach, Laura and Kathryn Edin. 2017. "The Social Safety Net after Welfare Reform: Recent Developments and Consequences for Household Dynamics." *Annual Review of Sociology* 43(1):541–61.

Taniguchi, Hiromi. 1999. "The Timing of Childbearing and Women's Wages." *Journal of Marriage and Family* 61(4):1008–19.

Thompson, Derek. 2009. "It's Not Just a Recession. It's a Mancession!" *The Atlantic*, July 9.

Thompson, William E. and Joseph V. Hickey. 2007. *Society in Focus: An Introduction to Sociology.* Boston: Allyn & Bacon

Thornton, Arland and Linda Young-DeMarco. 2001. "Four Decades of Trends in Attitudes toward Family Issues in the United States: The 1960s through the 1990s." *Journal of Marriage and Family* 63(4):1009–37.

Tolbert, Pamela S. and Phyllis Moen. 1998. "Men's and Women's Definitions of 'Good' Jobs: Similarities and Differences by Age and across Time." *Work and Occupations* 25(2):168–94.

Tuchman, Gaye. 2011. *Wannabe U: Inside the Corporate University.* Reprint edition. Chicago: University of Chicago Press.

US Department of Labor, Women's Bureau. N.d. *Women in the Labor Force.* Retrieved November 2, 2020(https://www.dol.gov/agencies/wb/data/facts-over-time/women-in-the-labor-force#labor-force-participation-rate-by-sex-race-and-hispanic-ethnicity).

US Bureau of Labor Statistics. N.d. *Occupational Outlook Handbook.* Retrieved November 2, 2020 (https://www.bls.gov/ooh/).

US Bureau of Labor Statistics. 2007. *Monthly Labor Review* 130(11). Retrieved May 1, 2009 (https://fraser.stlouisfed.org/title/6130/item/598245).

US Bureau of Labor Statistics. 2015a. "Median Weekly Earnings by Educational Attainment in 2014." *TED: The Economics Daily*, January 23. Retrieved May 20, 2020 (https://www.bls.gov/opub/ted/2015/median-weekly-earnings-by-education-gender-race-and-ethnicity-in-2014.htm)

US Bureau of Labor Statistics. 2015b. *Occupational Outlook Handbook: Nurse Anesthetists*. Washington, DC: United States Department of Labor. Retrieved March 15, 2016 (https://www.bls.gov/ooh/healthcare/home.htm).

US Bureau of Labor Statistics. 2018. *Women in the Labor Force*. BLS Report no. 1077 Retrieved May 26, 2019 (https://www.bls.gov/opub/reports/womens-databook/2018/home.htm).

US Bureau of Labor Statistics. 2021. *Occupational Outlook Handbook: Healthcare Occupations*. Washington, DC: United States Department of Labor. Retrieved September 16, 2021 (https://www.bls.gov/ooh/healthcare/home.htm).

US Department of Education, National Center for Education Statistics. 2020. "Undergraduate Retention and Graduation Rates." In *The Condition of Education 2020* (NCES 2020-144).

US Senate Committee on Health, Education, Labor and Pensions. 2012. *For Profit Higher Education: The Failure to Safeguard the Federal Investment and Ensure Student Success*. Vol. 1, No. 1-3. Washington, DC: US Government Printing Office.

Vaisey, Stephen. 2010. "What People Want: Rethinking Poverty, Culture, and Educational Attainment." *The ANNALS of the American Academy of Political and Social Science* 629(1):75–101.

Valletta, Robert G. 2018. *Recent Flattening in the Higher Education Wage Premium: Polarization, Skill Downgrading, or Both?* (NBER Working Paper No. 22935). Cambridge, MA: National Bureau of Economic Research.

Visher, Christy A. 1983. "Gender, Police Arrest Decisions, and Notions of Chivalry." *Criminology* 21(1):5–28.

Walpole, MaryBeth. 2003. "Socioeconomic Status and College: How SES Affects College Experiences and Outcomes." *The Review of Higher Education* 27(1):45–73.

Wang, Marian, Beckie Supiano, and Andrea Fuller. 2012. "The Parent Loan Trap." *Chronicle of Higher Education*, October 12. Retrieved June 2, 2020 (https://www.chronicle.com/article/the-parent-loan-trap/#:~:text=A%20joint%20examination%20by%20ProPublica,for%20families%20who've%20overreached).

Warner, Darrell B. and Katie Koeppel. 2009. "General Education Requirements: A Comparative Analysis." *The Journal of General Education* 58(4):241–58.

Wathen, C. Nadine, Jennifer C. D. MacGregor, and Barbara J. MacQuarrie. 2018. "Relationships among Intimate Partner Violence, Work, and Health." *Journal of Interpersonal Violence* 33(14):2268–90.

Weaver, Vesla M., Andrew Papachristos, and Michael Zanger-Tishler. 2019. "The Great Decoupling: The Disconnection Between Criminal Offending and Experience of Arrest across Two Cohorts." *RSF: The Russell Sage Foundation Journal of the Social Sciences* 5(1):89–123.

Webster, Juliet. 2016. "Microworkers of the Gig Economy: Separate and Precarious." *New Labor Forum* 25(3):56–64.

Western, Bruce and Becky Pettit. 2010. "Incarceration & Social Inequality." *Daedalus* 139(3):8–19.

Wiemers, Emily E. 2014. "The Effect of Unemployment on Household Composition and Doubling Up." *Demography* 51(6):2155–78.

Wight, Vanessa, Michelle M. Chau, Yumiko Aratani, Susan Wile Schwarz, and Kalyani Thampi. 2010. *A Profile of Disconnected Young Adults in 2010*. New York: National Center for Children in Poverty.

Williams, David R. 2008. "The Health of Men: Structured Inequalities and Opportunities." *American Journal of Public Health* 98(Supplement 1): S150–57.

Williams, Joan C. 2001. *Unbending Gender: Why Family and Work Conflict and What to Do about It*. New York: Oxford University Press.

Williams, Trish, Jennifer Connolly, Debra Pepler, and Wendy Craig. 2005. "Peer Victimization, Social Support, and Psychosocial Adjustment of Sexual Minority Adolescents." *Journal of Youth and Adolescence* 34(5):471–82.

Winston, Gordon C. 1999. "Subsidies, Hierarchy and Peers: The Awkward Economics of Higher Education." *Journal of Economic Perspectives* 13(1):13–36.

World Bank. N.d. "Rail Lines (Total Route—km)—United States." Retrieved February 24, 2022 (https://data.worldbank.org/indicator/IS.RRS.TOTL.KM?locations=US&view=chart).

Wright, Erik Olin. 1997. *Class Counts: Comparative Studies in Class Analysis*. New York: Cambridge University Press.

Yavorsky, Jill E., Claire M. Kamp Dush, and Sarah J. Schoppe-Sullivan. 2015. "The Production of Inequality: The Gender Division of Labor across the Transition to Adulthood." *Journal of Marriage and Family* 77(3):662–79.

Index

Founded in 1893,
UNIVERSITY OF CALIFORNIA PRESS
publishes bold, progressive books and journals
on topics in the arts, humanities, social sciences,
and natural sciences—with a focus on social
justice issues—that inspire thought and action
among readers worldwide.

The UC PRESS FOUNDATION
raises funds to uphold the press's vital role
as an independent, nonprofit publisher, and
receives philanthropic support from a wide
range of individuals and institutions—and from
committed readers like you. To learn more, visit
ucpress.edu/supportus.